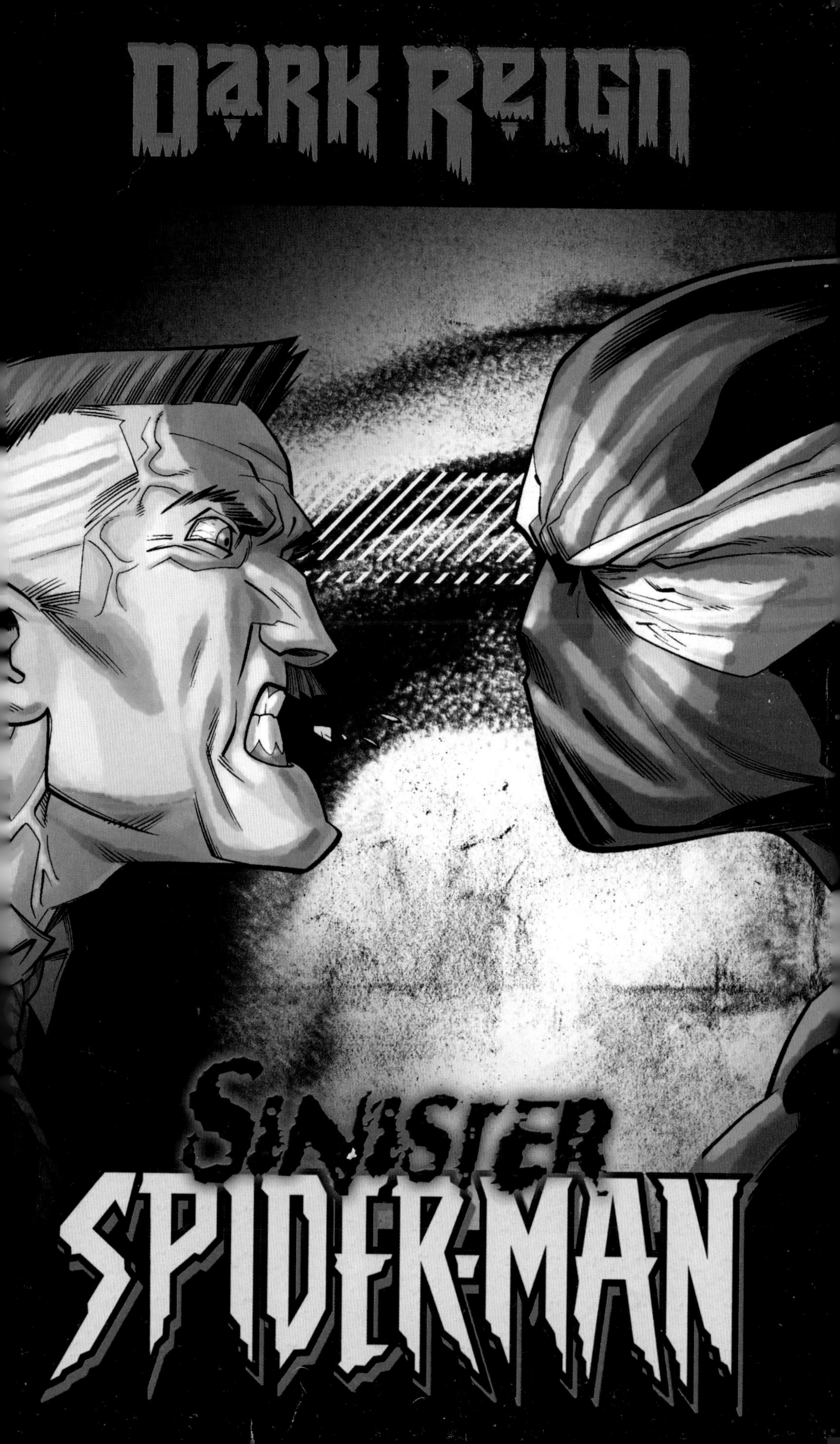
DARK REIGN
SINISTER
SPIDER-MAN

DARK REIGN

Sinister SPIDER-MAN

Writer: **BRIAN REED**
Pencilers: **CHRIS BACHALO & ROB DISALVO**
Inkers: **TIM TOWNSEND, JAIME MENDOZA, JON SIBAL,
ROB DISALVO, MARK IRWIN & WALDEN WONG**
Colorists: **CHRIS BACHALO** WITH **ANTONIO FABELA & ANDRES MOSSA**
Letterer: **JARED K. FLETCHER**
Cover Artist: **CHRIS BACHALO**
Editor: **TOM BRENNAN**
Supervising Editor: **STEPHEN WACKER**
Executive Editor: **TOM BREVOORT**

"DARK REFLECTION"
Writer: **MARC SUMERAK**
Artist: **JAVIER PULIDO**
Colorist: **JAVIER RODRIGUEZ**
Letterer: **DAVE LANPHEAR**
Cover Artist: **NUNO PLATI**
Assistant Editor: **TOM BRENNAN**
Editor: **STEPHEN WACKER**

Collection Editor: **CORY LEVINE**
Assistant Editors: **ALEX STARBUCK & JOHN DENNING**
Editors, Special Projects: **JENNIFER GRÜNWALD & MARK D. BEAZLEY**
Senior Editor, Special Projects: **JEFF YOUNGQUIST**
Senior Vice President of Sales: **DAVID GABRIEL**
Book Design: **RODOLFO MURAGUCHI**

Editor in Chief: **JOE QUESADA**
Publisher: **DAN BUCKLEY**
Executive Producer: **ALAN FINE**

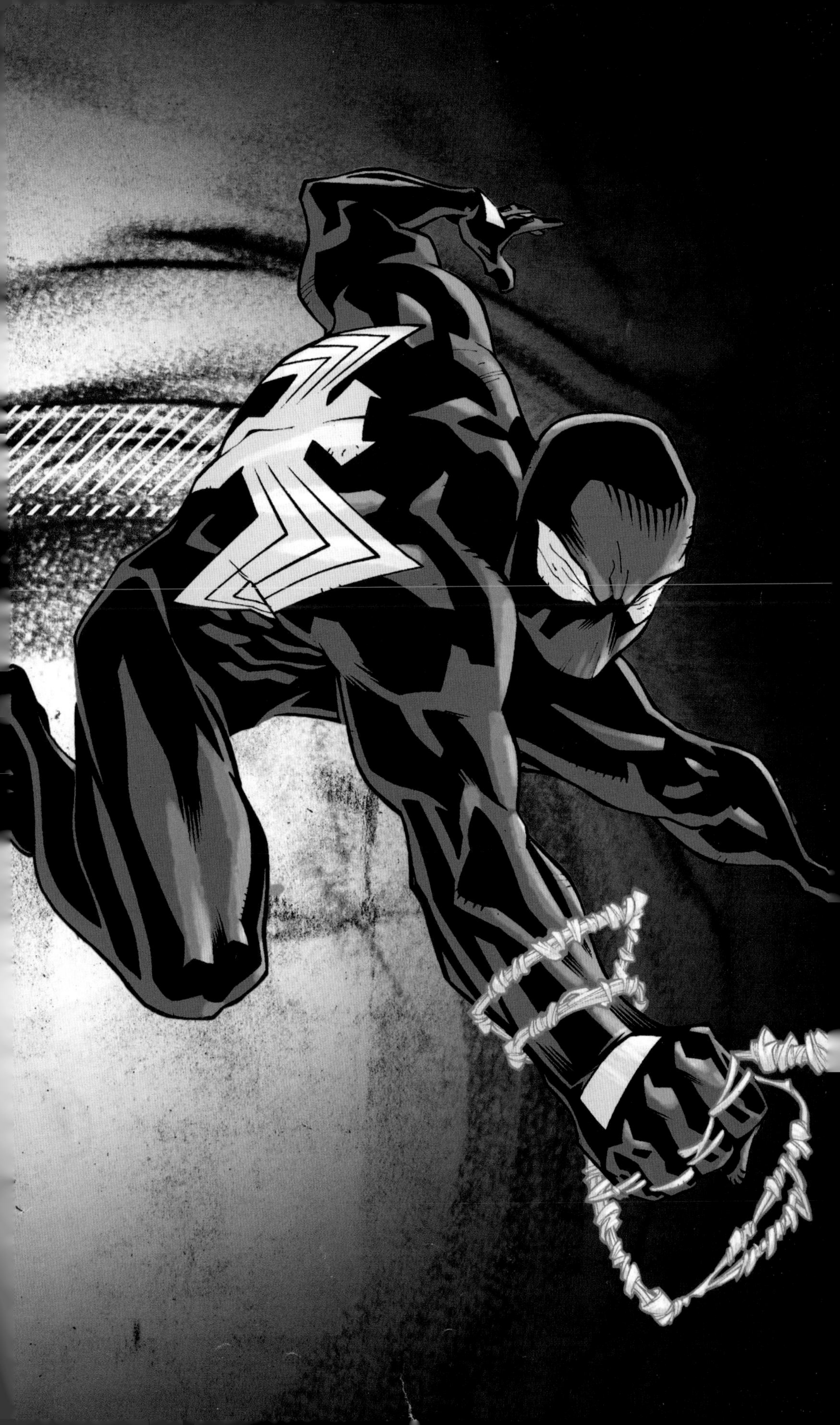

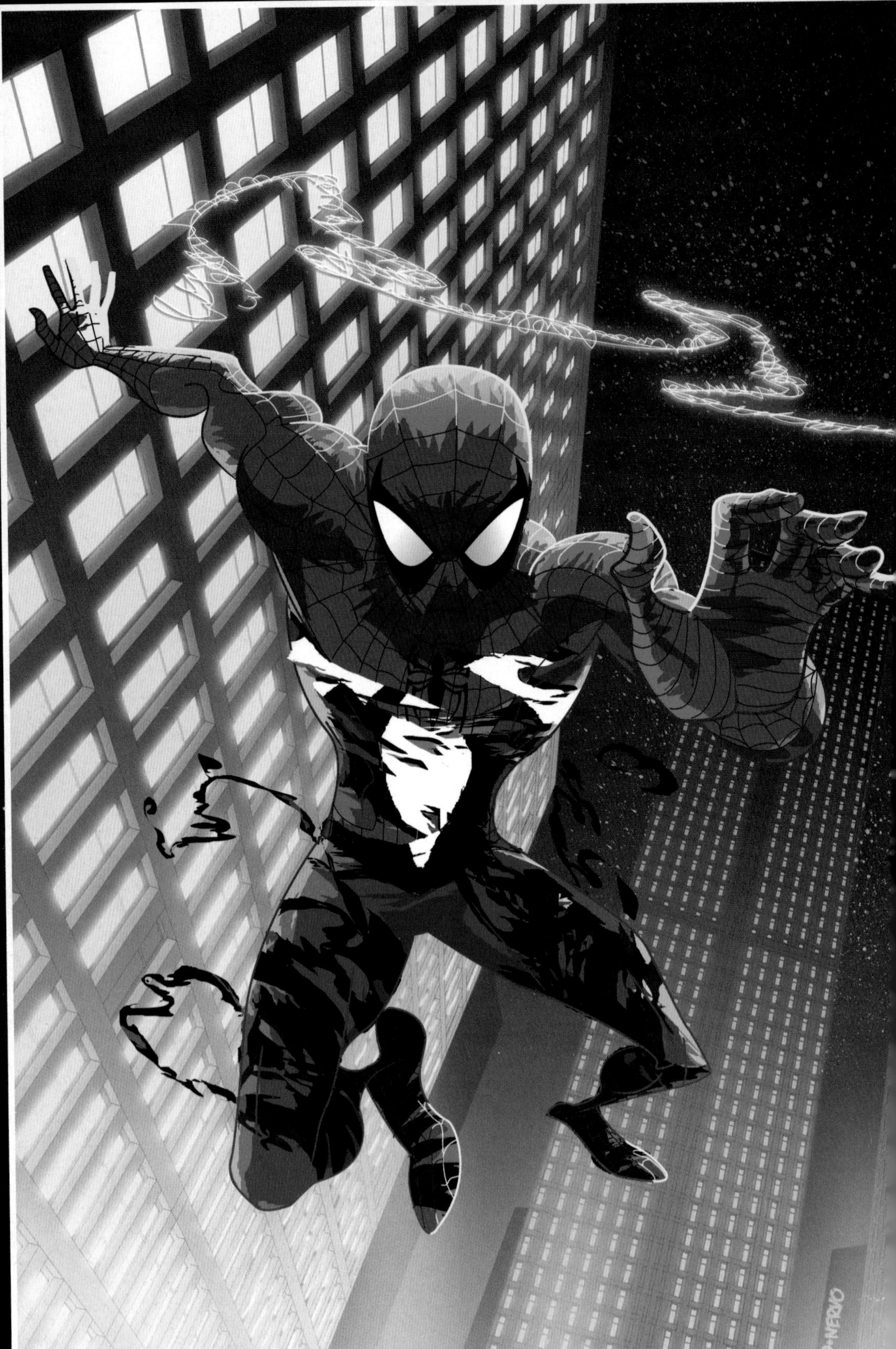

AMAZING SPIDER-MAN FAMILY #8

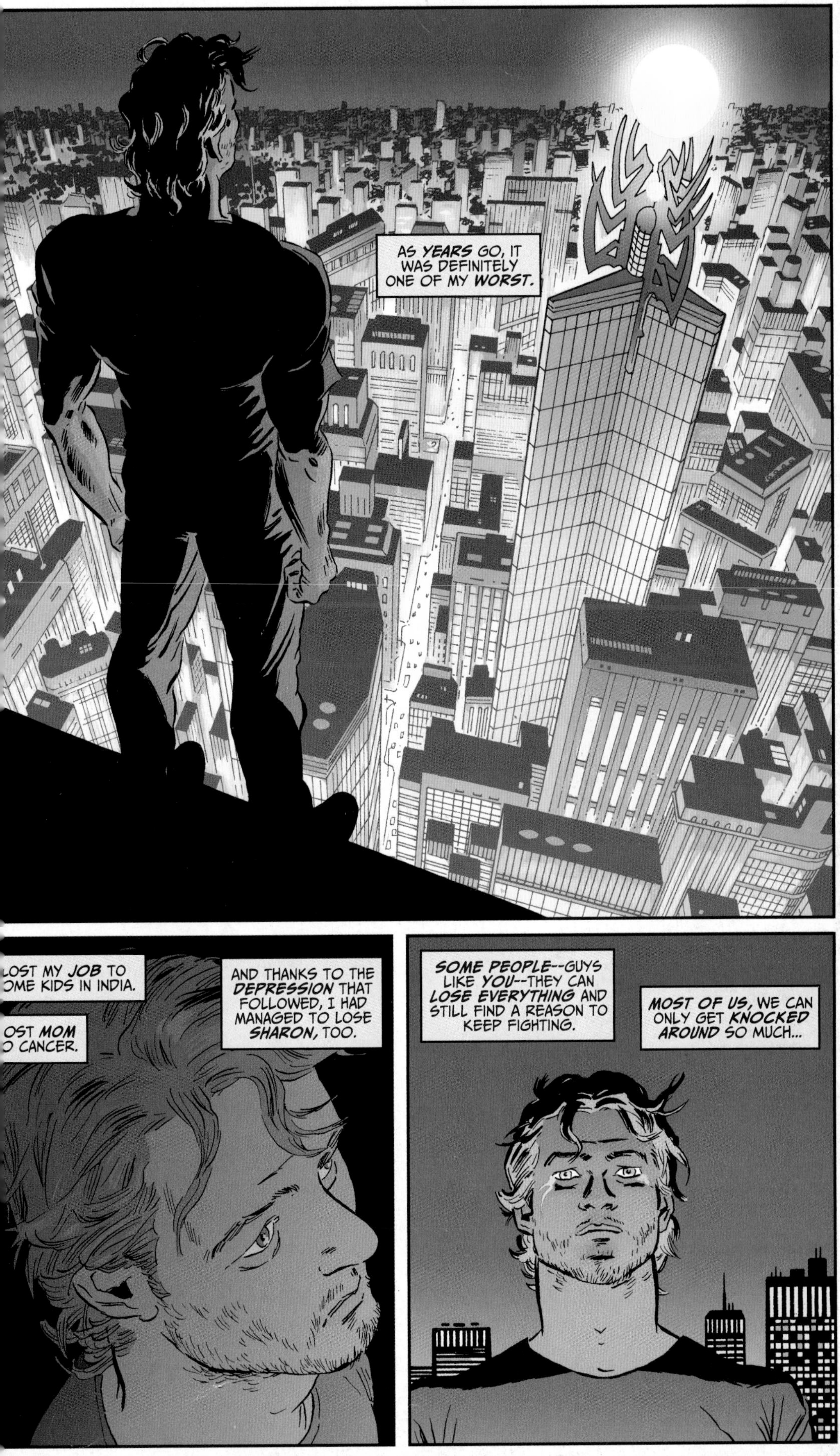
AS YEARS GO, IT WAS DEFINITELY ONE OF MY WORST.
LOST MY JOB TO
OME KIDS IN INDIA.
OST MOM
O CANCER.
AND THANKS TO THE DEPRESSION THAT FOLLOWED, I HAD MANAGED TO LOSE SHARON, TOO.
SOME PEOPLE--GUYS LIKE YOU--THEY CAN LOSE EVERYTHING AND STILL FIND A REASON TO KEEP FIGHTING.
MOST OF US, WE CAN ONLY GET KNOCKED AROUND SO MUCH...

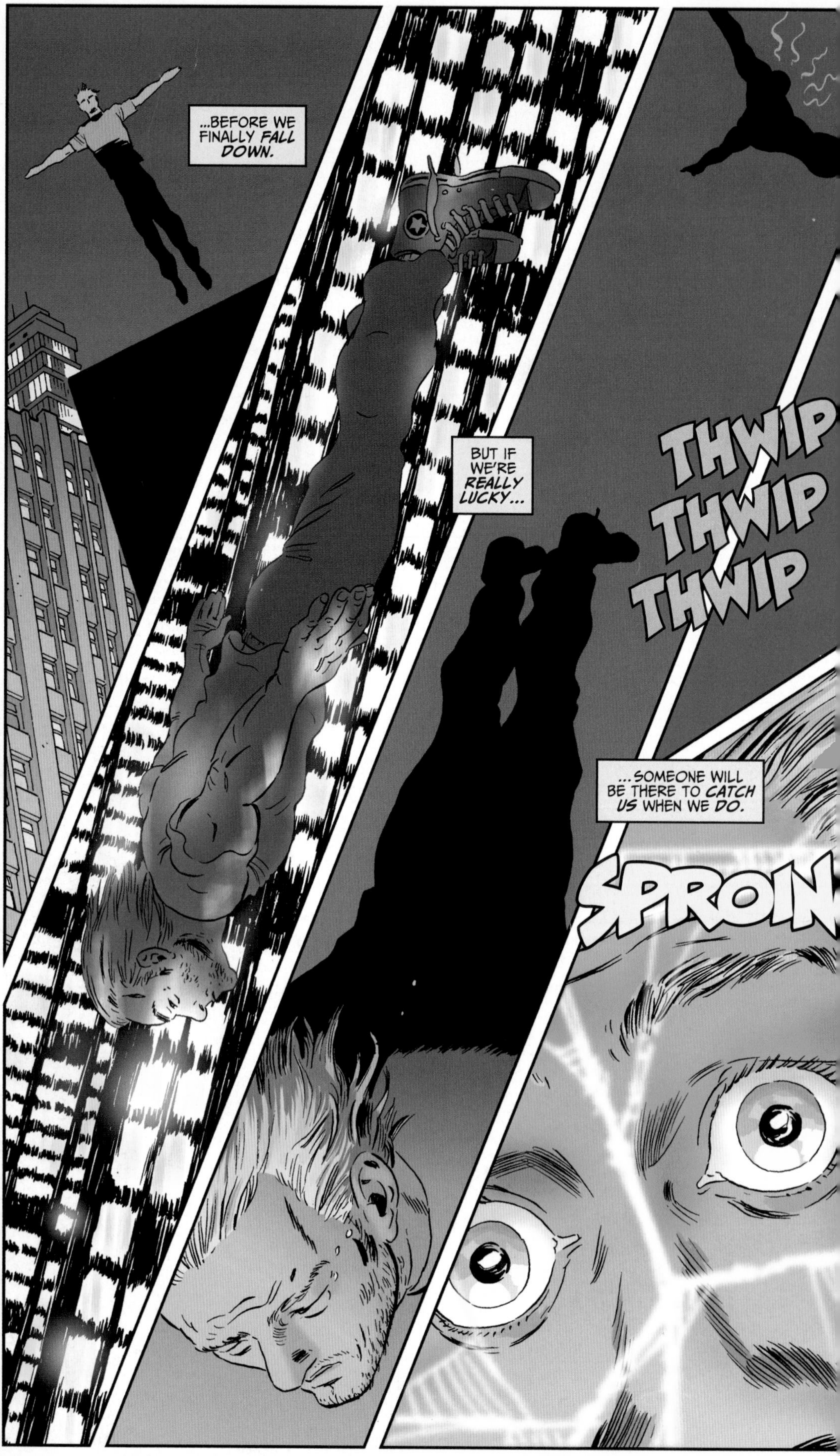
...BEFORE WE FINALLY FALL DOWN.
BUT IF WE'RE REALLY LUCKY...
THWIP THWIP THWIP
...SOMEONE WILL BE THERE TO CATCH US WHEN WE DO.
SPROIN

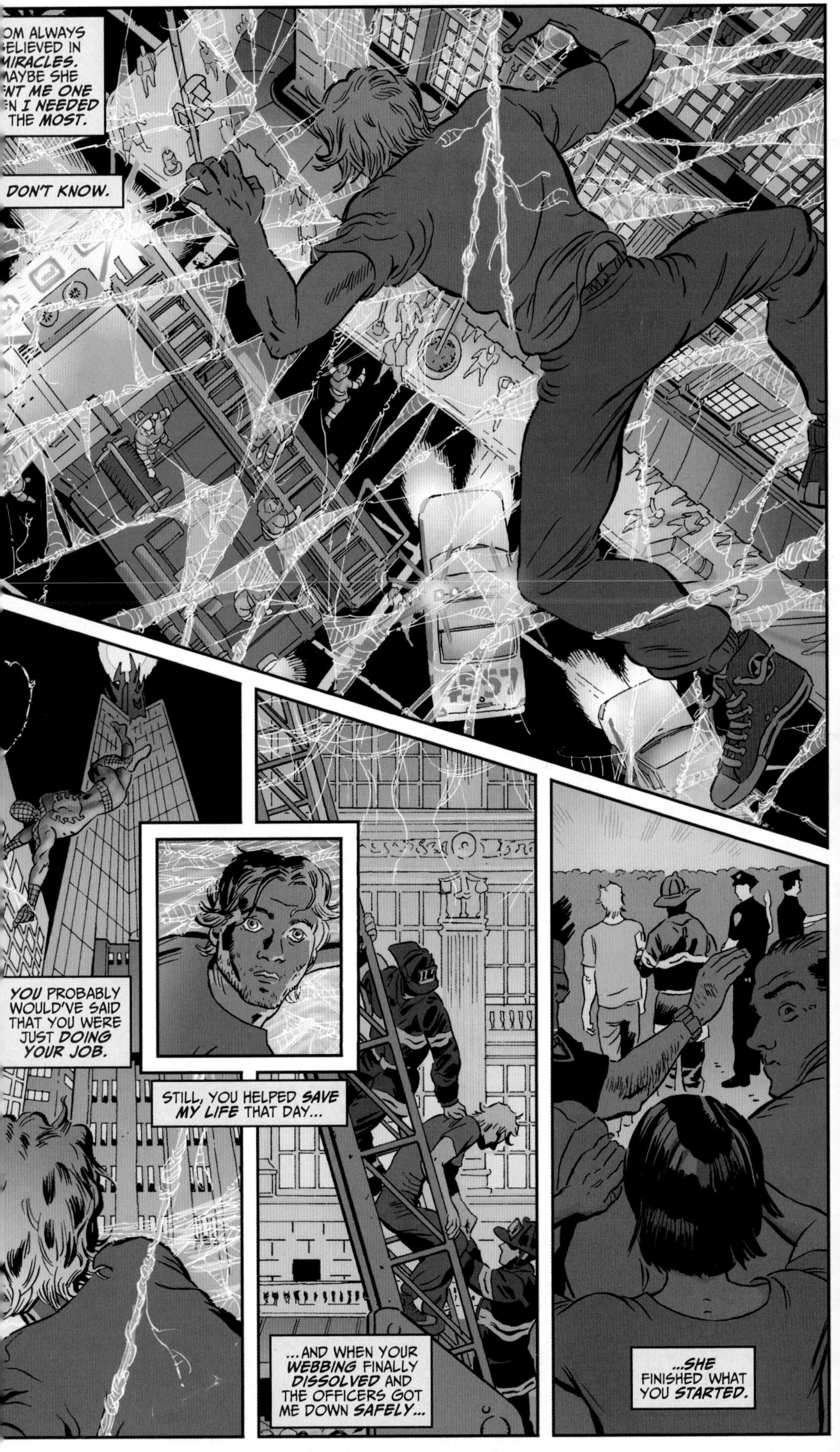
OM ALWAYS
ELIEVED IN
MIRACLES.
MAYBE SHE
NT ME ONE
N I NEEDED
THE MOST.
DON'T KNOW.
YOU PROBABLY WOULD'VE SAID THAT YOU WERE JUST DOING YOUR JOB.
STILL, YOU HELPED SAVE MY LIFE THAT DAY...
...AND WHEN YOUR WEBBING FINALLY DISSOLVED AND THE OFFICERS GOT ME DOWN SAFELY...
...SHE FINISHED WHAT YOU STARTED.

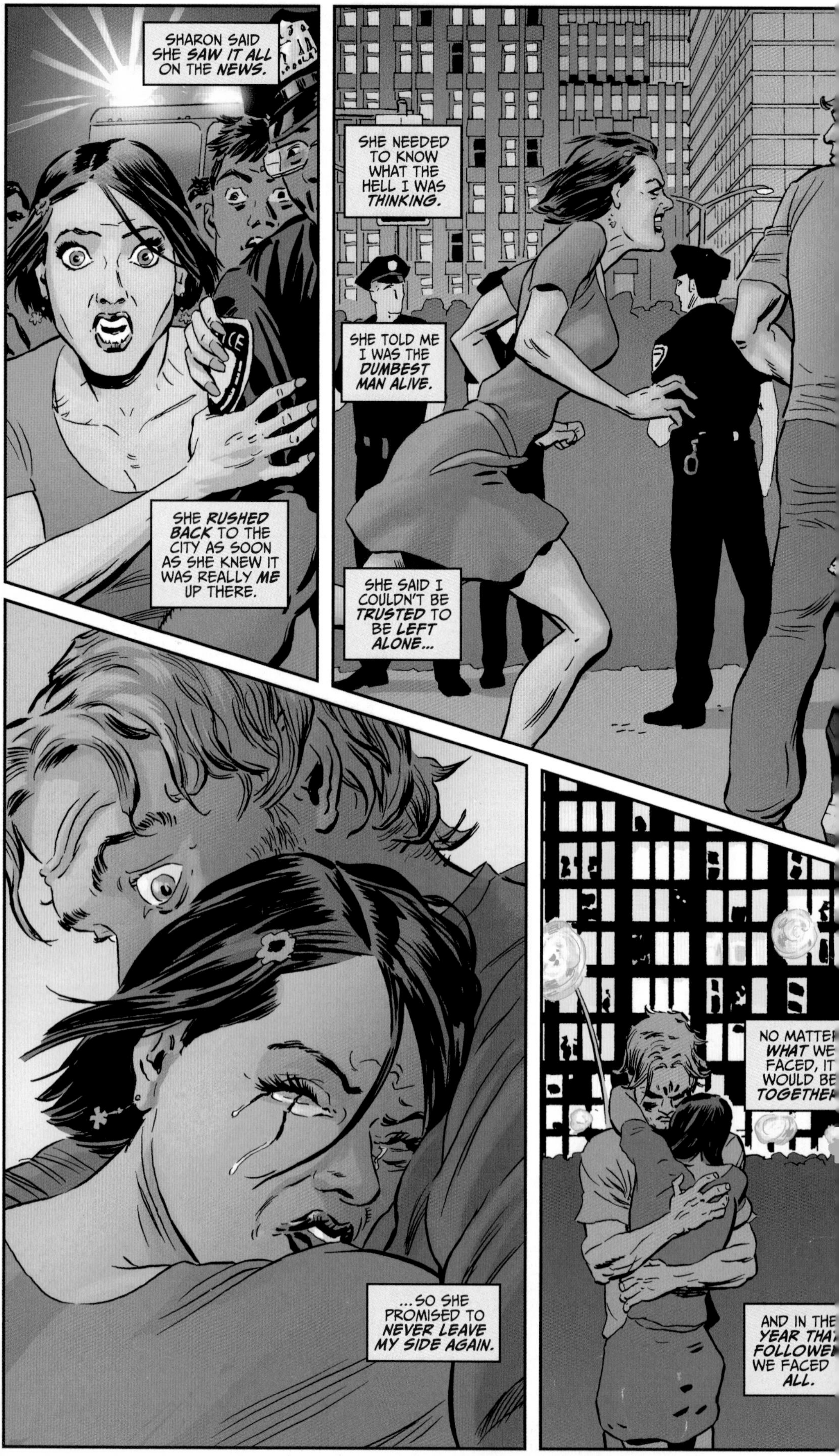
SHARON SAID SHE *SAW IT ALL* ON THE *NEWS.*
SHE *RUSHED BACK* TO THE CITY AS SOON AS SHE KNEW IT WAS REALLY *ME* UP THERE.
SHE NEEDED TO KNOW WHAT THE HELL I WAS *THINKING.*
SHE TOLD ME I WAS THE *DUMBEST MAN ALIVE.*
SHE SAID I COULDN'T BE *TRUSTED* TO BE *LEFT ALONE...*
...SO SHE PROMISED TO *NEVER LEAVE MY SIDE AGAIN.*
NO MATTE
WHAT WE
FACED, IT
WOULD BE
TOGETHE
AND IN THE
YEAR THA
FOLLOWE
WE FACED
ALL.

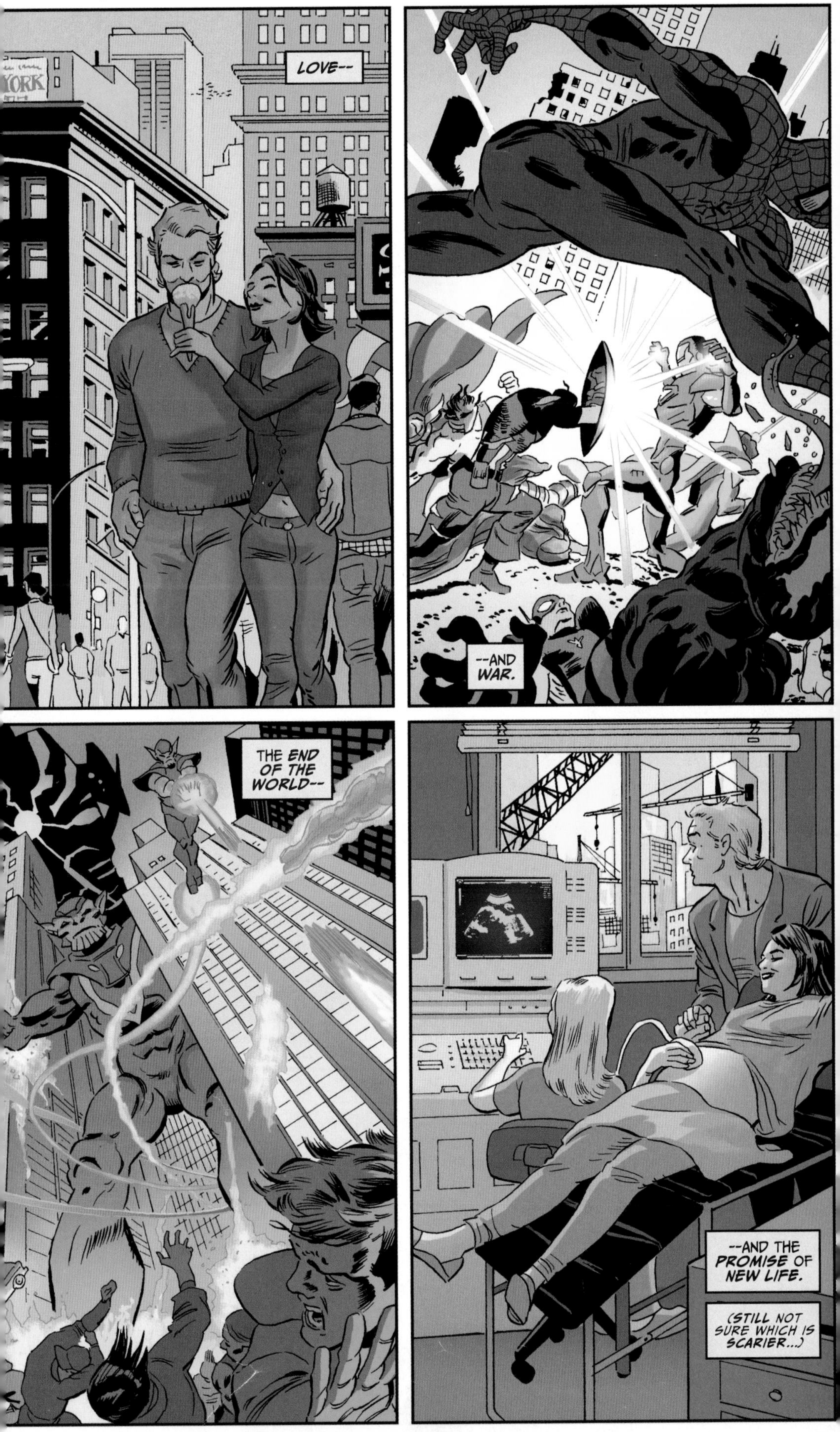
LOVE--
--AND WAR.
THE END OF THE WORLD--
--AND THE PROMISE OF NEW LIFE.
(STILL NOT SURE WHICH IS SCARIER...)

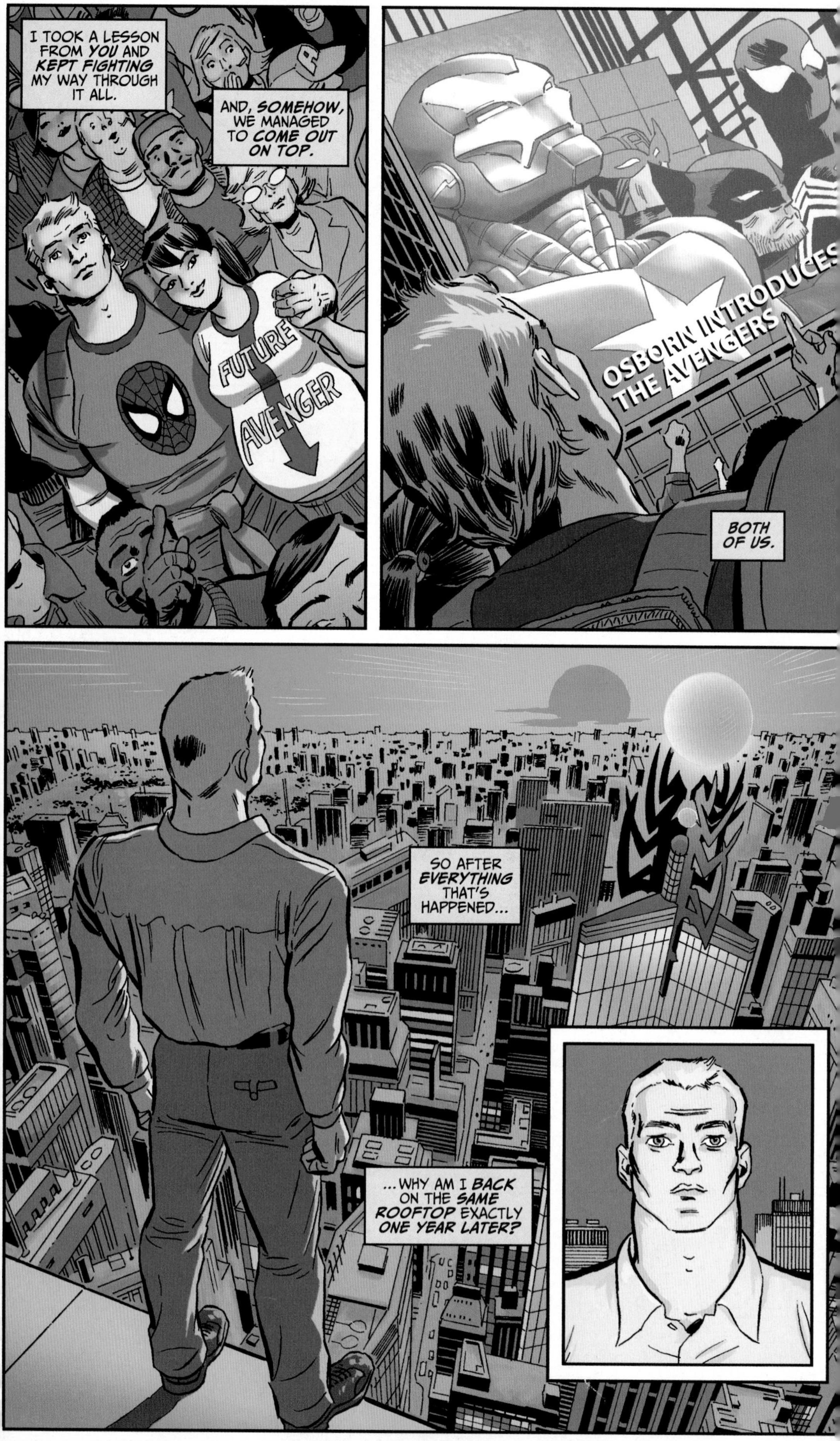
I TOOK A LESSON FROM YOU AND KEPT FIGHTING MY WAY THROUGH IT ALL.
AND, SOMEHOW, WE MANAGED TO COME OUT ON TOP.
FUTURE AVENGER
OSBORN INTRODUCES THE AVENGERS
BOTH OF US.
SO AFTER EVERYTHING THAT'S HAPPENED...
...WHY AM I BACK ON THE SAME ROOFTOP EXACTLY ONE YEAR LATER?

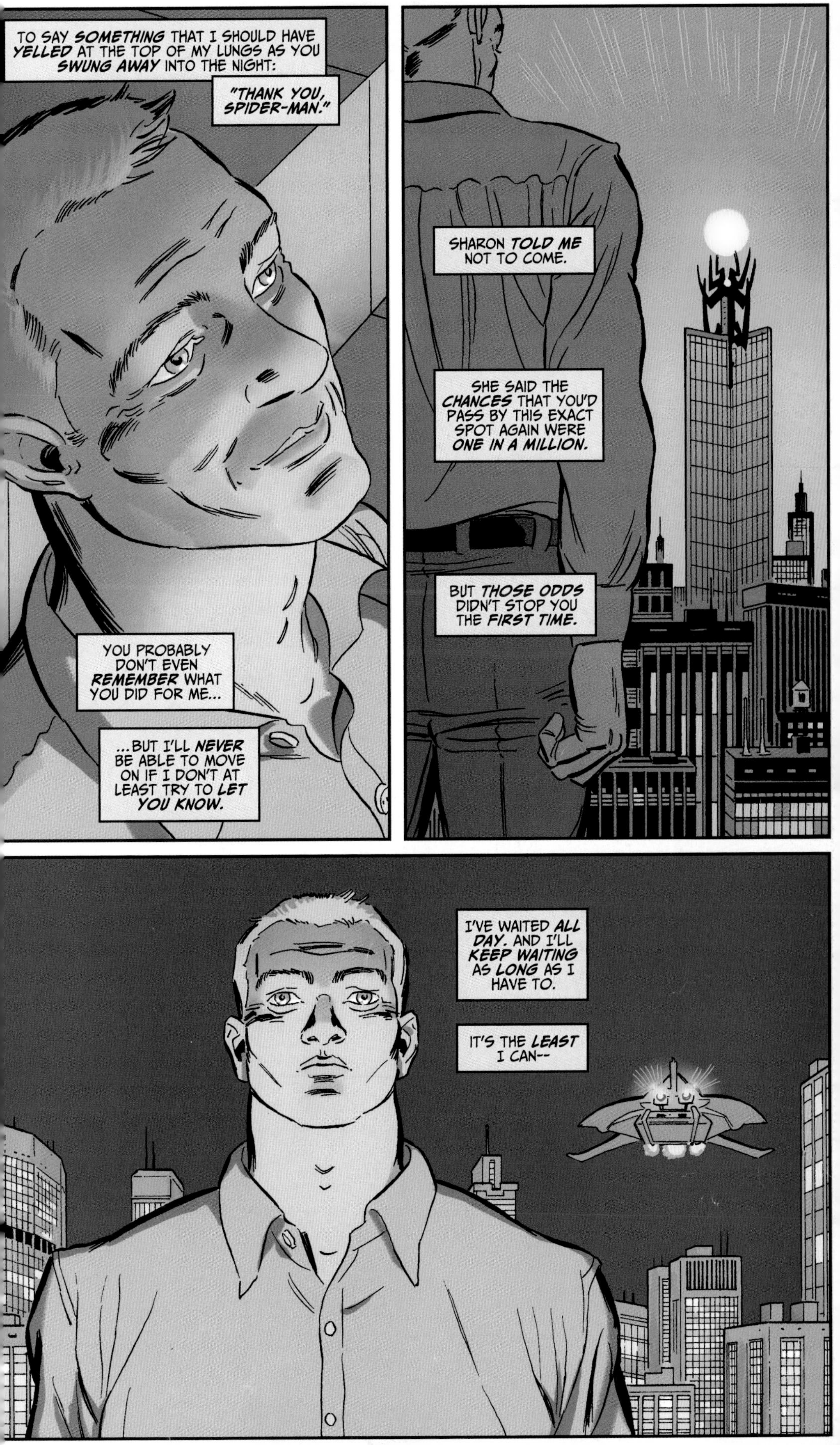
TO SAY SOMETHING THAT I SHOULD HAVE YELLED AT THE TOP OF MY LUNGS AS YOU SWUNG AWAY INTO THE NIGHT:
"THANK YOU, SPIDER-MAN."
YOU PROBABLY DON'T EVEN REMEMBER WHAT YOU DID FOR ME...
...BUT I'LL NEVER BE ABLE TO MOVE ON IF I DON'T AT LEAST TRY TO LET YOU KNOW.
SHARON TOLD ME NOT TO COME.
SHE SAID THE CHANCES THAT YOU'D PASS BY THIS EXACT SPOT AGAIN WERE ONE IN A MILLION.
BUT THOSE ODDS DIDN'T STOP YOU THE FIRST TIME.
I'VE WAITED ALL DAY. AND I'LL KEEP WAITING AS LONG AS I HAVE TO.
IT'S THE LEAST I CAN--

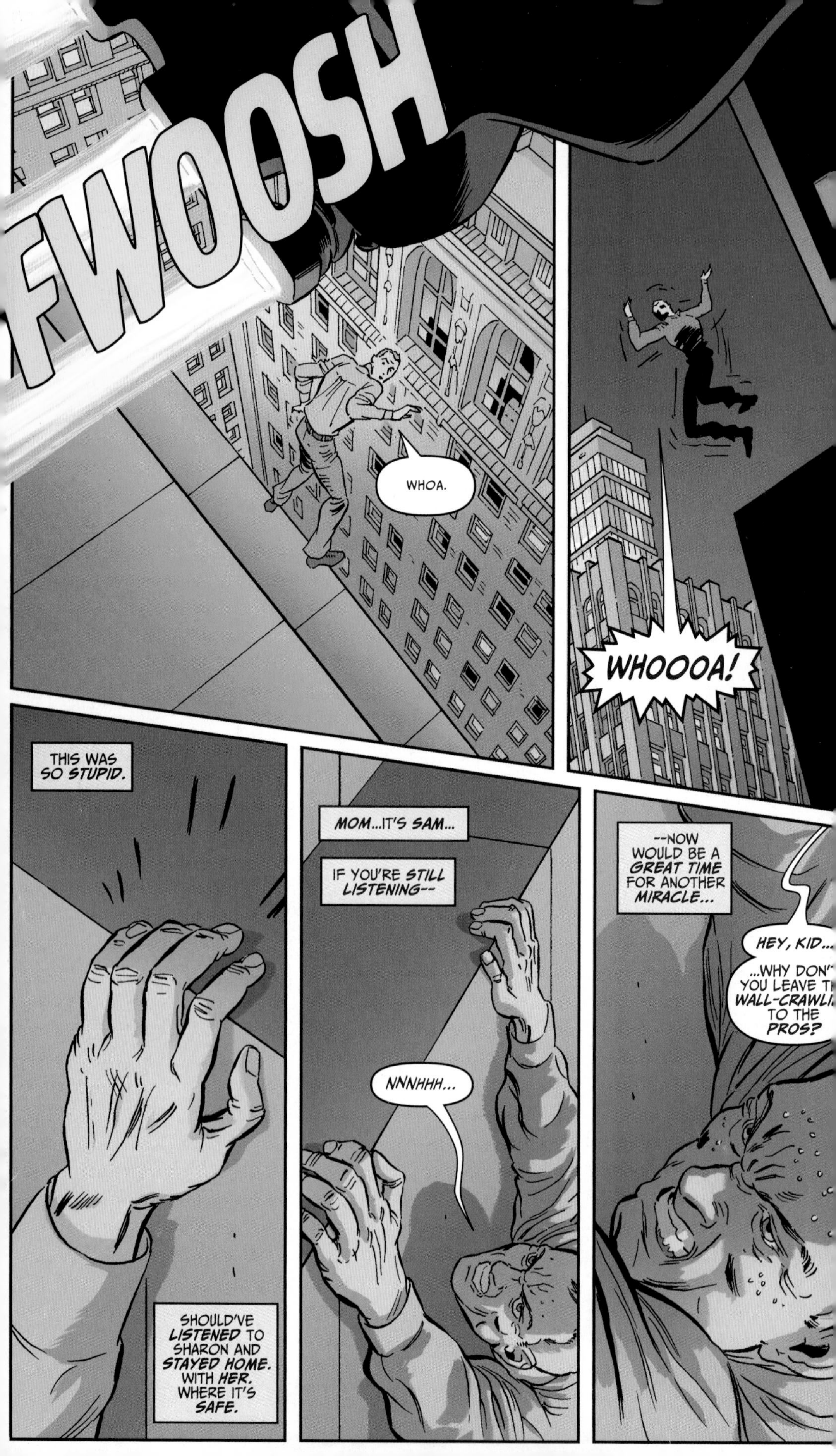
FWOOSH
WHOA.
WHOOOA!
THIS WAS SO STUPID.
SHOULD'VE LISTENED TO SHARON AND STAYED HOME. WITH HER. WHERE IT'S SAFE.
MOM...IT'S SAM...
IF YOU'RE STILL LISTENING--
NNNHHH...
--NOW WOULD BE A GREAT TIME FOR ANOTHER MIRACLE...
HEY, KID...
...WHY DON' YOU LEAVE T WALL-CRAWLI TO THE PROS?

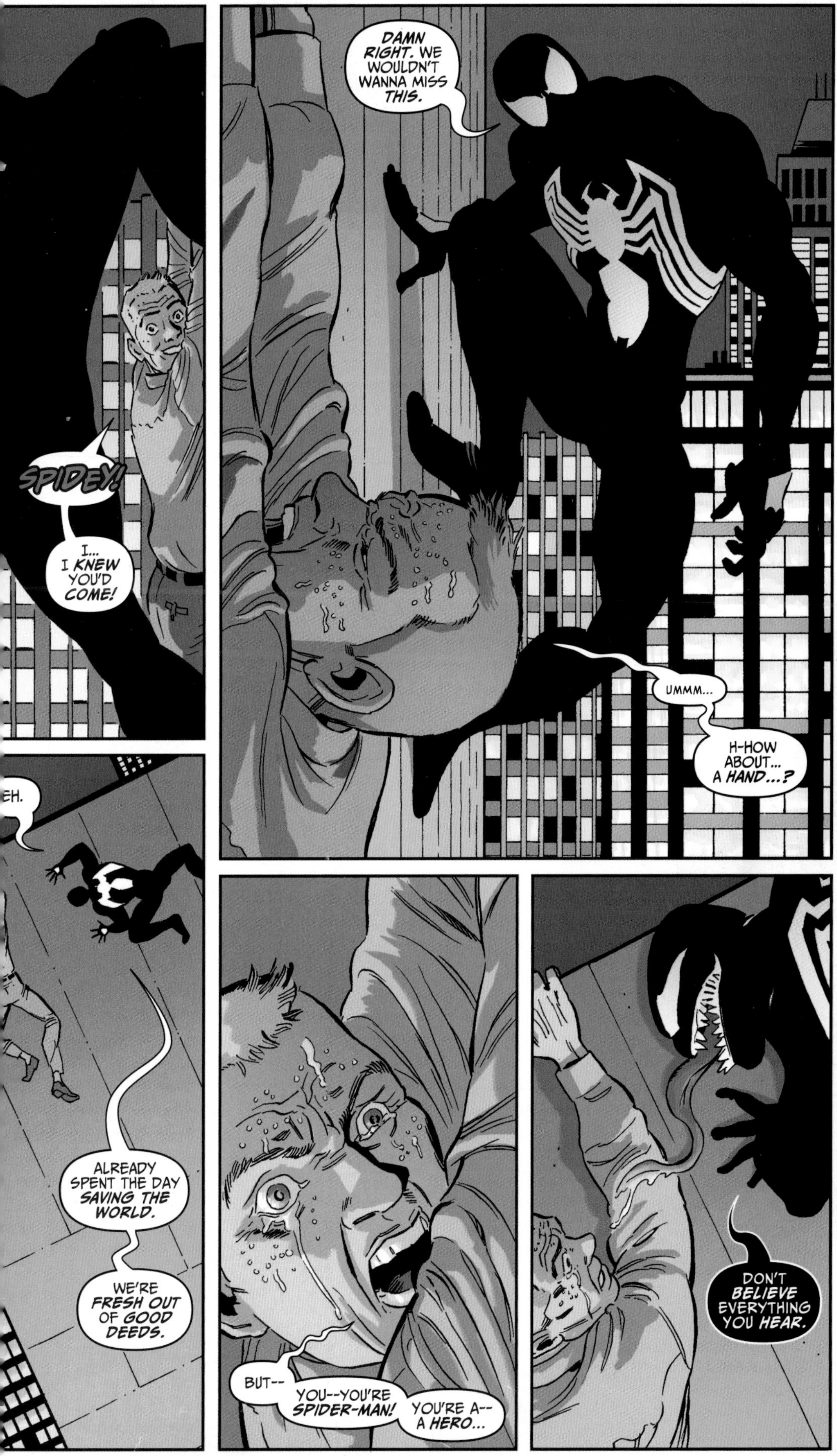
SPIDEY!
I... I KNEW YOU'D COME!
DAMN RIGHT. WE WOULDN'T WANNA MISS THIS.
UMMM...
H-HOW ABOUT... A HAND...?
EH.
ALREADY SPENT THE DAY SAVING THE WORLD.
WE'RE FRESH OUT OF GOOD DEEDS.
BUT--
YOU--YOU'RE SPIDER-MAN!
YOU'RE A--A HERO...
DON'T BELIEVE EVERYTHING YOU HEAR.

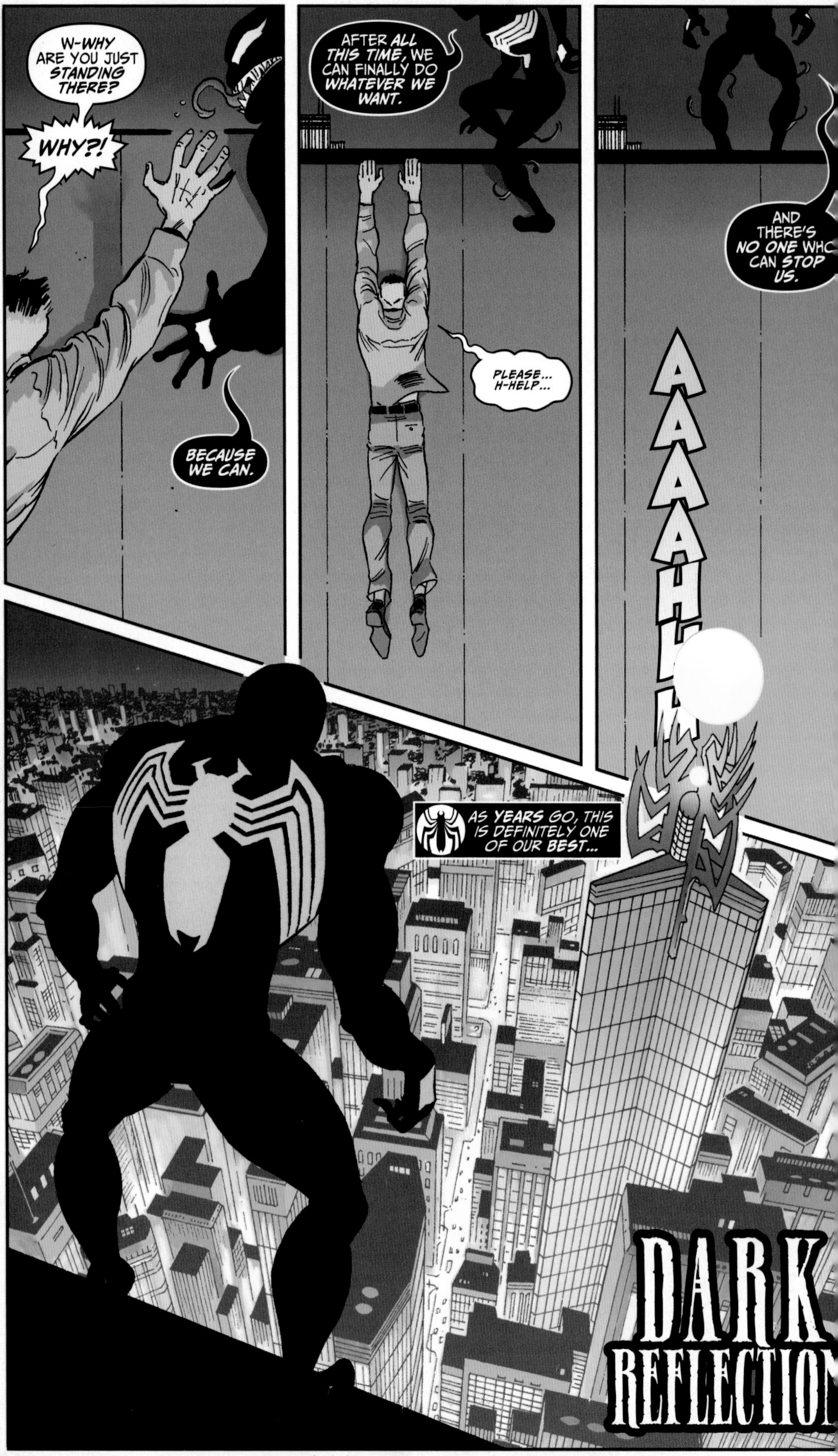
W-WHY ARE YOU JUST STANDING THERE?
WHY?!
BECAUSE WE CAN.
AFTER ALL THIS TIME, WE CAN FINALLY DO WHATEVER WE WANT.
PLEASE... H-HELP...
AND THERE'S NO ONE WHO CAN STOP US.
AAAAAHH
AS YEARS GO, THIS IS DEFINITELY ONE OF OUR BEST...
DARK REFLECTION

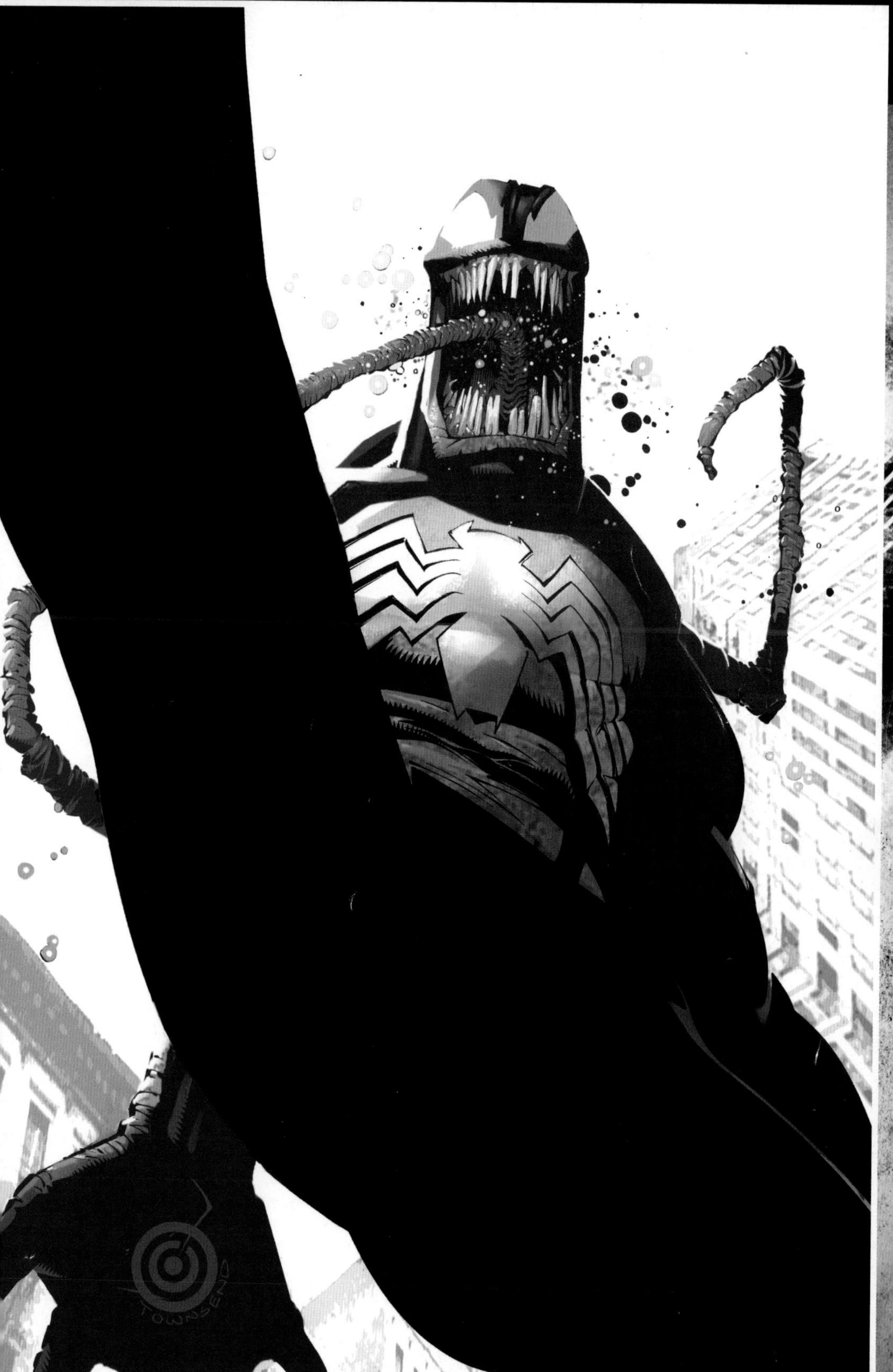
TOWNSEND

DARK REIGN: SINISTER SPIDER-MAN #1

WANTED

DEAD OR ~~DEAD~~ ~~OR~~ ALIVE

NAME: MacDonald "Mac" Gargan

ALIASES: The Scorpion, Venom

HEIGHT: Variable

WEIGHT: Variable

IF SEEN, PLEASE CONTACT:
ANTHONY DIAL
PRODUCTION

Gargan's one of the all-time great lowli
an unscrupulous private eye who volunte
to get genetically engineered into the su
human Scorpion, Gargan got locked in a vic
cycle of low-impact crime and high-im
beatdowns from Spider-Man.

All that changed when he bonded
the Venom symbiote and became a new V
— one with even more power than its prev
incarnation, Eddie Brock — and none of Bro
conscience. Gargan was recruited by th
Government to hunt down superhumans
didn't comply with the Superhuman Regis
tion Act.

Serving under the leadership of No
Osborn, (the former Green Goblin and
around sociopathic billionaire), Gargan be
increasingly unhinged and violent, devou
limbs and sometimes whole people in the
of combat. When Osborn ascended to leade
of all things superhuman in the United St
he brought Gargan along to be a member o
Avengers team in the guise of Spider-Man.

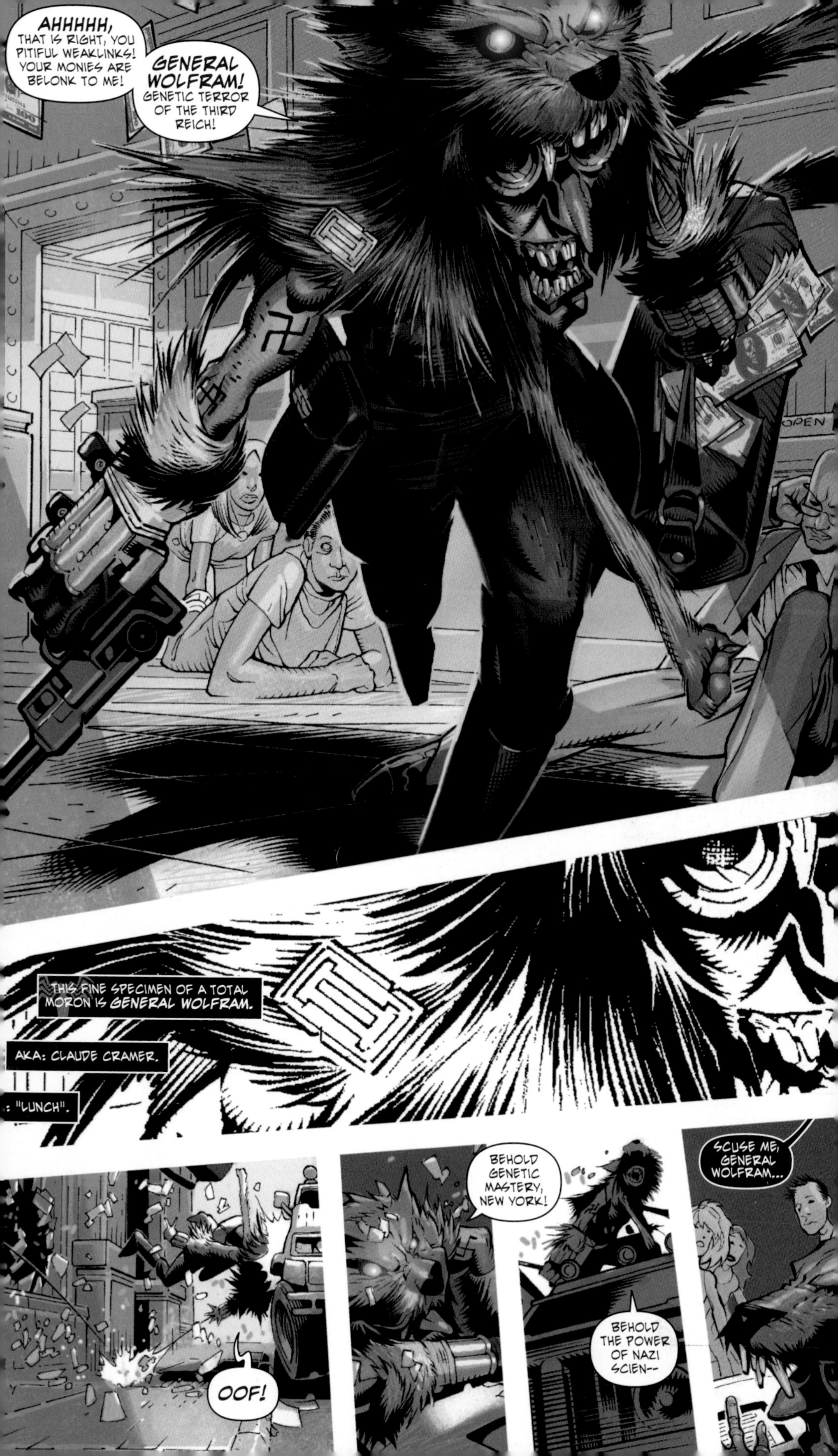
AHHHHH, THAT IS RIGHT, YOU PITIFUL WEAKLINKS! YOUR MONIES ARE BELONK TO ME!
GENERAL WOLFRAM! GENETIC TERROR OF THE THIRD REICH!
OPEN
THIS FINE SPECIMEN OF A TOTAL MORON IS GENERAL WOLFRAM.
AKA: CLAUDE CRAMER.
: "LUNCH".
OOF!
BEHOLD GENETIC MASTERY, NEW YORK!
BEHOLD THE POWER OF NAZI SCIEN--
SCUSE ME, GENERAL WOLFRAM...

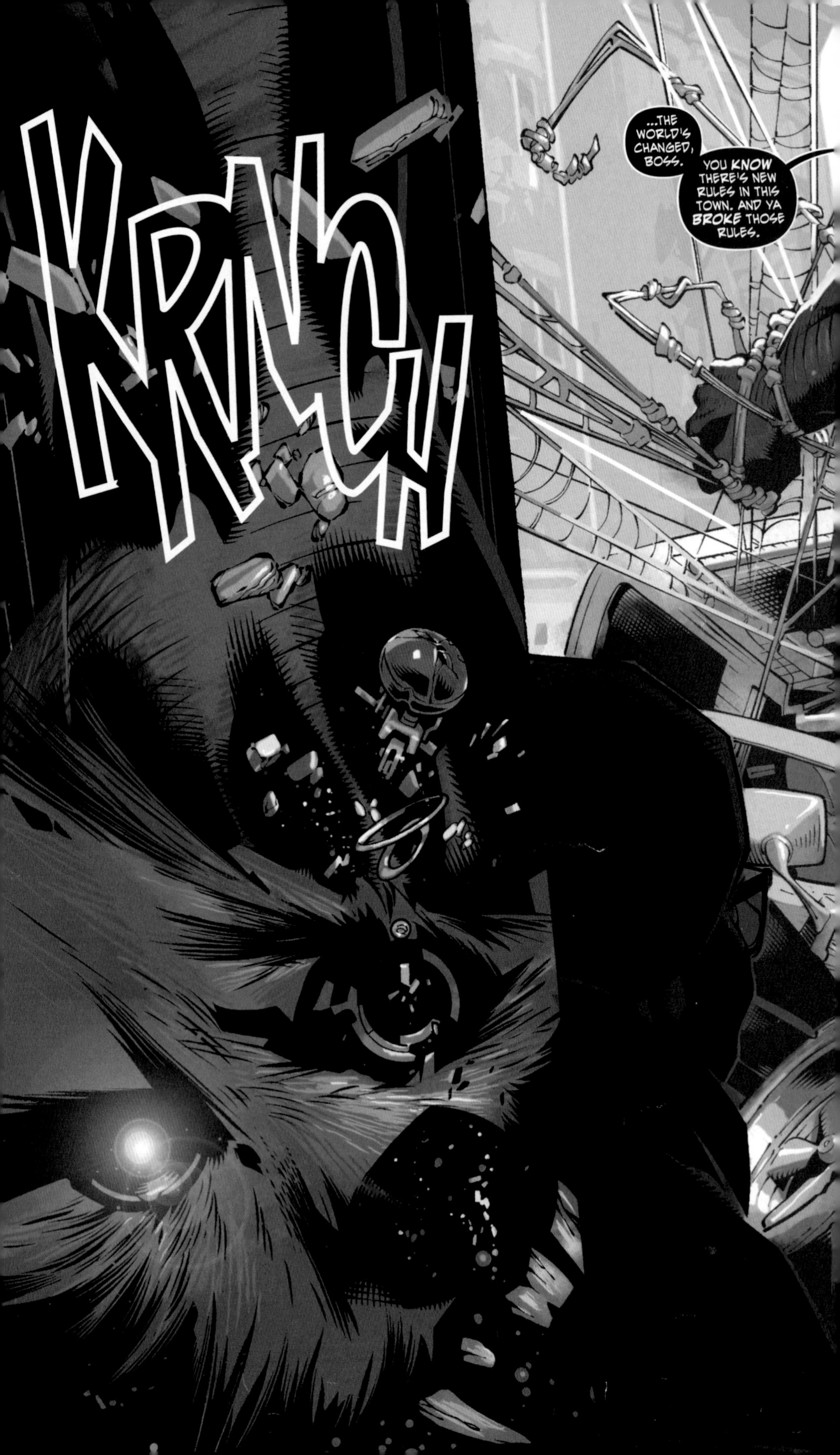
KRNCH
...THE WORLD'S CHANGED, BOSS.
YOU KNOW THERE'S NEW RULES IN THIS TOWN. AND YA BROKE THOSE RULES.

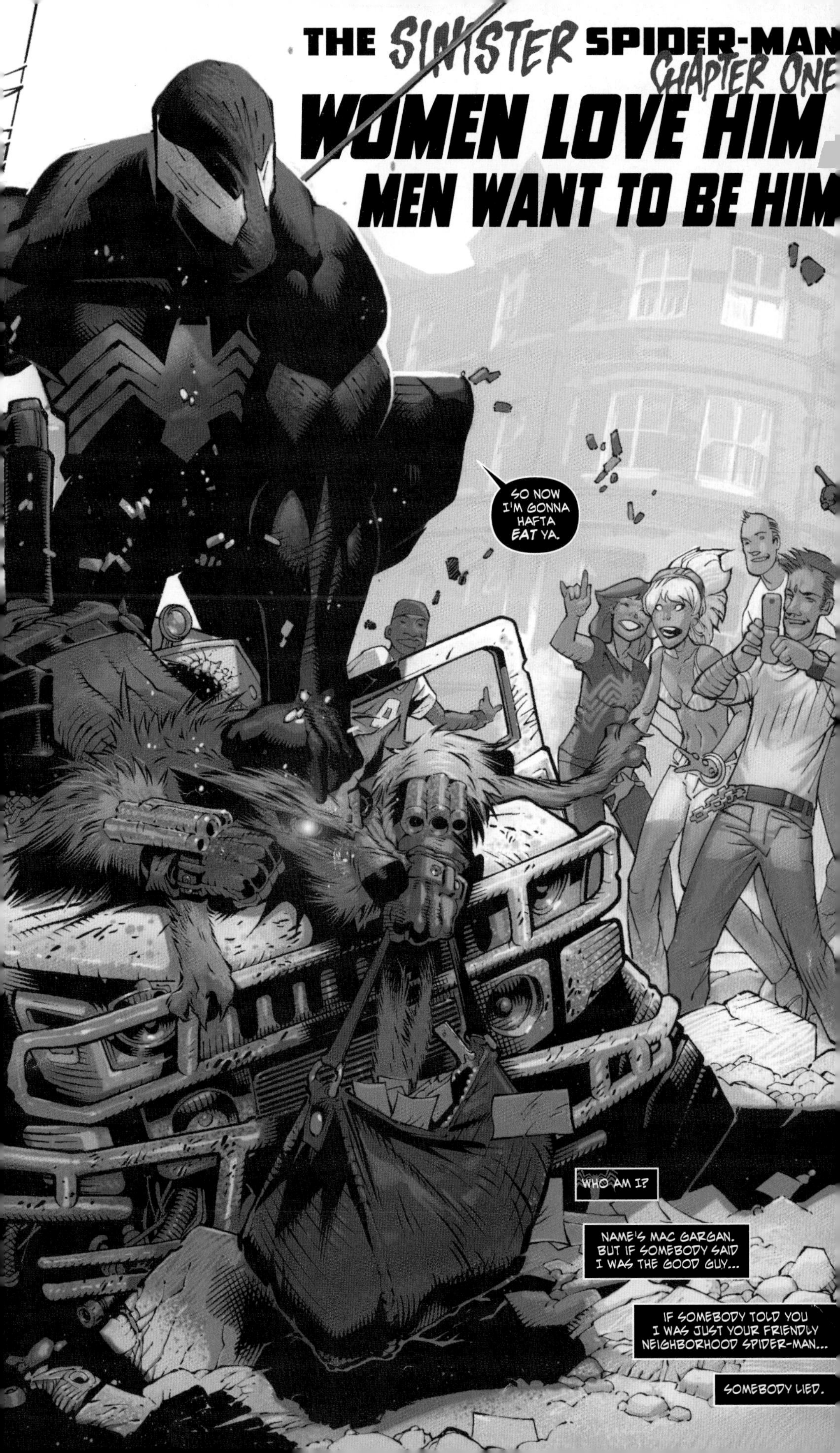
THE SINISTER SPIDER-MAN
CHAPTER ONE
WOMEN LOVE HIM
MEN WANT TO BE HIM
SO NOW I'M GONNA HAFTA EAT YA.
WHO AM I?
NAME'S MAC GARGAN. BUT IF SOMEBODY SAID I WAS THE GOOD GUY...
IF SOMEBODY TOLD YOU I WAS JUST YOUR FRIENDLY NEIGHBORHOOD SPIDER-MAN...
SOMEBODY LIED.

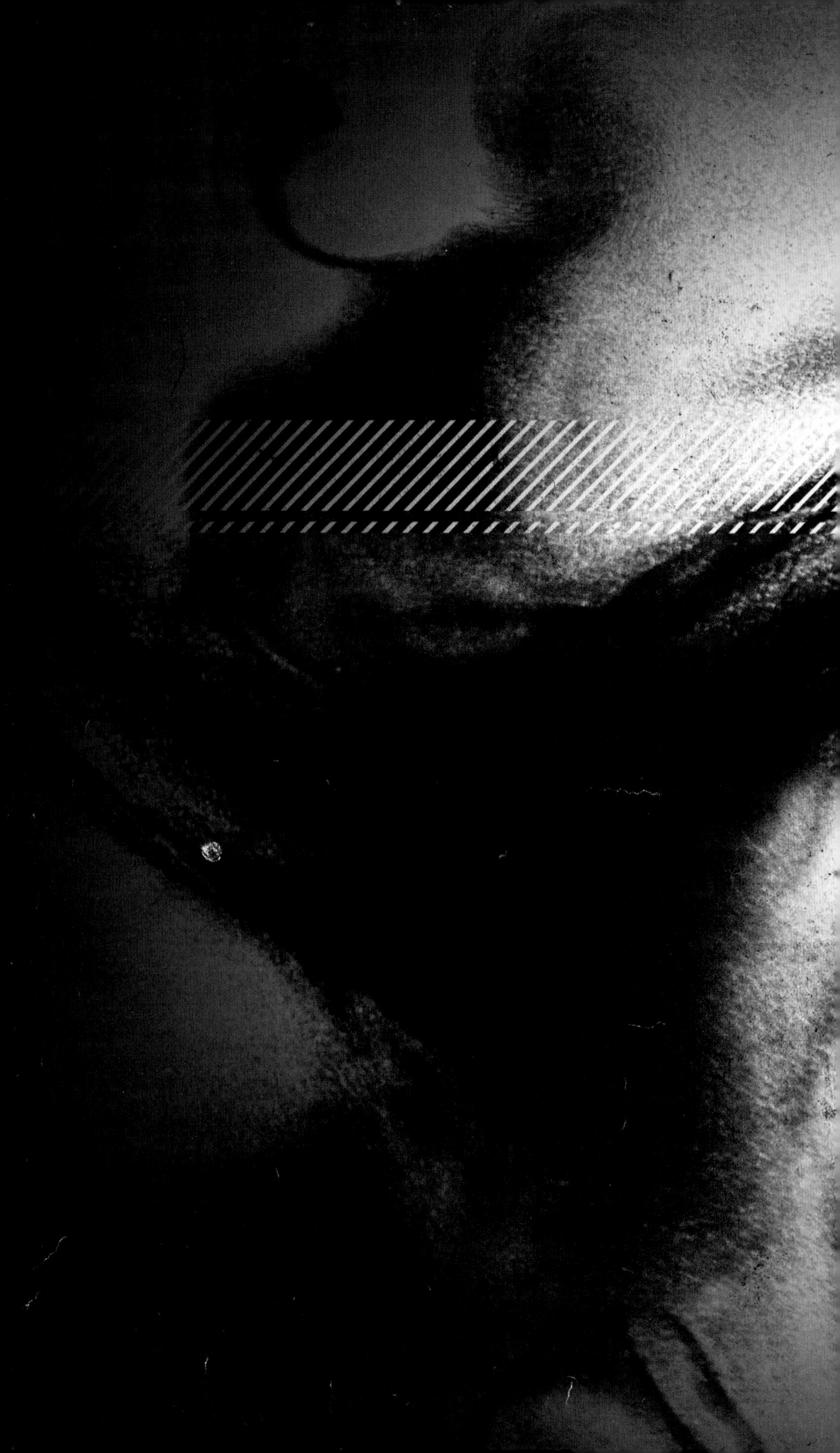

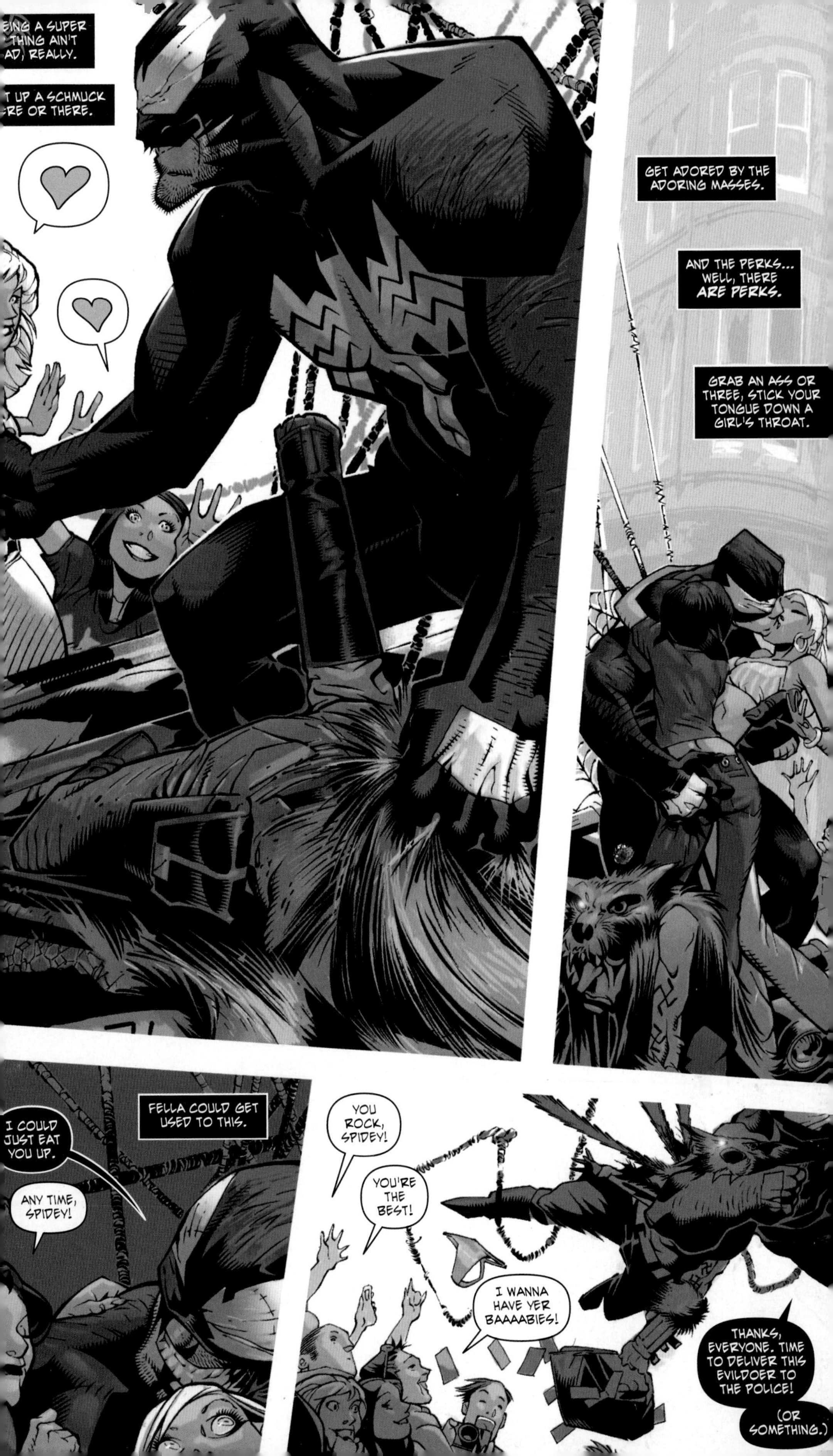
EING A SUPER
THING AIN'T
AD, REALLY.
T UP A SCHMUCK
RE OR THERE.
GET ADORED BY THE ADORING MASSES.
AND THE PERKS... WELL, THERE ARE PERKS.
GRAB AN ASS OR THREE, STICK YOUR TONGUE DOWN A GIRL'S THROAT.
FELLA COULD GET USED TO THIS.
I COULD JUST EAT YOU UP.
ANY TIME, SPIDEY!
YOU ROCK, SPIDEY!
YOU'RE THE BEST!
I WANNA HAVE YER BAAAABIES!
THANKS, EVERYONE. TIME TO DELIVER THIS EVILDOER TO THE POLICE!
(OR SOMETHING.)

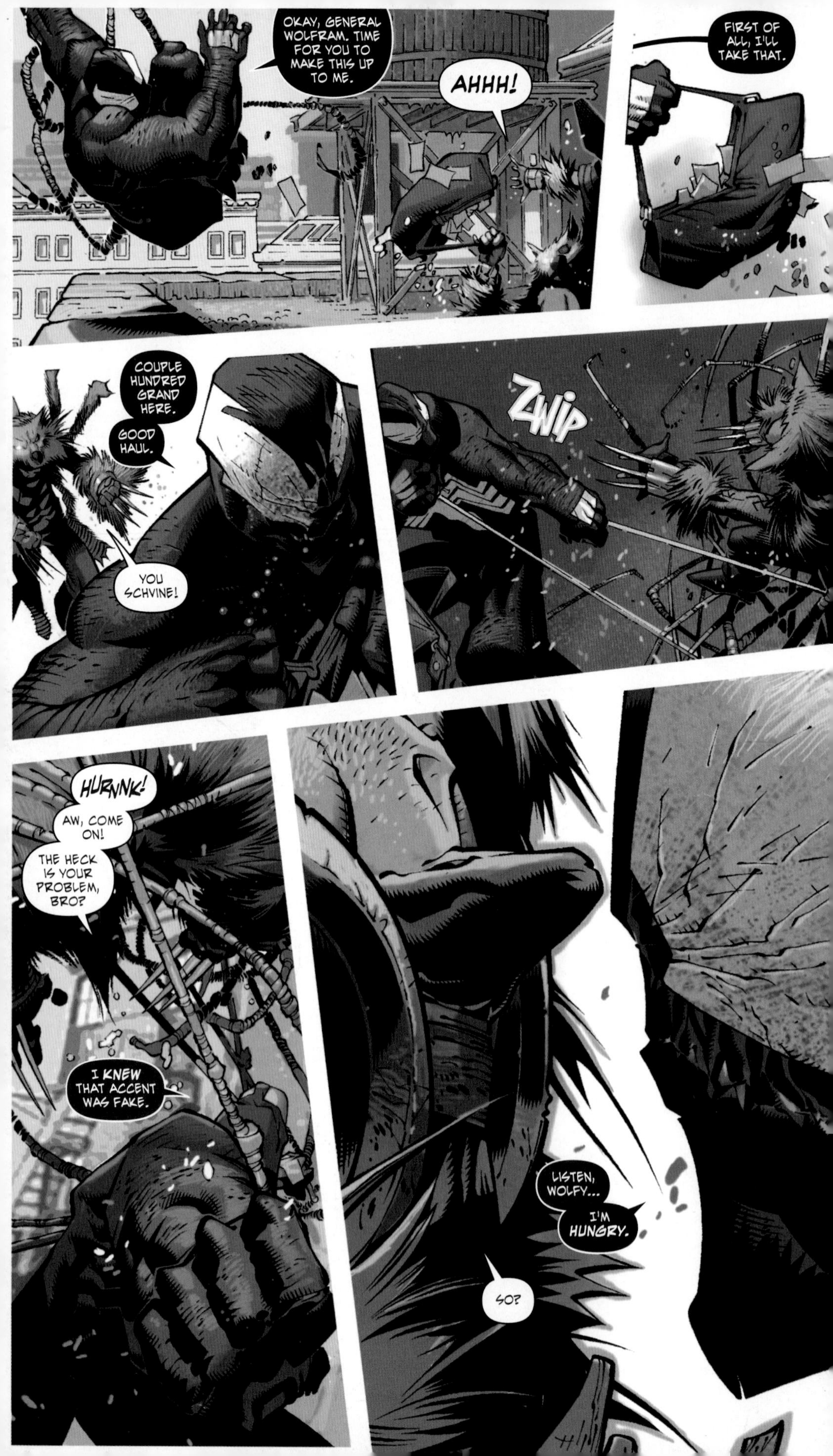
OKAY, GENERAL WOLFRAM. TIME FOR YOU TO MAKE THIS UP TO ME.
AHHH!
FIRST OF ALL, I'LL TAKE THAT.
COUPLE HUNDRED GRAND HERE.
GOOD HAUL.
YOU SCHVINE!
ZWIP
HURNNK!
AW, COME ON!
THE HECK IS YOUR PROBLEM, BRO?
I KNEW THAT ACCENT WAS FAKE.
LISTEN, WOLFY...
I'M HUNGRY.
SO?

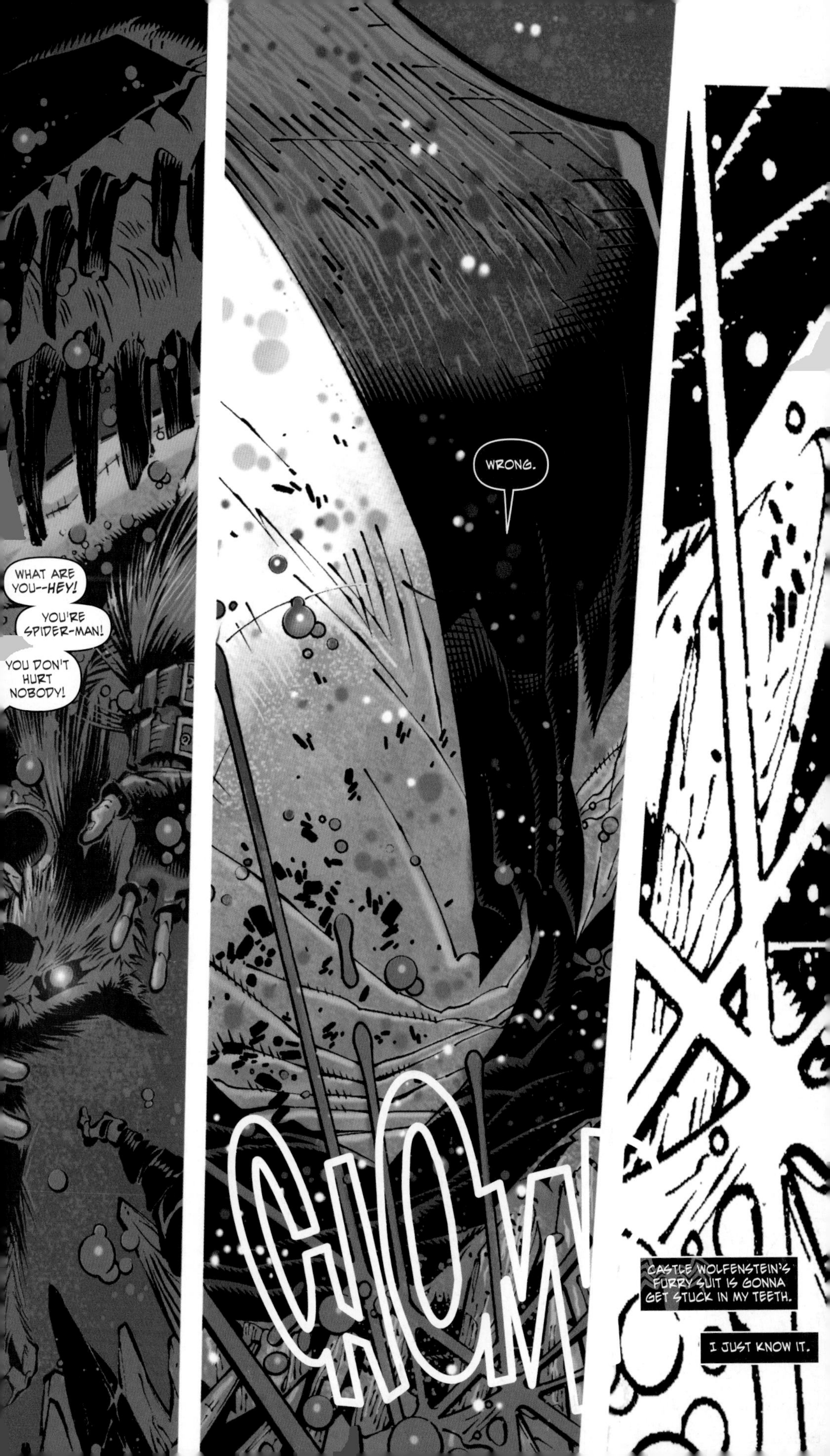

WHAT ARE YOU--HEY!
YOU'RE SPIDER-MAN!
YOU DON'T HURT NOBODY!
WRONG.
CHOW
CASTLE WOLFENSTEIN'S FURRY SUIT IS GONNA GET STUCK IN MY TEETH.
I JUST KNOW IT.

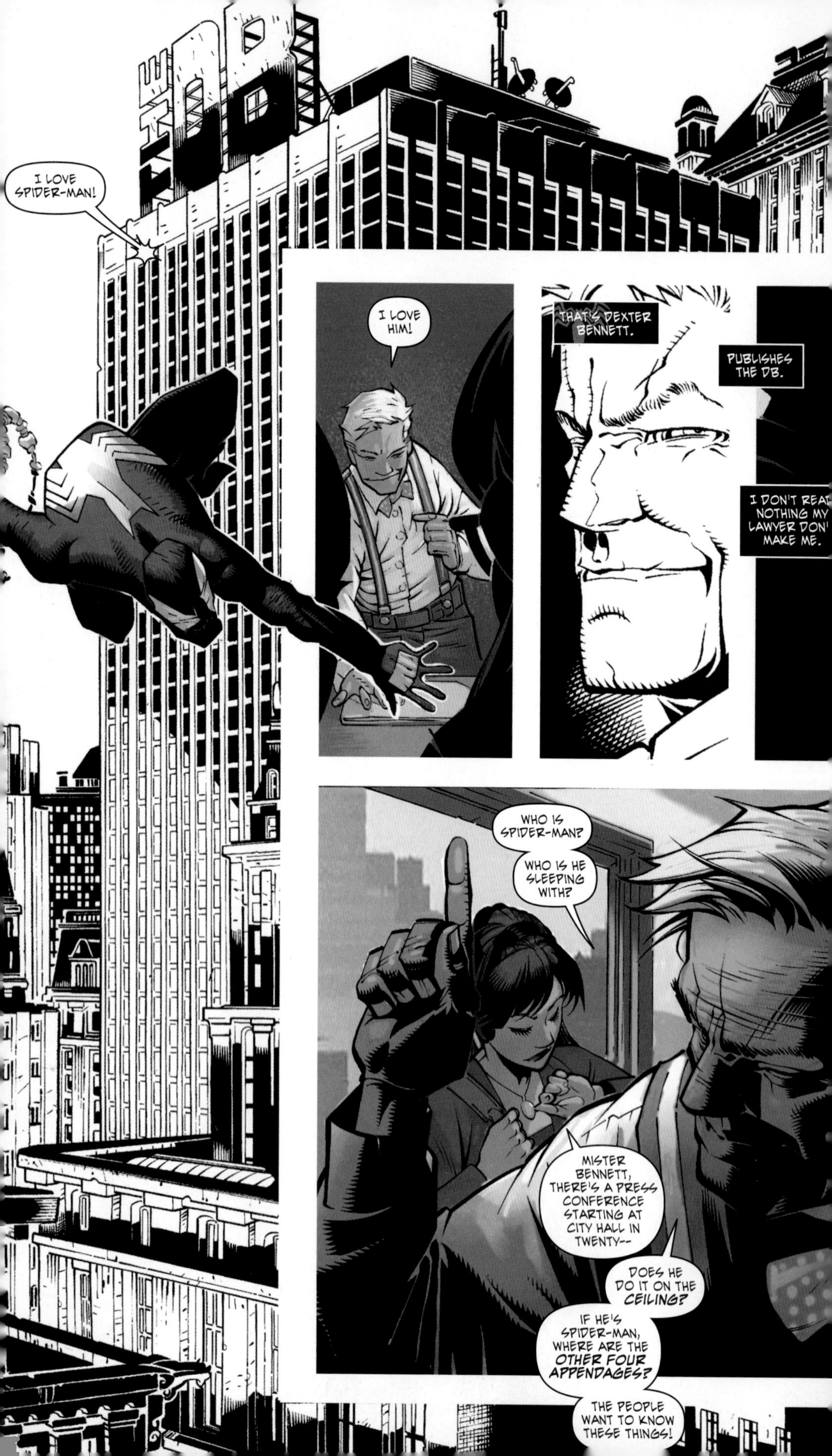

I LOVE SPIDER-MAN!
I LOVE HIM!
THAT'S DEXTER BENNETT.
PUBLISHES THE DB.
I DON'T REA NOTHING MY LAWYER DON' MAKE ME.
WHO IS SPIDER-MAN?
WHO IS HE SLEEPING WITH?
MISTER BENNETT, THERE'S A PRESS CONFERENCE STARTING AT CITY HALL IN TWENTY--
DOES HE DO IT ON THE CEILING?
IF HE'S SPIDER-MAN, WHERE ARE THE OTHER FOUR APPENDAGES?
THE PEOPLE WANT TO KNOW THESE THINGS!

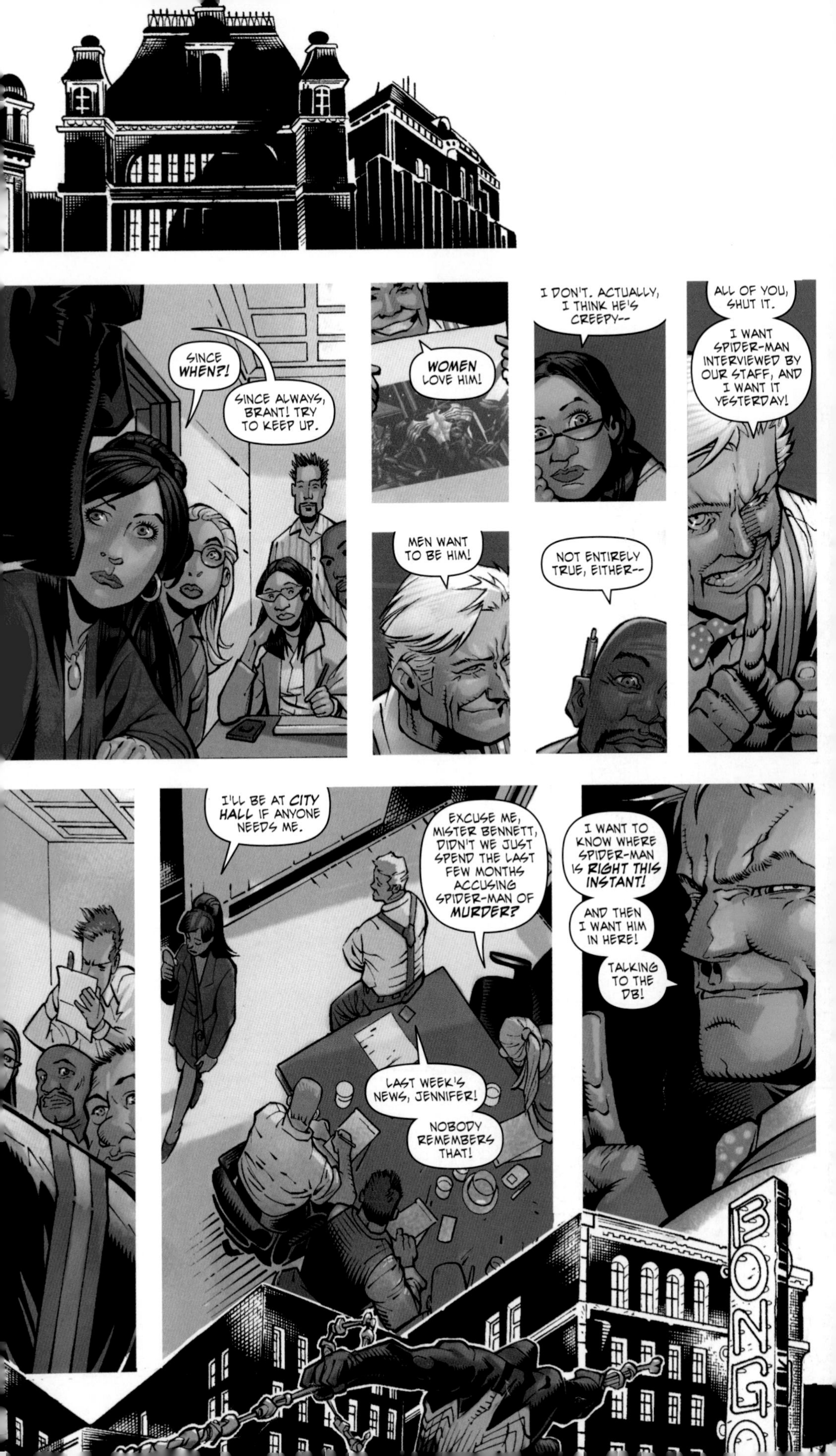
SINCE WHEN?!
SINCE ALWAYS, BRANT! TRY TO KEEP UP.
WOMEN LOVE HIM!
I DON'T. ACTUALLY, I THINK HE'S CREEPY--
MEN WANT TO BE HIM!
NOT ENTIRELY TRUE, EITHER--
ALL OF YOU, SHUT IT.
I WANT SPIDER-MAN INTERVIEWED BY OUR STAFF, AND I WANT IT YESTERDAY!
I'LL BE AT CITY HALL IF ANYONE NEEDS ME.
EXCUSE ME, MISTER BENNETT, DIDN'T WE JUST SPEND THE LAST FEW MONTHS ACCUSING SPIDER-MAN OF MURDER?
LAST WEEK'S NEWS, JENNIFER!
NOBODY REMEMBERS THAT!
I WANT TO KNOW WHERE SPIDER-MAN IS RIGHT THIS INSTANT!
AND THEN I WANT HIM IN HERE!
TALKING TO THE DB!
BONGO

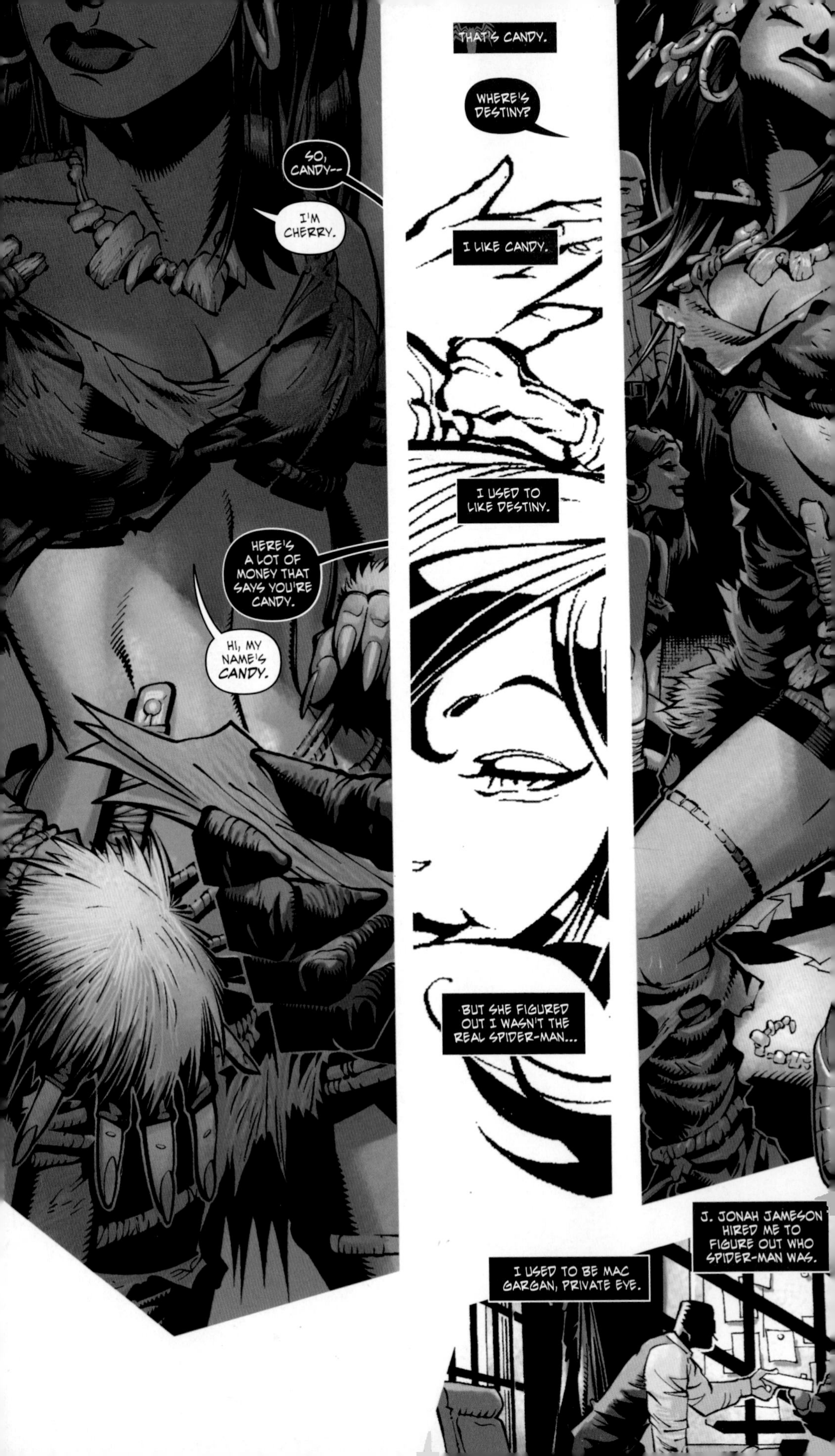

SO, CANDY--
I'M CHERRY.
HERE'S A LOT OF MONEY THAT SAYS YOU'RE CANDY.
HI, MY NAME'S CANDY.
THAT'S CANDY.
WHERE'S DESTINY?
I LIKE CANDY.
I USED TO LIKE DESTINY.
BUT SHE FIGURED OUT I WASN'T THE REAL SPIDER-MAN...
I USED TO BE MAC GARGAN, PRIVATE EYE.
J. JONAH JAMESON HIRED ME TO FIGURE OUT WHO SPIDER-MAN WAS.

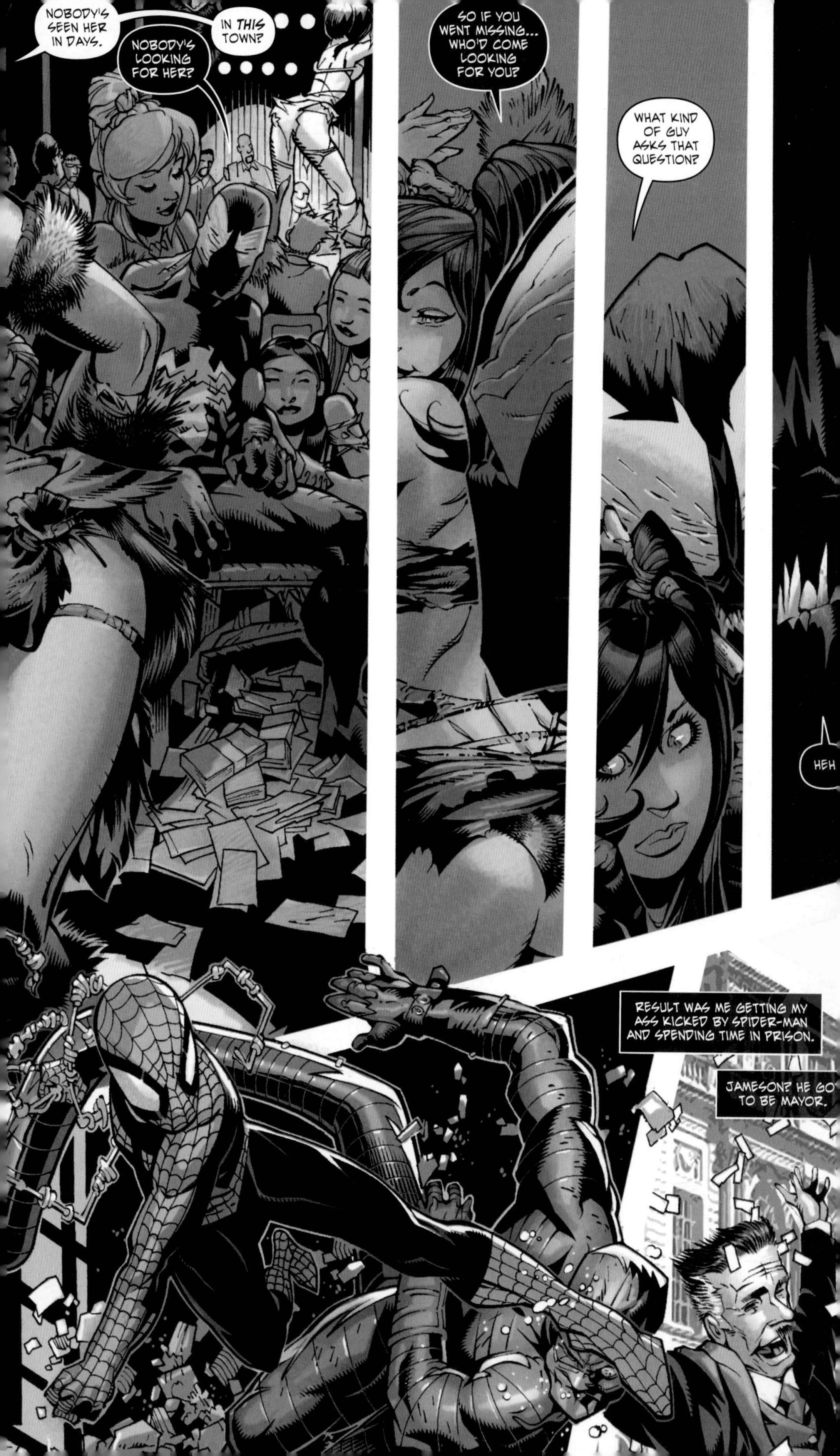
NOBODY'S SEEN HER IN DAYS.
IN THIS TOWN?
NOBODY'S LOOKING FOR HER?
SO IF YOU WENT MISSING... WHO'D COME LOOKING FOR YOU?
WHAT KIND OF GUY ASKS THAT QUESTION?
HEH
RESULT WAS ME GETTING MY ASS KICKED BY SPIDER-MAN AND SPENDING TIME IN PRISON.
JAMESON? HE GOT TO BE MAYOR.

EVENTUALLY, I WAS FUSED WITH THE ALIEN SYMBIOTE VENOM...

BUT NOW I'M AN AVENGER, AND EVERYBODY THINKS I'M SPIDER-MAN.

SO I FIGURE IT'S TIME TO PUT J. JONAH JAMESON IN HIS PLACE.

CITY HALL...

SINCE YOU WERE ELECTED, MAYOR JAMESON, CRIME HAS RISEN 7%.

THAT'S NONSENSE AND YOU KNOW IT.

LOOK AT HIM. A GROWN MAN-- MAYOR OF THE *WORLD'S GREATEST CITY*--WITH THAT *HAIRCUT*.

WITH THAT *MUSTACHE!*

I LITERALLY *EAT PEOPLE* FOR *BREAKFAST* AND I DON'T HAVE THE CAJONES TO GROW A *HITLER 'STACHE*.

IT'S IN THE NUMBERS DISTRIBUTED BY *YOUR* OFFICE.

AH. RIGHT. THOSE NUMBERS WERE PRELIMINARY DATA.

PROJECTIONS, IF YOU WILL, OF, UH, A *WORST CASE SCENARIO* IF WE WERE TO DO *NOTHING*.

BUT WE *ARE* DOING SOMETHING. SO THOSE NUMBERS ARE NOTHING TO WORRY ABOUT.

FAIR ENOUGH...

WHAT A[R]E YOU DOI[NG] EXACTL[Y]

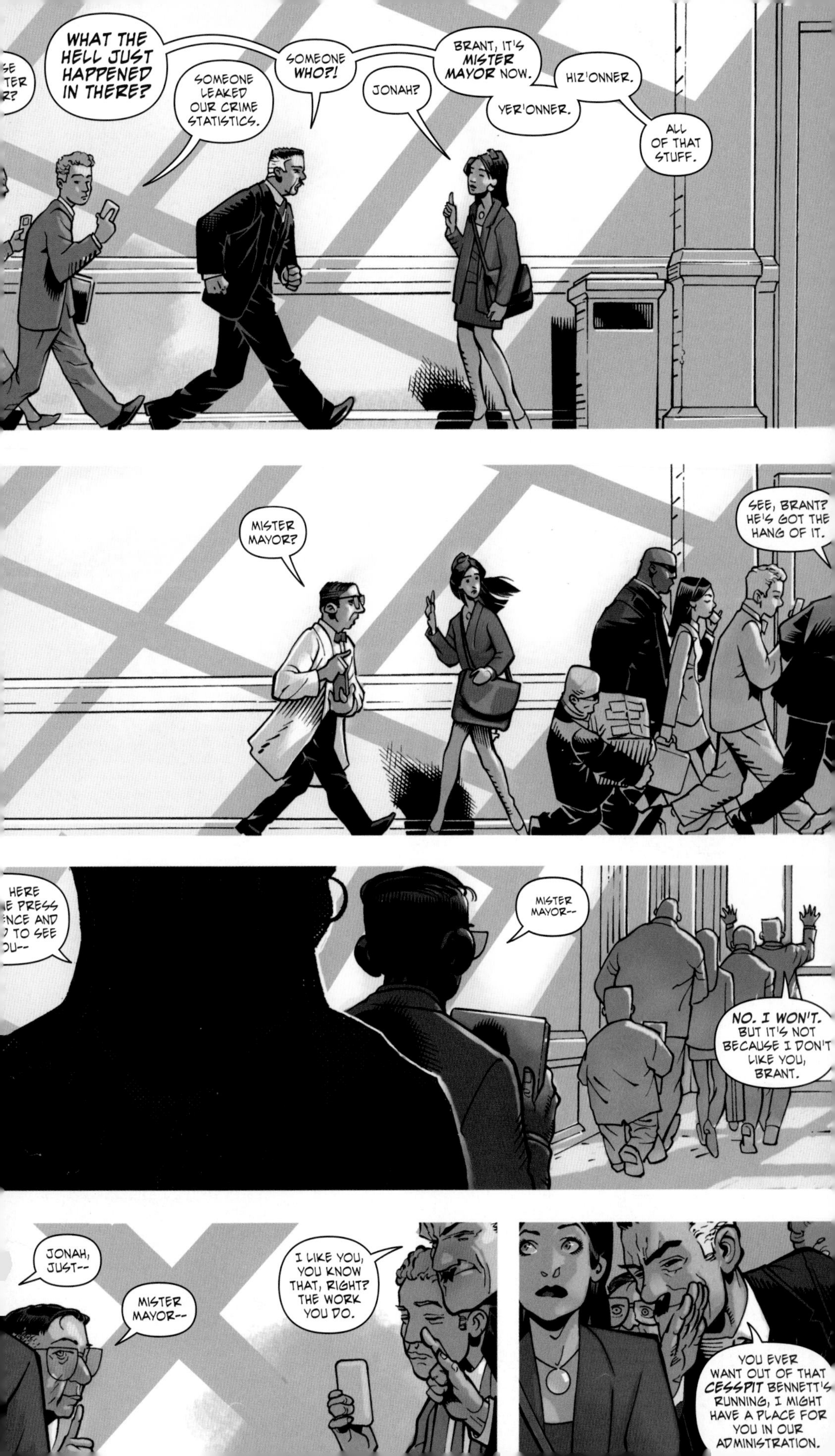

WHAT THE HELL JUST HAPPENED IN THERE?
SOMEONE LEAKED OUR CRIME STATISTICS.
SOMEONE WHO?!
JONAH?
BRANT, IT'S MISTER MAYOR NOW.
YER'ONNER.
HIZ'ONNER.
ALL OF THAT STUFF.
MISTER MAYOR?
SEE, BRANT? HE'S GOT THE HANG OF IT.
MISTER MAYOR--
NO. I WON'T. BUT IT'S NOT BECAUSE I DON'T LIKE YOU, BRANT.
JONAH, JUST--
MISTER MAYOR--
I LIKE YOU, YOU KNOW THAT, RIGHT? THE WORK YOU DO.
YOU EVER WANT OUT OF THAT CESSPIT BENNETT'S RUNNING, I MIGHT HAVE A PLACE FOR YOU IN OUR ADMINISTRATION.

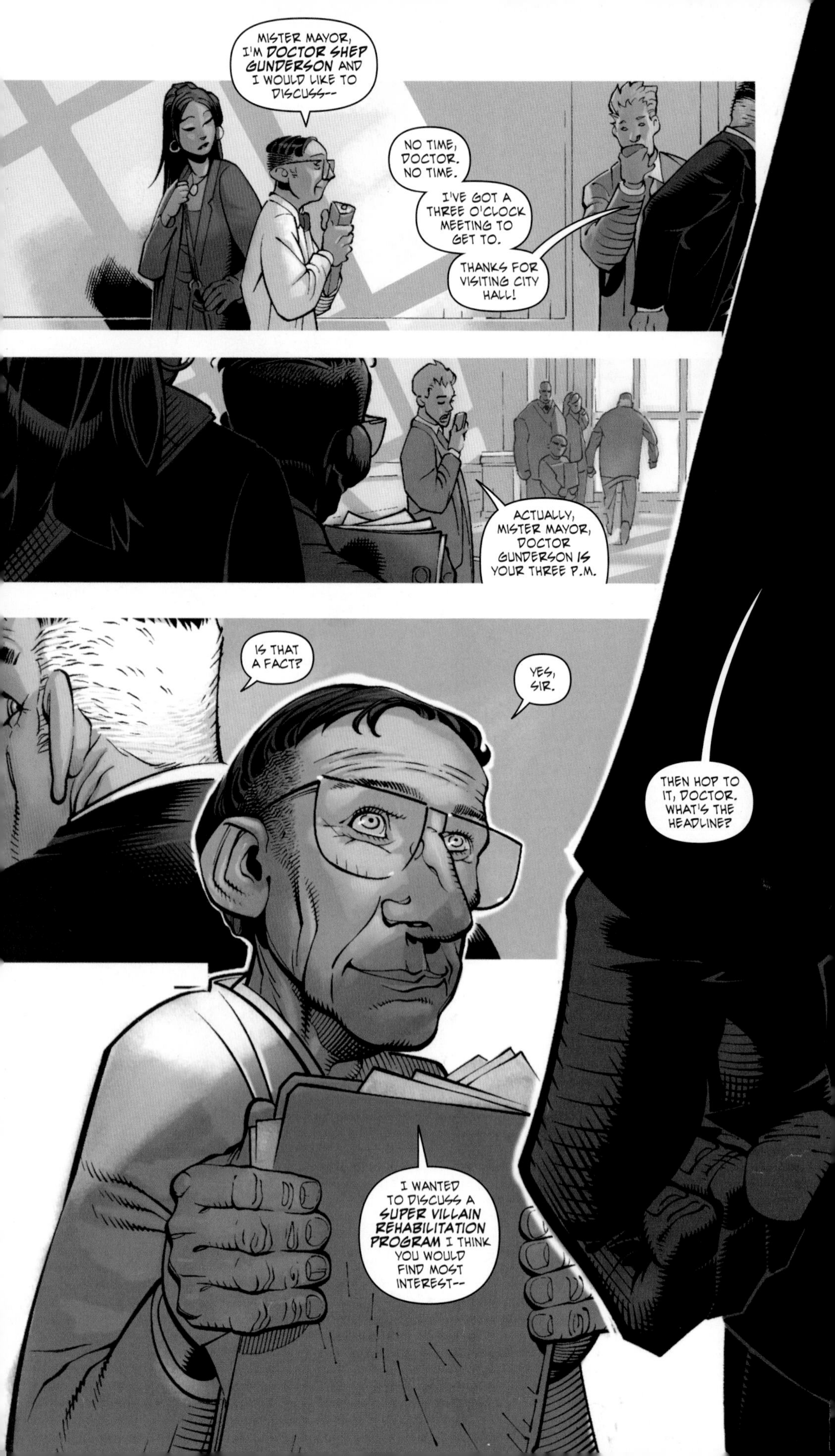
MISTER MAYOR, I'M DOCTOR SHEP GUNDERSON AND I WOULD LIKE TO DISCUSS--
NO TIME, DOCTOR. NO TIME.
I'VE GOT A THREE O'CLOCK MEETING TO GET TO.
THANKS FOR VISITING CITY HALL!
ACTUALLY, MISTER MAYOR, DOCTOR GUNDERSON IS YOUR THREE P.M.
IS THAT A FACT?
YES, SIR.
THEN HOP TO IT, DOCTOR. WHAT'S THE HEADLINE?
I WANTED TO DISCUSS A SUPER VILLAIN REHABILITATION PROGRAM I THINK YOU WOULD FIND MOST INTEREST--

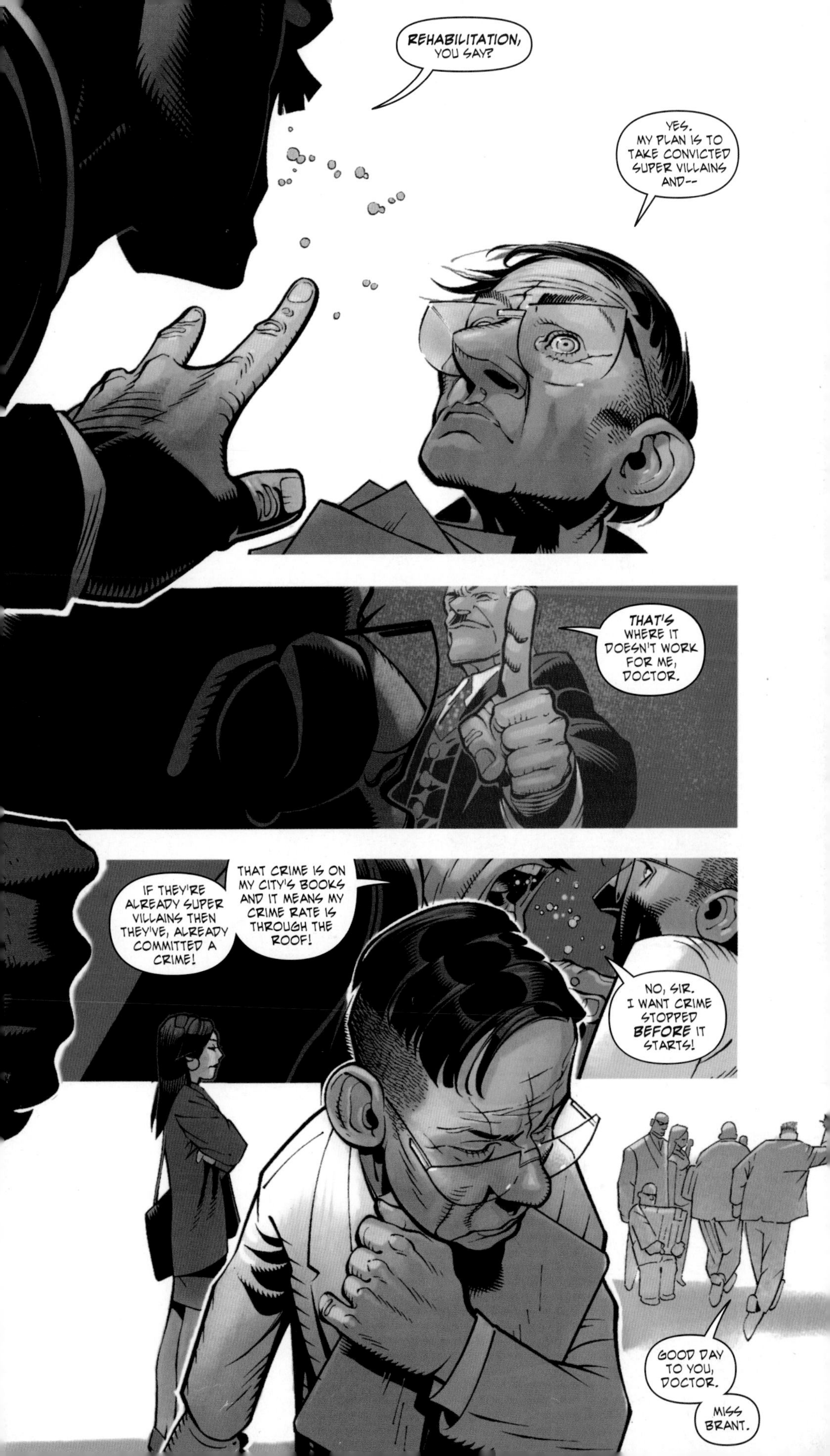
REHABILITATION, YOU SAY?
YES. MY PLAN IS TO TAKE CONVICTED SUPER VILLAINS AND--
THAT'S WHERE IT DOESN'T WORK FOR ME, DOCTOR.
IF THEY'RE ALREADY SUPER VILLAINS THEN THEY'VE, ALREADY COMMITTED A CRIME!
THAT CRIME IS ON MY CITY'S BOOKS AND IT MEANS MY CRIME RATE IS THROUGH THE ROOF!
NO, SIR. I WANT CRIME STOPPED BEFORE IT STARTS!
GOOD DAY TO YOU, DOCTOR.
MISS BRANT.

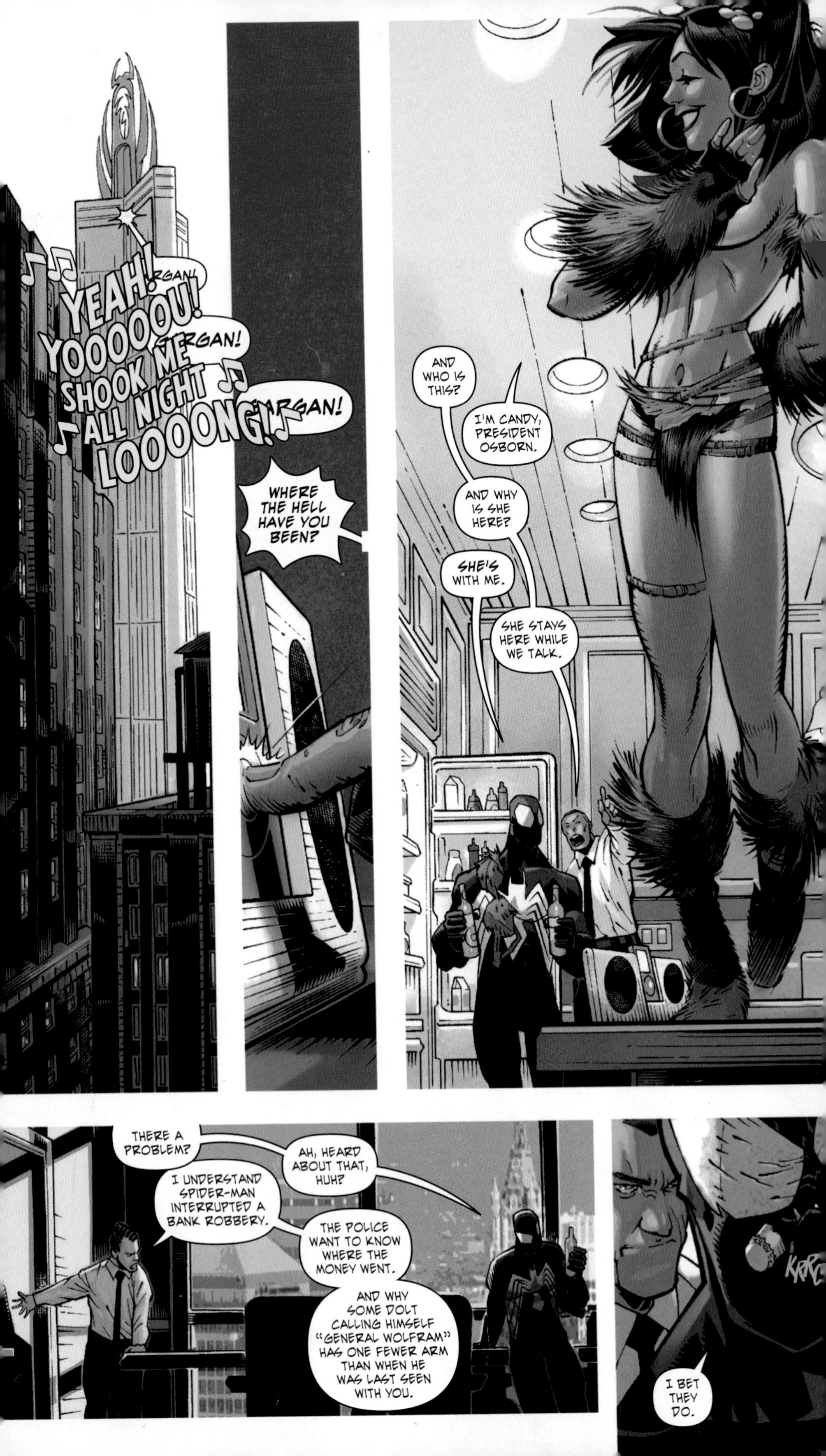
YEAH! YOOOOOU! SHOOK ME ALL NIGHT LOOOONG!
WHERE THE HELL HAVE YOU BEEN?
AND WHO IS THIS?
I'M CANDY, PRESIDENT OSBORN.
AND WHY IS SHE HERE?
SHE'S WITH ME.
SHE STAYS HERE WHILE WE TALK.
THERE A PROBLEM?
AH, HEARD ABOUT THAT, HUH?
I UNDERSTAND SPIDER-MAN INTERRUPTED A BANK ROBBERY.
THE POLICE WANT TO KNOW WHERE THE MONEY WENT.
AND WHY SOME DOLT CALLING HIMSELF "GENERAL WOLFRAM" HAS ONE FEWER ARM THAN WHEN HE WAS LAST SEEN WITH YOU.
KRRC
I BET THEY DO.

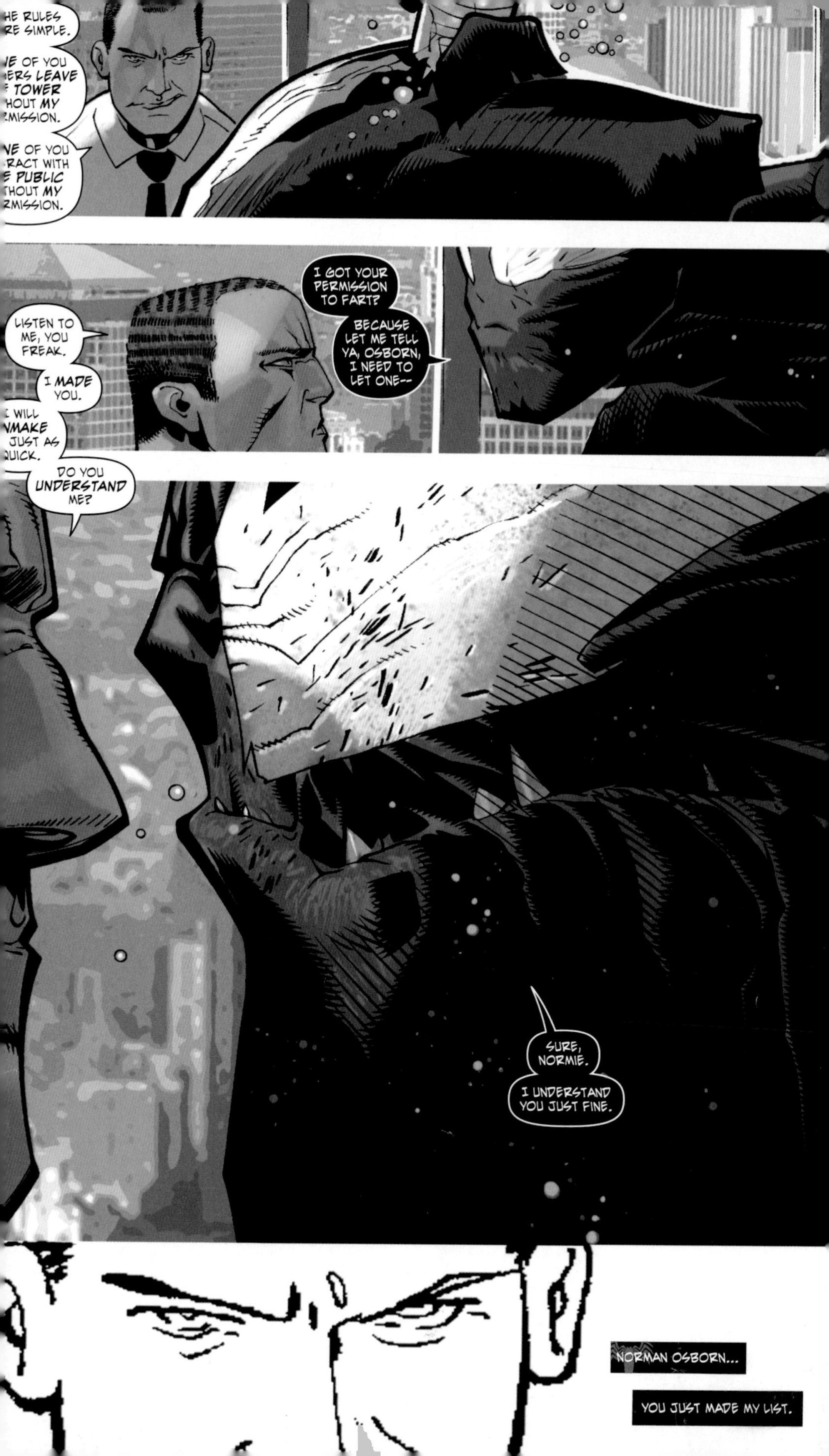

HE RULES RE SIMPLE.
NE OF YOU ERS LEAVE TOWER HOUT MY RMISSION.
NE OF YOU RACT WITH PUBLIC THOUT MY RMISSION.
LISTEN TO ME, YOU FREAK.
I MADE YOU.
WILL NMAKE JUST AS UICK.
I GOT YOUR PERMISSION TO FART?
BECAUSE LET ME TELL YA, OSBORN, I NEED TO LET ONE--
DO YOU UNDERSTAND ME?
SURE, NORMIE.
I UNDERSTAND YOU JUST FINE.
NORMAN OSBORN...
YOU JUST MADE MY LIST.

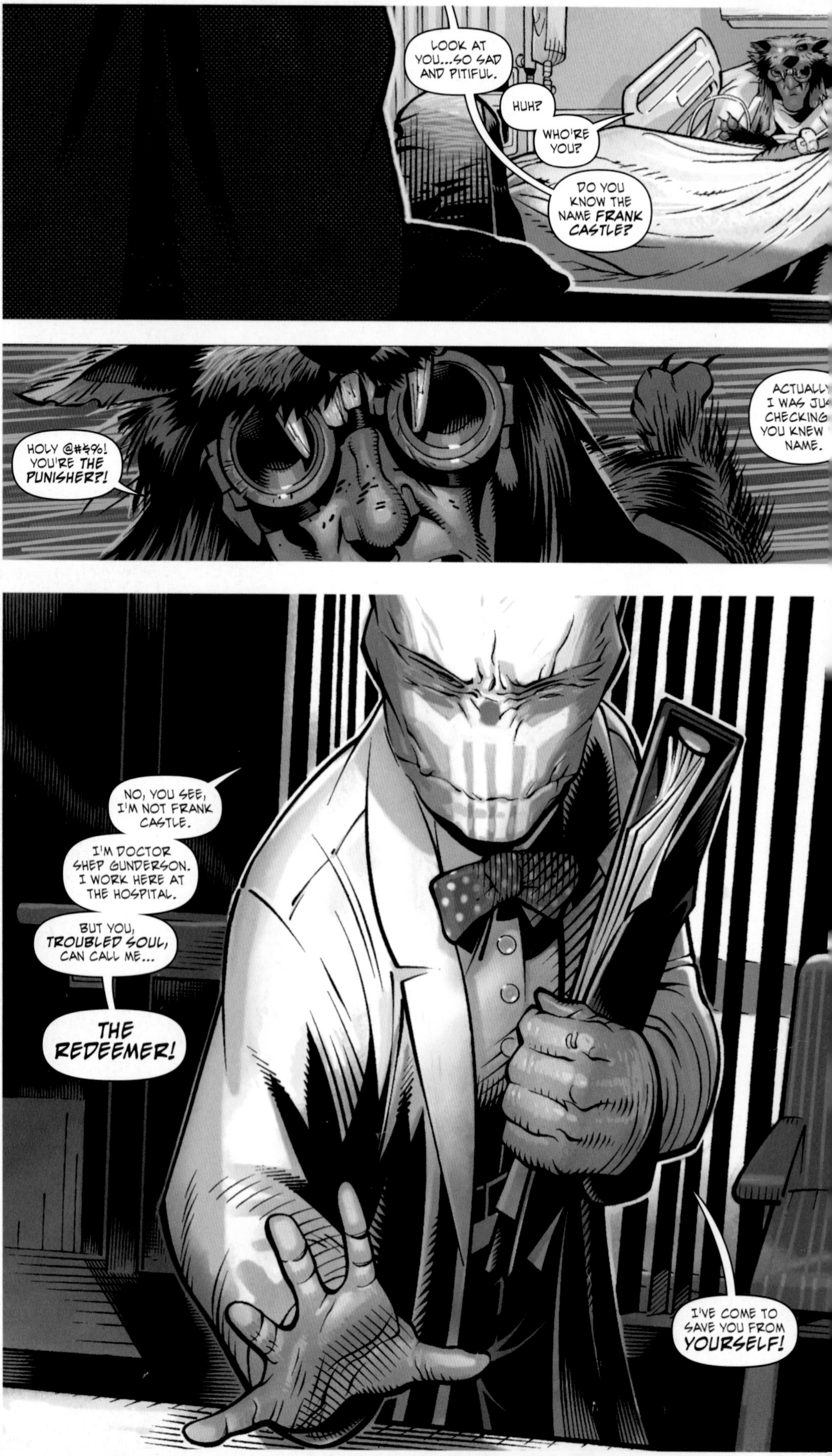
LOOK AT YOU...SO SAD AND PITIFUL.
HUH?
WHO'RE YOU?
DO YOU KNOW THE NAME FRANK CASTLE?
HOLY @#$%! YOU'RE THE PUNISHER?!
ACTUALLY I WAS JU CHECKING YOU KNEW NAME.
NO, YOU SEE, I'M NOT FRANK CASTLE.
I'M DOCTOR SHEP GUNDERSON. I WORK HERE AT THE HOSPITAL.
BUT YOU, TROUBLED SOUL, CAN CALL ME...
THE REDEEMER!
I'VE COME TO SAVE YOU FROM YOURSELF!

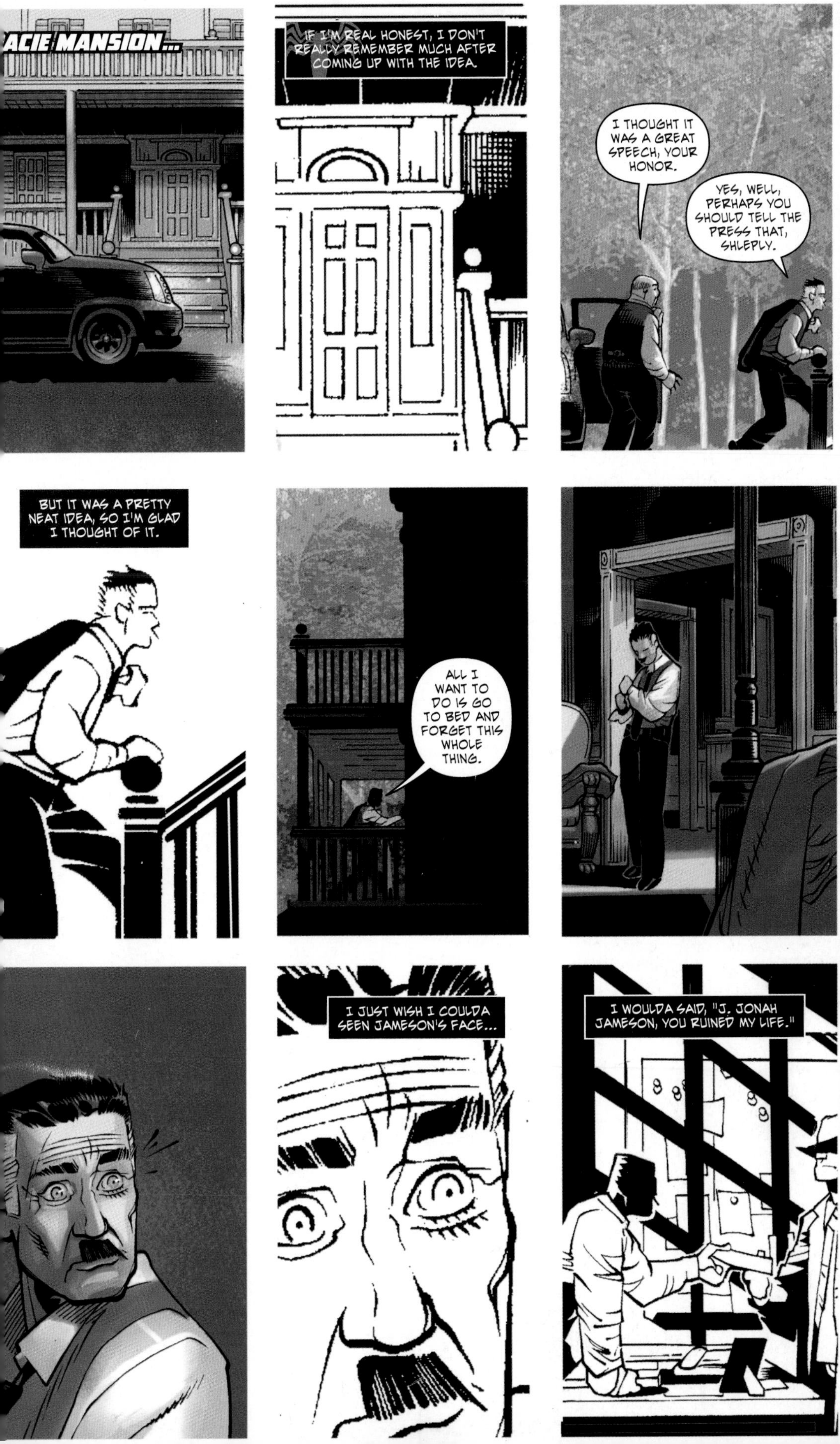
ACIE MANSION...
IF I'M REAL HONEST, I DON'T REALLY REMEMBER MUCH AFTER COMING UP WITH THE IDEA.
I THOUGHT IT WAS A GREAT SPEECH, YOUR HONOR.
YES, WELL, PERHAPS YOU SHOULD TELL THE PRESS THAT, SHLEPLY.
BUT IT WAS A PRETTY NEAT IDEA, SO I'M GLAD I THOUGHT OF IT.
ALL I WANT TO DO IS GO TO BED AND FORGET THIS WHOLE THING.
I JUST WISH I COULDA SEEN JAMESON'S FACE...
I WOULDA SAID, "J. JONAH JAMESON, YOU RUINED MY LIFE."

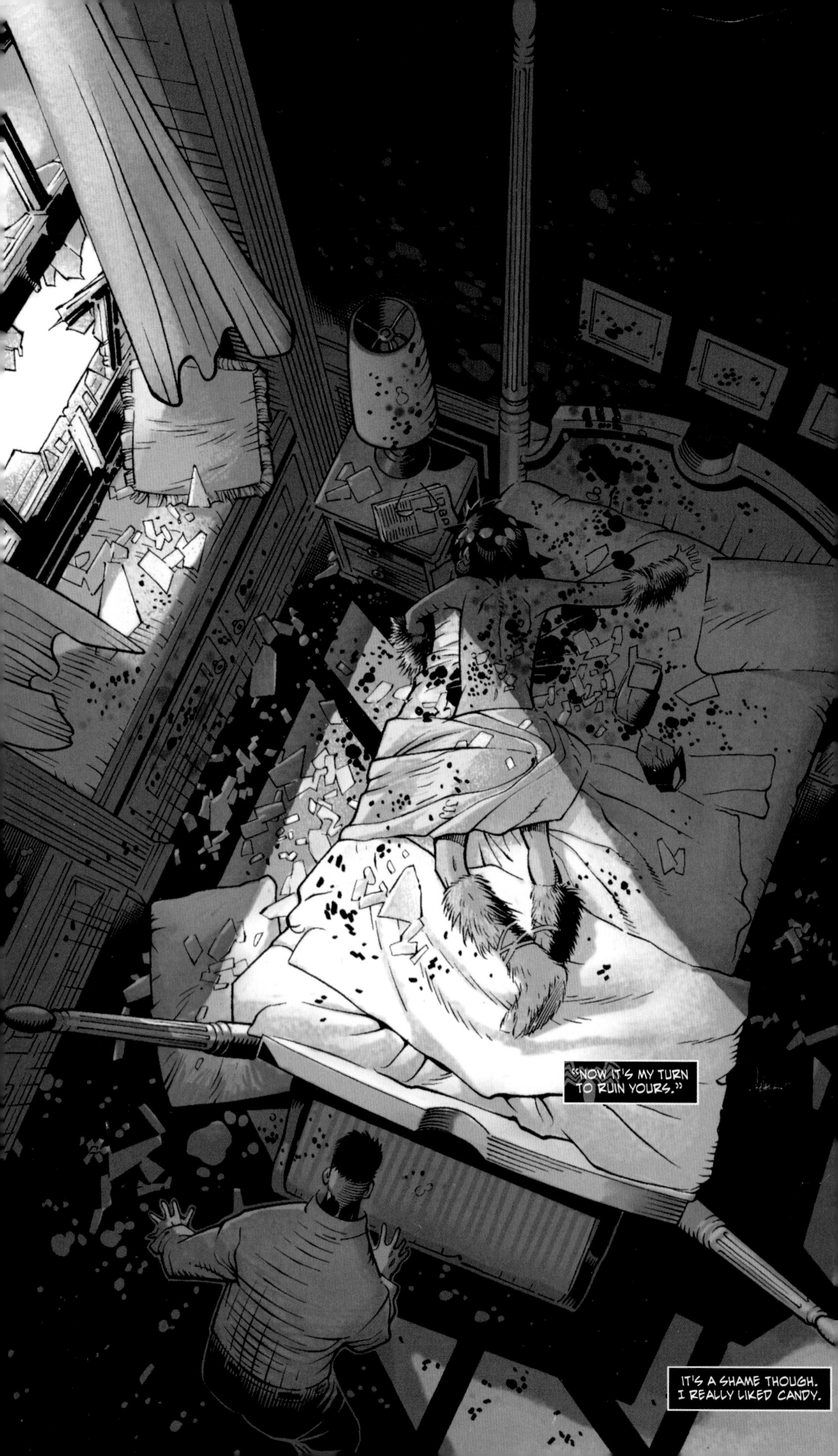
"NOW IT'S MY TURN TO RUIN YOURS."
IT'S A SHAME THOUGH. I REALLY LIKED CANDY.

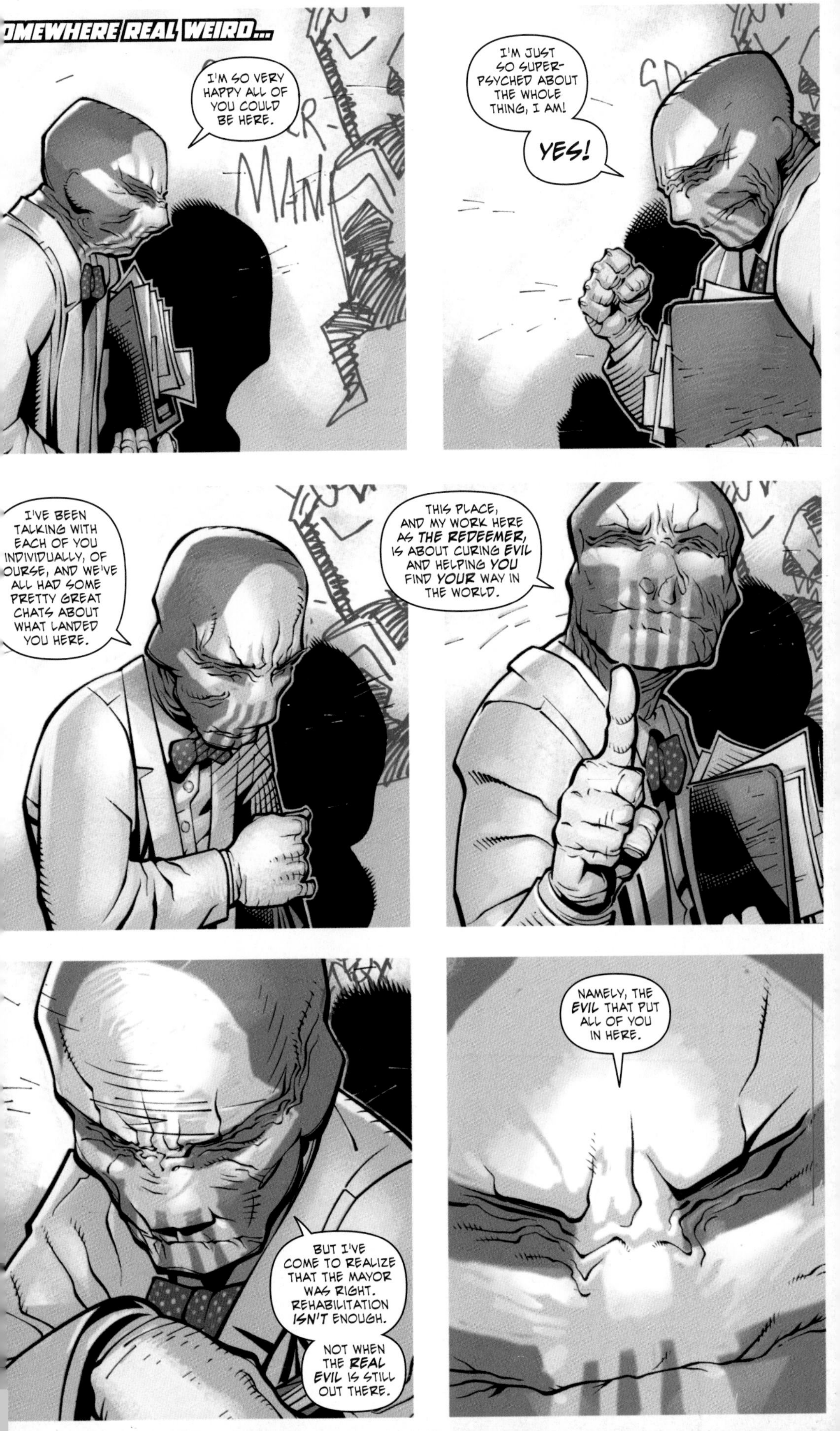
OMEWHERE REAL WEIRD...
I'M SO VERY HAPPY ALL OF YOU COULD BE HERE.
I'M JUST SO SUPER-PSYCHED ABOUT THE WHOLE THING, I AM!
YES!
I'VE BEEN TALKING WITH EACH OF YOU INDIVIDUALLY, OF OURSE, AND WE'VE ALL HAD SOME PRETTY GREAT CHATS ABOUT WHAT LANDED YOU HERE.
THIS PLACE, AND MY WORK HERE AS THE REDEEMER, IS ABOUT CURING EVIL AND HELPING YOU FIND YOUR WAY IN THE WORLD.
BUT I'VE COME TO REALIZE THAT THE MAYOR WAS RIGHT. REHABILITATION ISN'T ENOUGH.
NOT WHEN THE REAL EVIL IS STILL OUT THERE.
NAMELY, THE EVIL THAT PUT ALL OF YOU IN HERE.

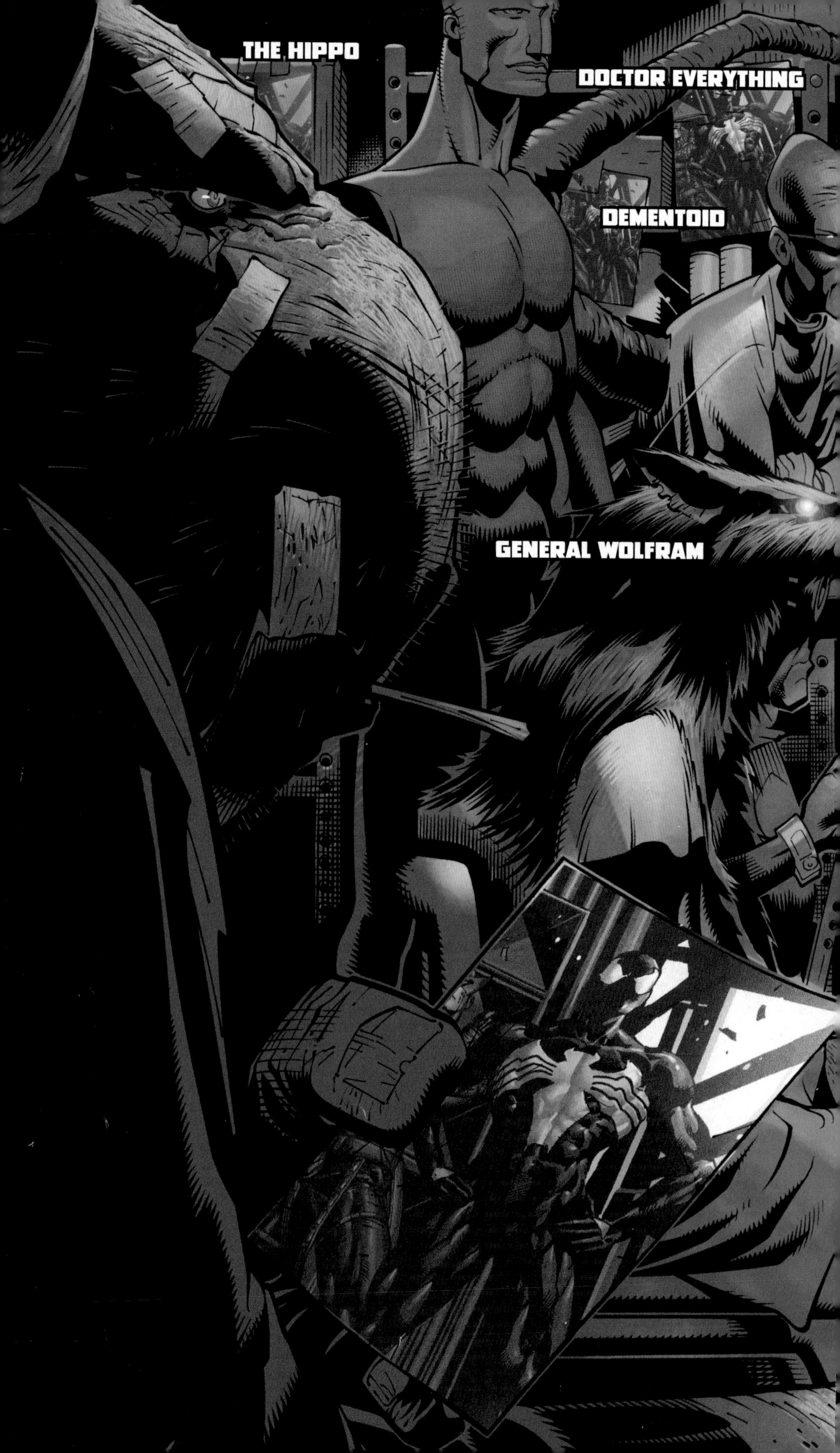
THE HIPPO
DOCTOR EVERYTHING
DEMENTOID
GENERAL WOLFRAM

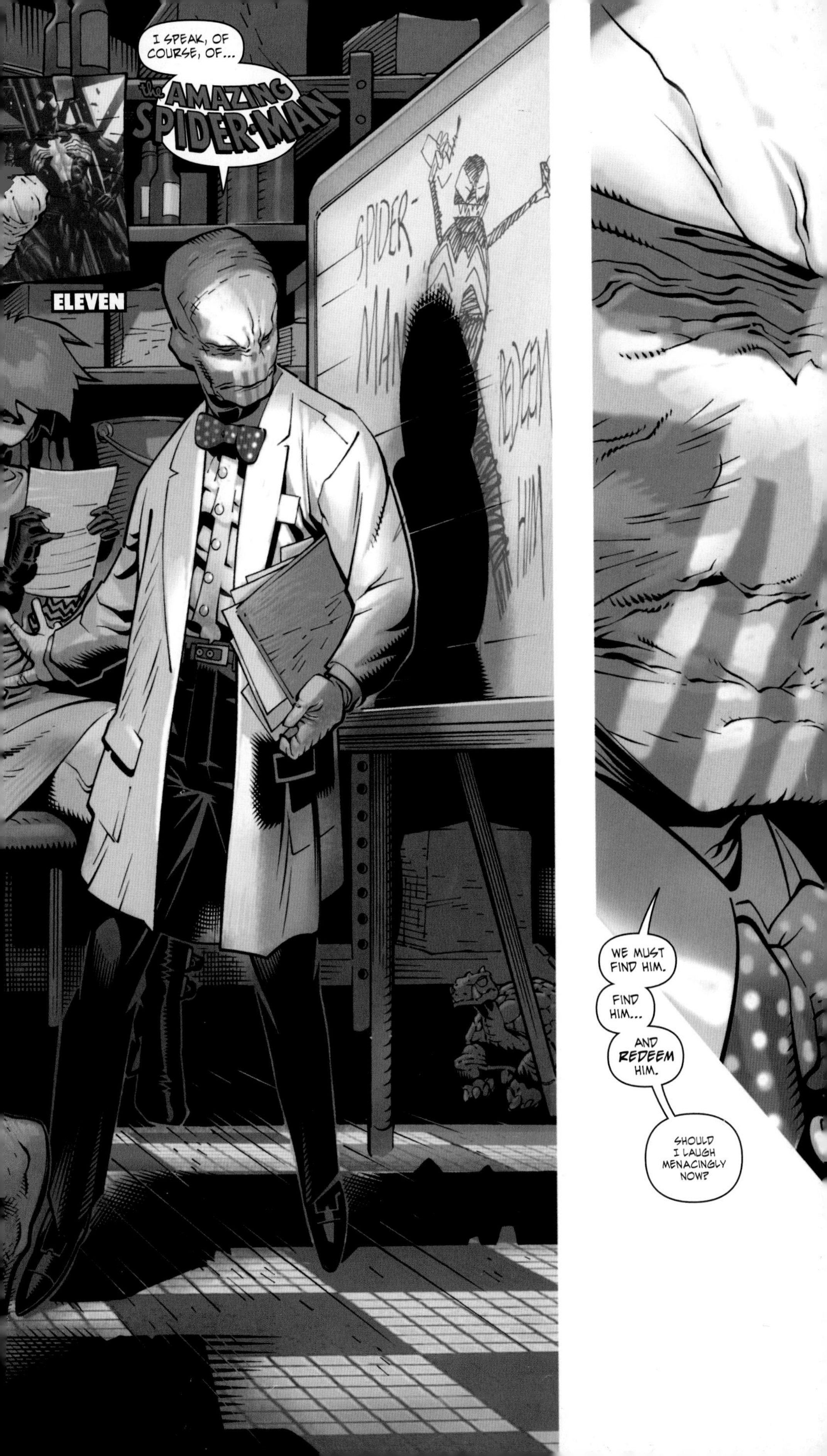
I SPEAK, OF COURSE, OF...
the AMAZING SPIDER-MAN
ELEVEN
SPIDER-MAN
REDEEM HIM
WE MUST FIND HIM.
FIND HIM...
AND REDEEM HIM.
SHOULD I LAUGH MENACINGLY NOW?

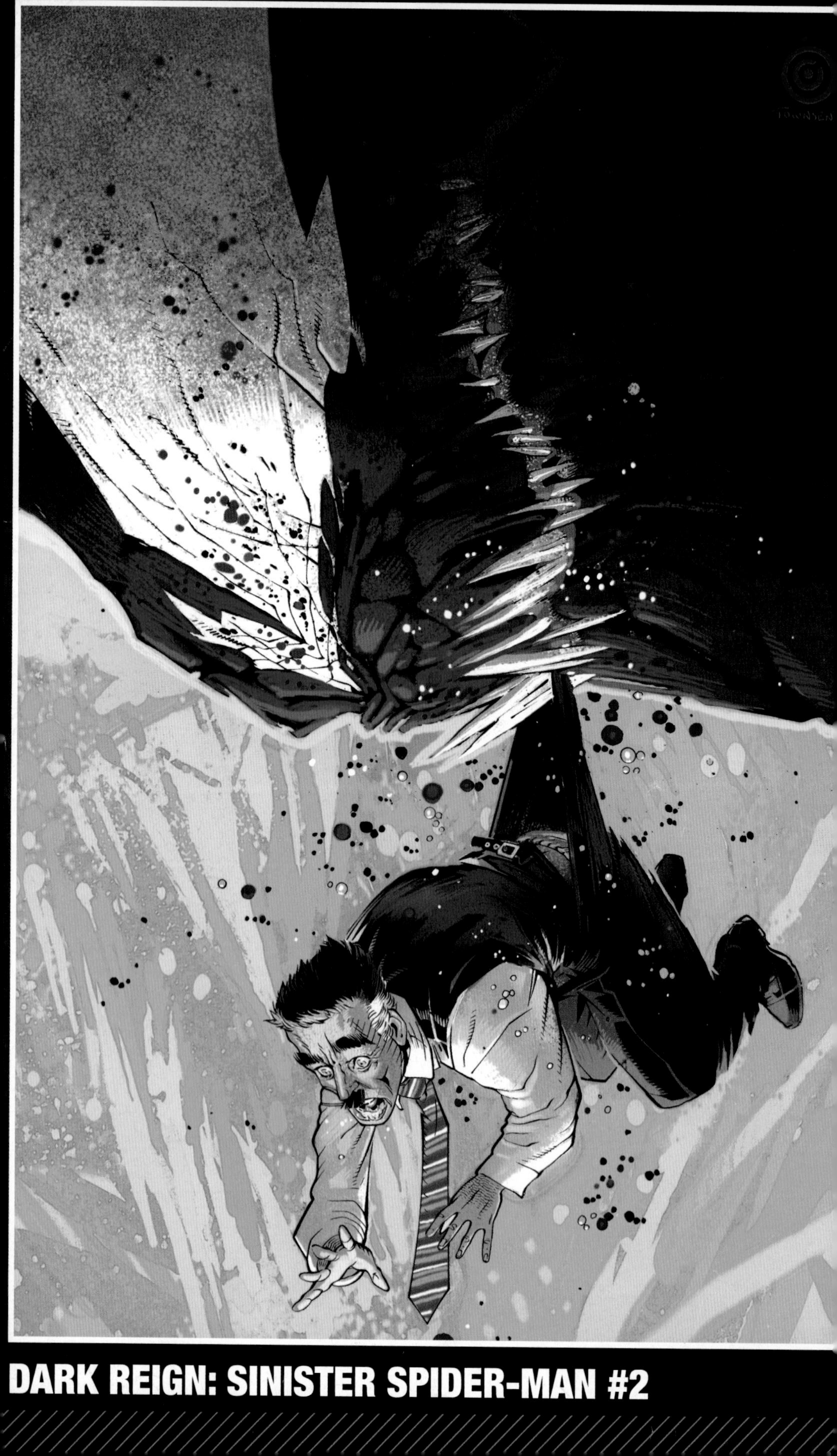

DARK REIGN: SINISTER SPIDER-MAN #2

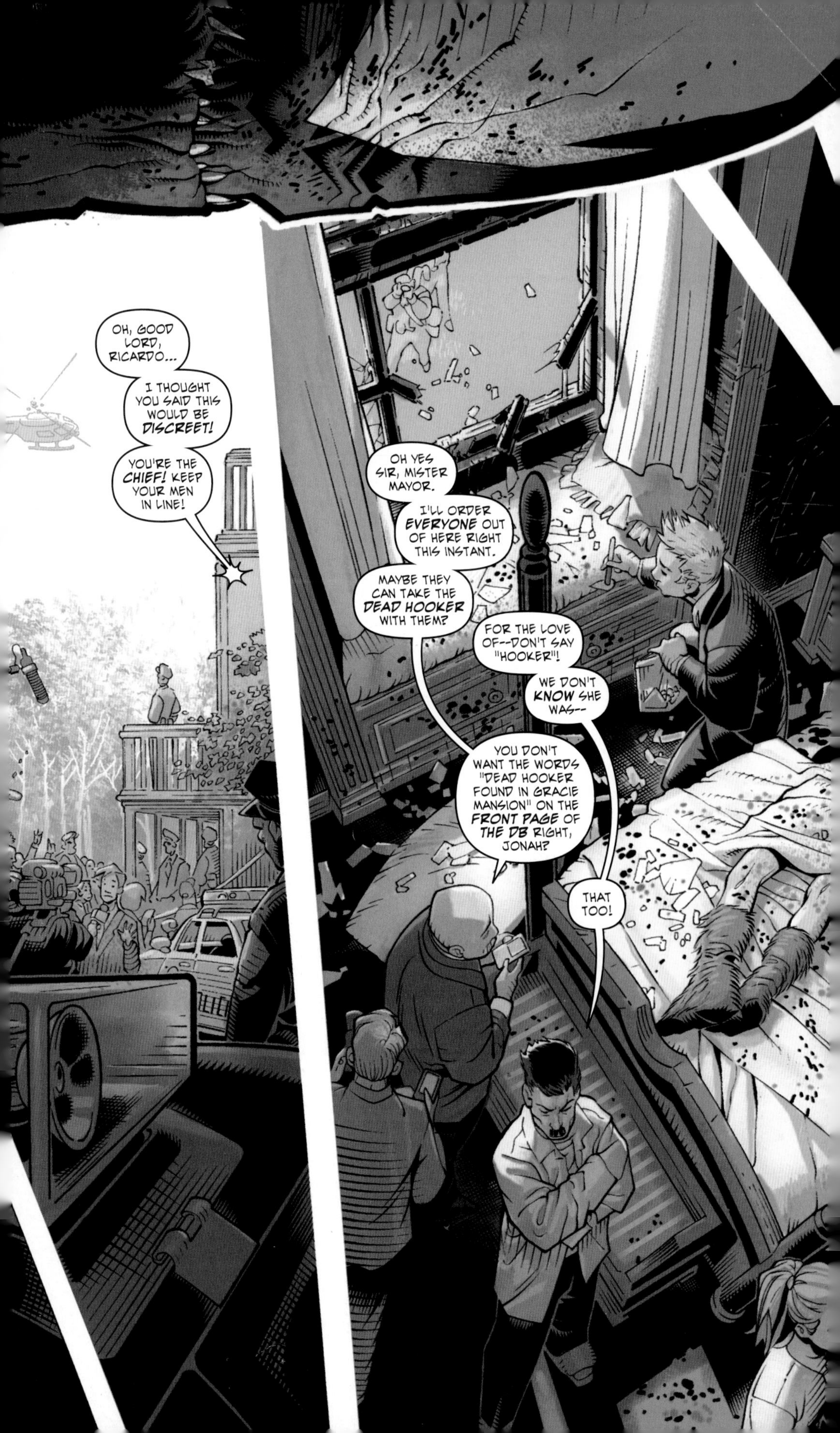
OH, GOOD LORD, RICARDO...
I THOUGHT YOU SAID THIS WOULD BE DISCREET!
YOU'RE THE CHIEF! KEEP YOUR MEN IN LINE!
OH YES SIR, MISTER MAYOR.
I'LL ORDER EVERYONE OUT OF HERE RIGHT THIS INSTANT.
MAYBE THEY CAN TAKE THE DEAD HOOKER WITH THEM?
FOR THE LOVE OF--DON'T SAY "HOOKER"!
WE DON'T KNOW SHE WAS--
YOU DON'T WANT THE WORDS "DEAD HOOKER FOUND IN GRACIE MANSION" ON THE FRONT PAGE OF THE DB RIGHT, JONAH?
THAT TOO!

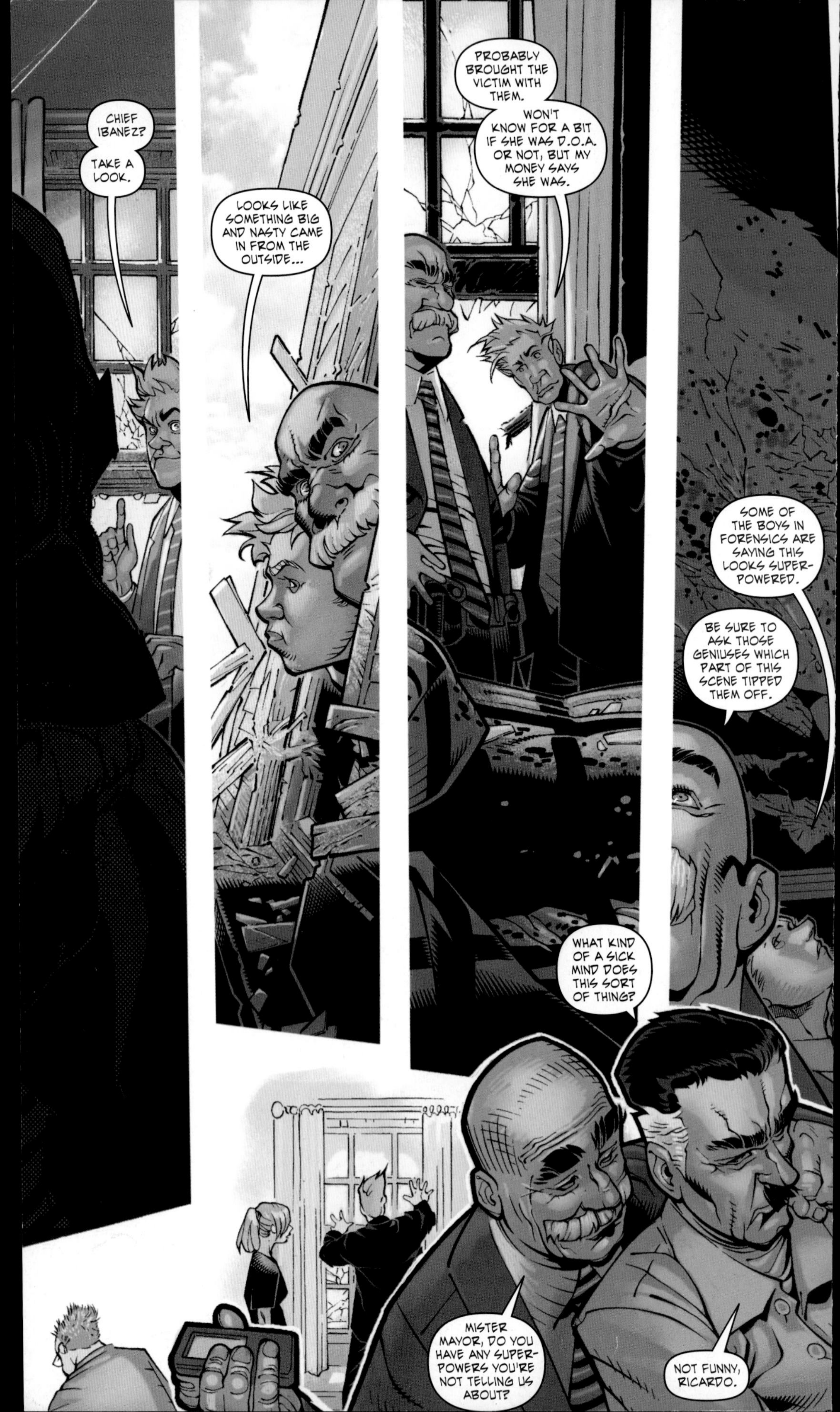
CHIEF IBANEZ?
TAKE A LOOK.
LOOKS LIKE SOMETHING BIG AND NASTY CAME IN FROM THE OUTSIDE...
PROBABLY BROUGHT THE VICTIM WITH THEM.
WON'T KNOW FOR A BIT IF SHE WAS D.O.A. OR NOT, BUT MY MONEY SAYS SHE WAS.
SOME OF THE BOYS IN FORENSICS ARE SAYING THIS LOOKS SUPER-POWERED.
BE SURE TO ASK THOSE GENIUSES WHICH PART OF THIS SCENE TIPPED THEM OFF.
WHAT KIND OF A SICK MIND DOES THIS SORT OF THING?
MISTER MAYOR, DO YOU HAVE ANY SUPER-POWERS YOU'RE NOT TELLING US ABOUT?
NOT FUNNY, RICARDO.

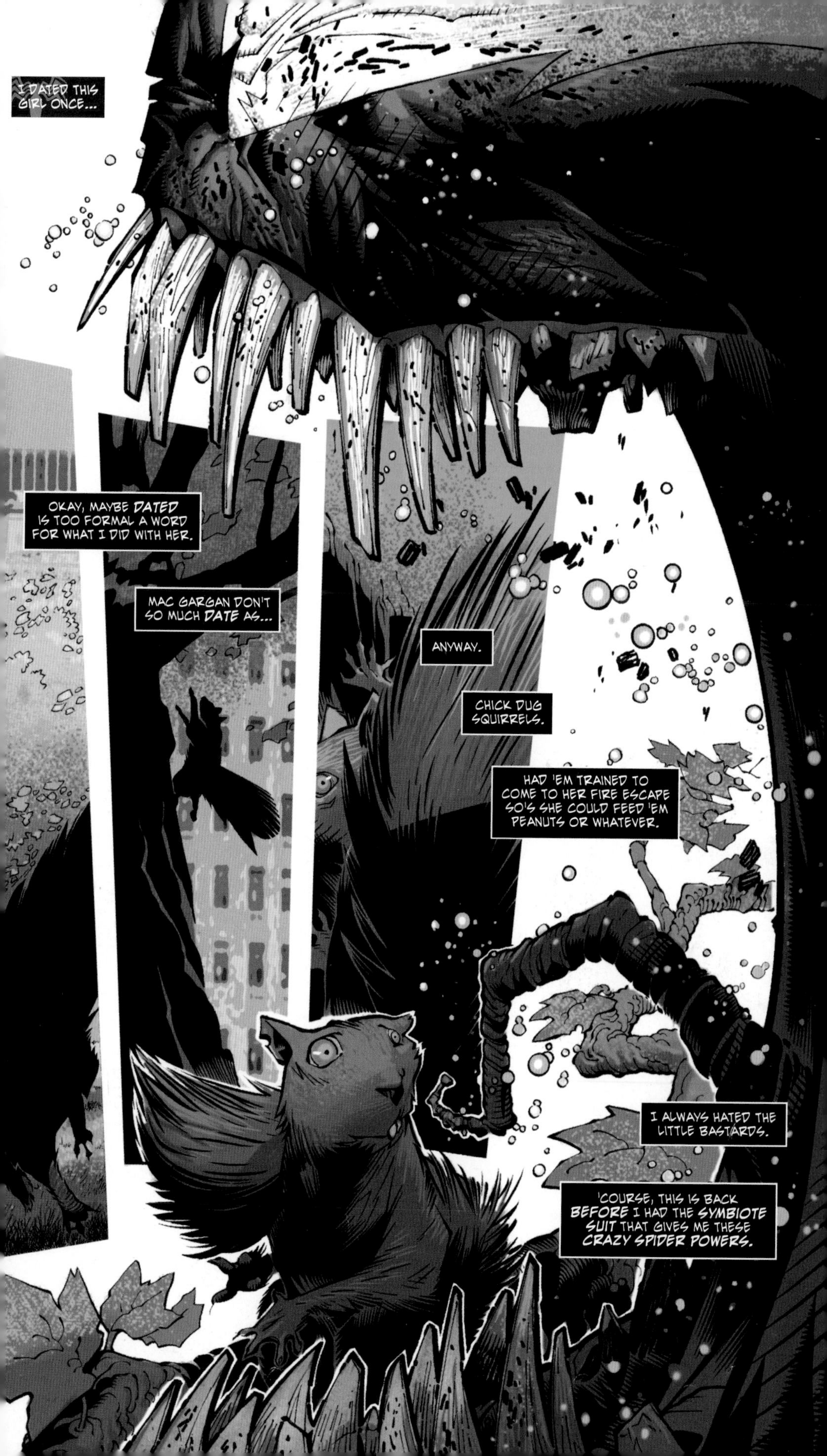
I DATED THIS GIRL ONCE...
OKAY, MAYBE DATED IS TOO FORMAL A WORD FOR WHAT I DID WITH HER.
MAC GARGAN DON'T SO MUCH DATE AS...
ANYWAY.
CHICK DUG SQUIRRELS.
HAD 'EM TRAINED TO COME TO HER FIRE ESCAPE SO'S SHE COULD FEED 'EM PEANUTS OR WHATEVER.
I ALWAYS HATED THE LITTLE BASTARDS.
'COURSE, THIS IS BACK BEFORE I HAD THE SYMBIOTE SUIT THAT GIVES ME THESE CRAZY SPIDER POWERS.

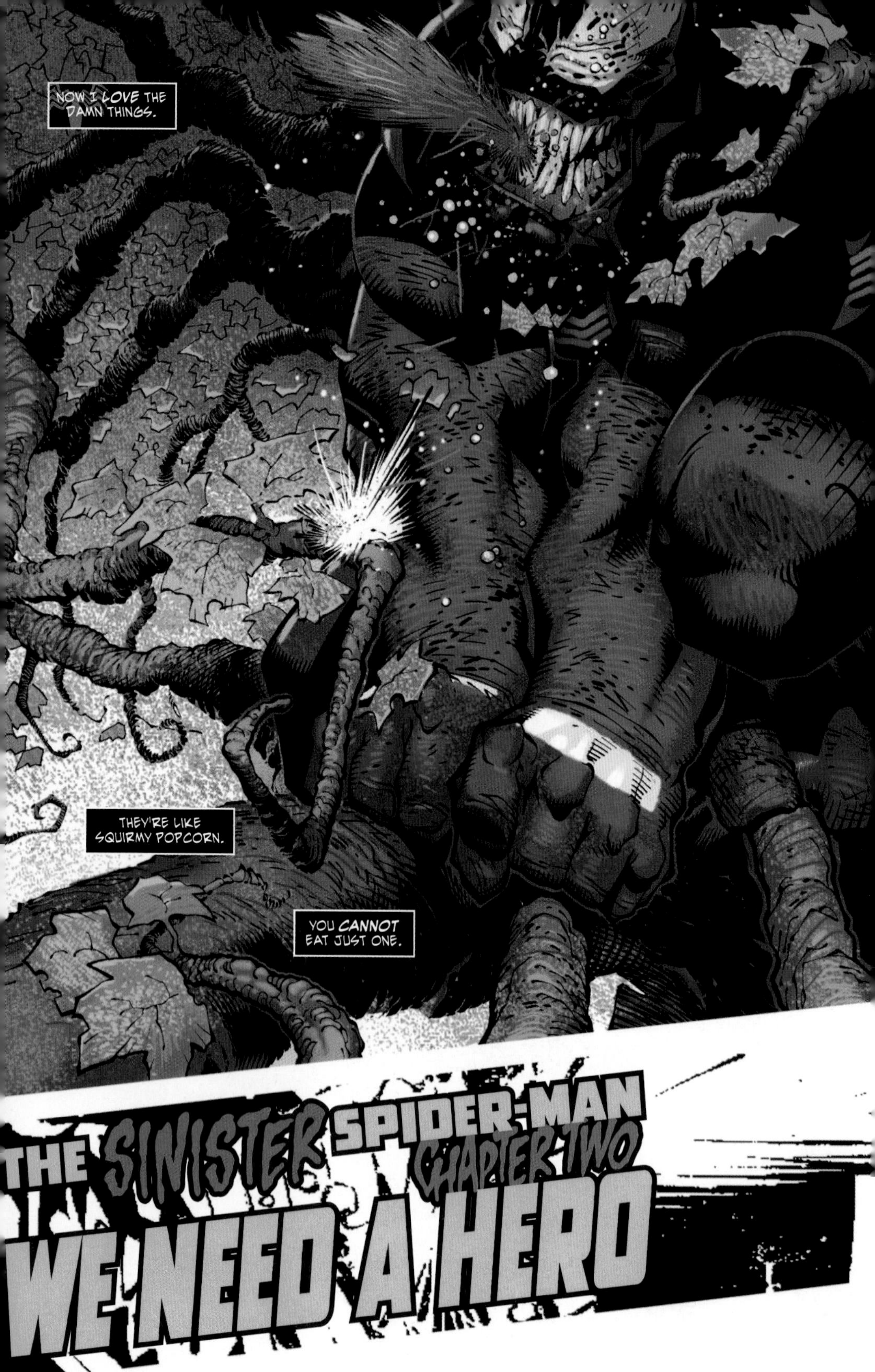

NOW I LOVE THE DAMN THINGS.
THEY'RE LIKE SQUIRMY POPCORN.
YOU CANNOT EAT JUST ONE.
THE SINISTER SPIDER-MAN CHAPTER TWO
WE NEED A HERO

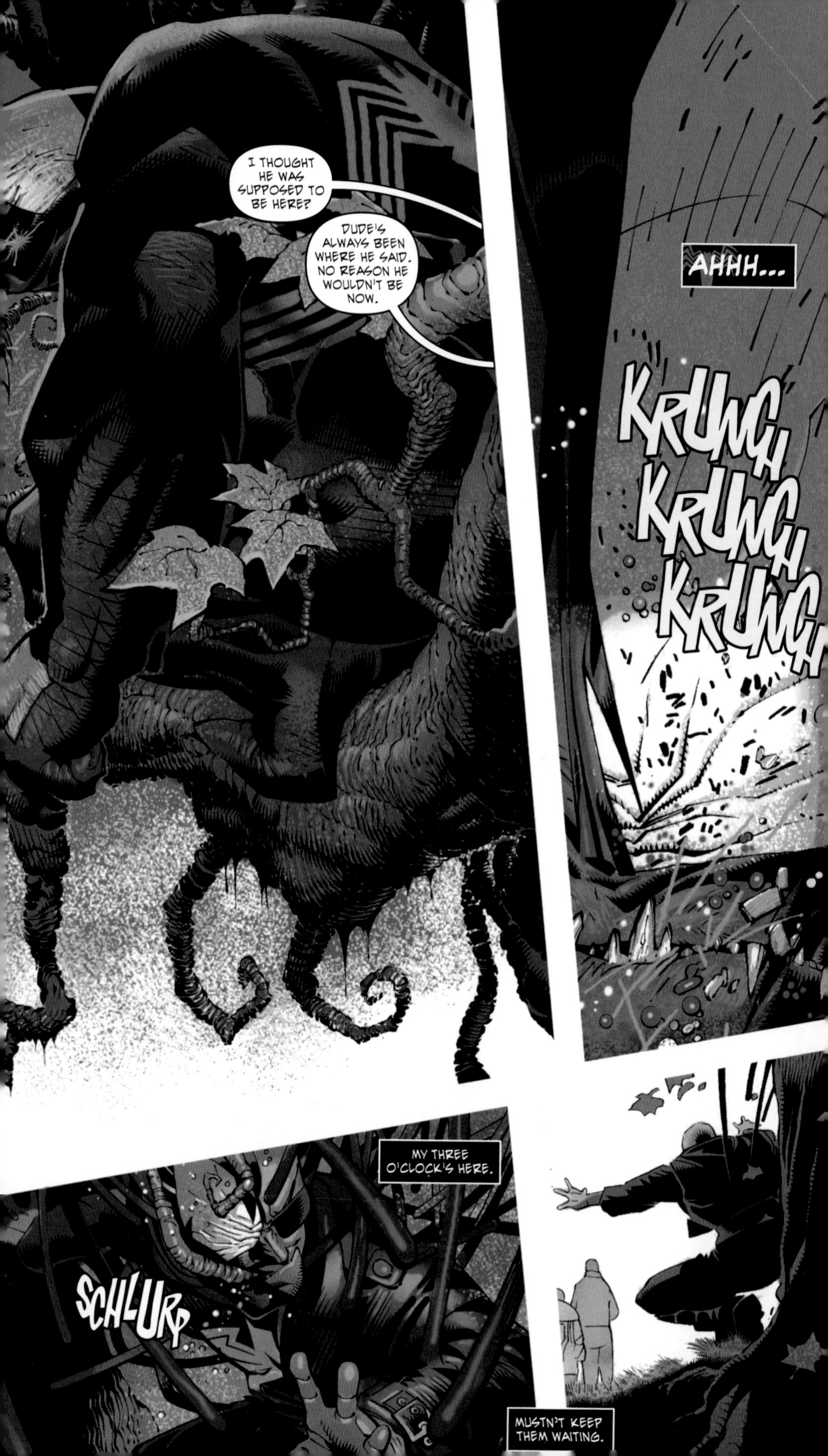

I THOUGHT HE WAS SUPPOSED TO BE HERE?
DUDE'S ALWAYS BEEN WHERE HE SAID. NO REASON HE WOULDN'T BE NOW.
AHHH...
KRUNCH KRUNCH KRUNCH
MY THREE O'CLOCK'S HERE.
SCHLURP
MUSTN'T KEEP THEM WAITING.

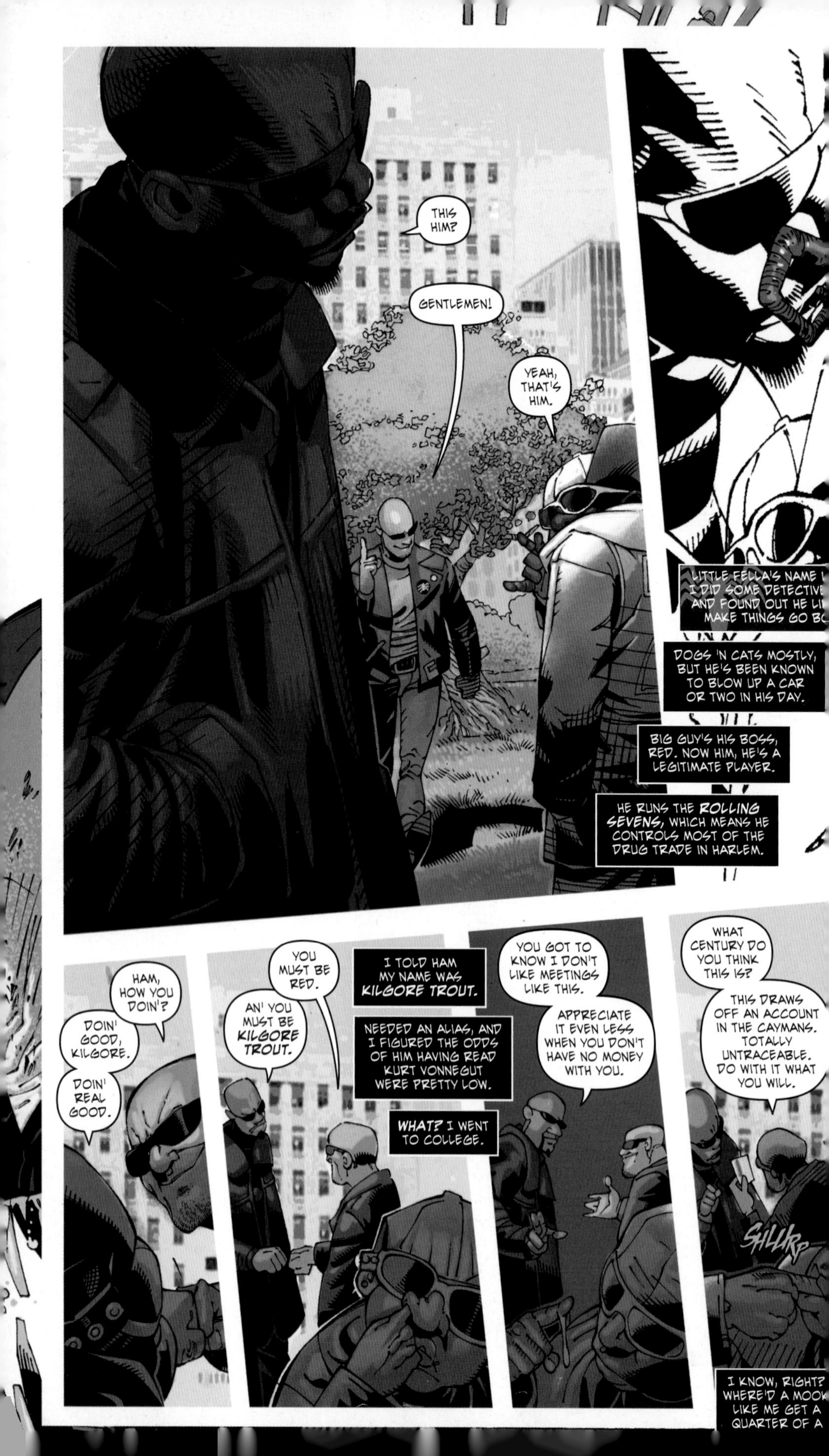

THIS HIM?
GENTLEMEN!
YEAH, THAT'S HIM.
LITTLE FELLA'S NAME I
I DID SOME DETECTIVE
AND FOUND OUT HE LI
MAKE THINGS GO BO
DOGS 'N CATS MOSTLY, BUT HE'S BEEN KNOWN TO BLOW UP A CAR OR TWO IN HIS DAY.
BIG GUY'S HIS BOSS, RED. NOW HIM, HE'S A LEGITIMATE PLAYER.
HE RUNS THE ROLLING SEVENS, WHICH MEANS HE CONTROLS MOST OF THE DRUG TRADE IN HARLEM.
HAM, HOW YOU DOIN'?
DOIN' GOOD, KILGORE.
DOIN' REAL GOOD.
YOU MUST BE RED.
AN' YOU MUST BE KILGORE TROUT.
I TOLD HAM MY NAME WAS KILGORE TROUT.
NEEDED AN ALIAS, AND I FIGURED THE ODDS OF HIM HAVING READ KURT VONNEGUT WERE PRETTY LOW.
WHAT? I WENT TO COLLEGE.
YOU GOT TO KNOW I DON'T LIKE MEETINGS LIKE THIS.
APPRECIATE IT EVEN LESS WHEN YOU DON'T HAVE NO MONEY WITH YOU.
WHAT CENTURY DO YOU THINK THIS IS?
THIS DRAWS OFF AN ACCOUNT IN THE CAYMANS. TOTALLY UNTRACEABLE. DO WITH IT WHAT YOU WILL.
SHLURP
I KNOW, RIGHT?
WHERE'D A MOOK
LIKE ME GET A
QUARTER OF A

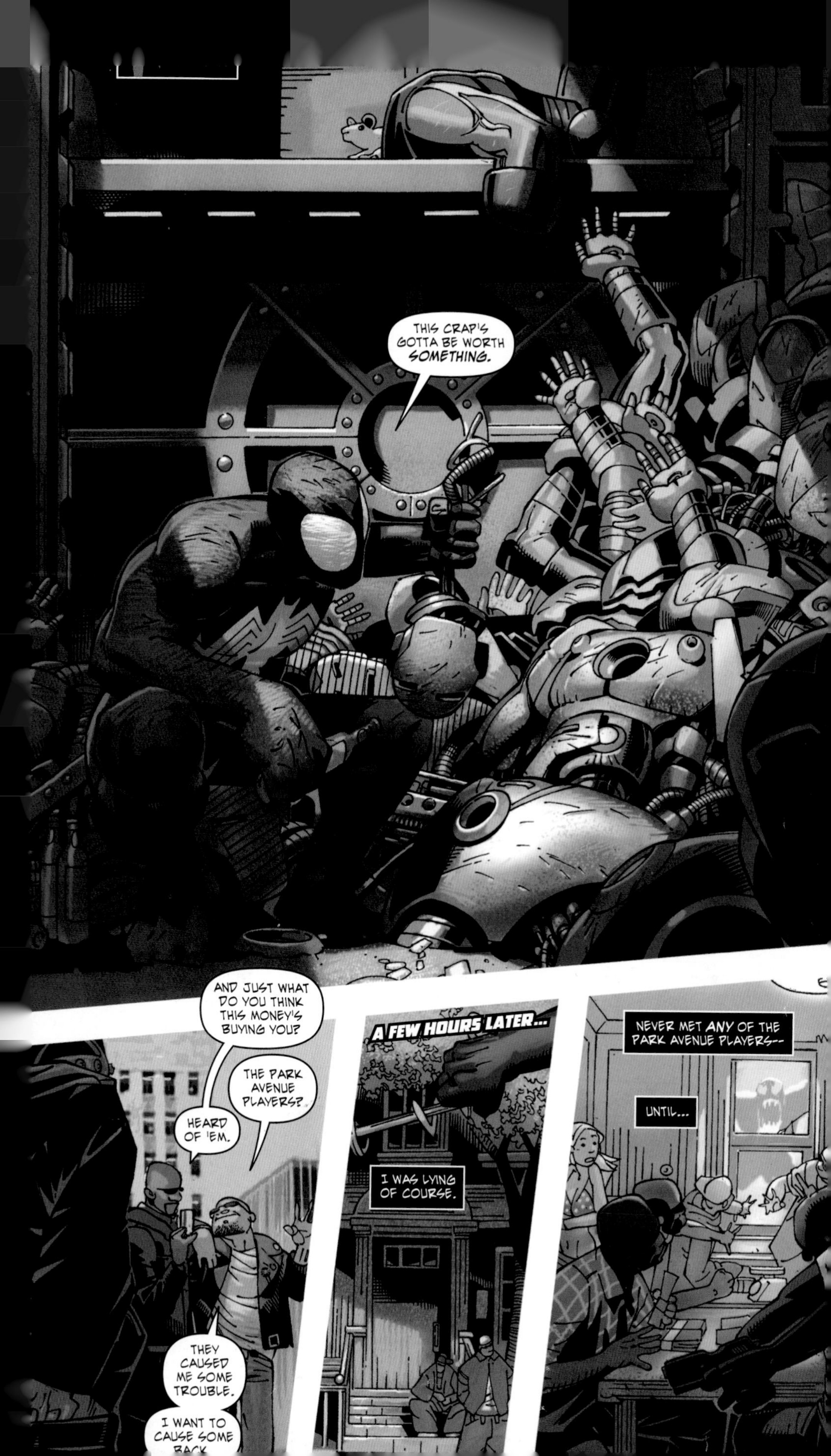
THIS CRAP'S GOTTA BE WORTH SOMETHING.
AND JUST WHAT DO YOU THINK THIS MONEY'S BUYING YOU?
THE PARK AVENUE PLAYERS?
HEARD OF 'EM.
THEY CAUSED ME SOME TROUBLE.
I WANT TO CAUSE SOME
A FEW HOURS LATER...
I WAS LYING OF COURSE.
NEVER MET ANY OF THE PARK AVENUE PLAYERS--
UNTIL...

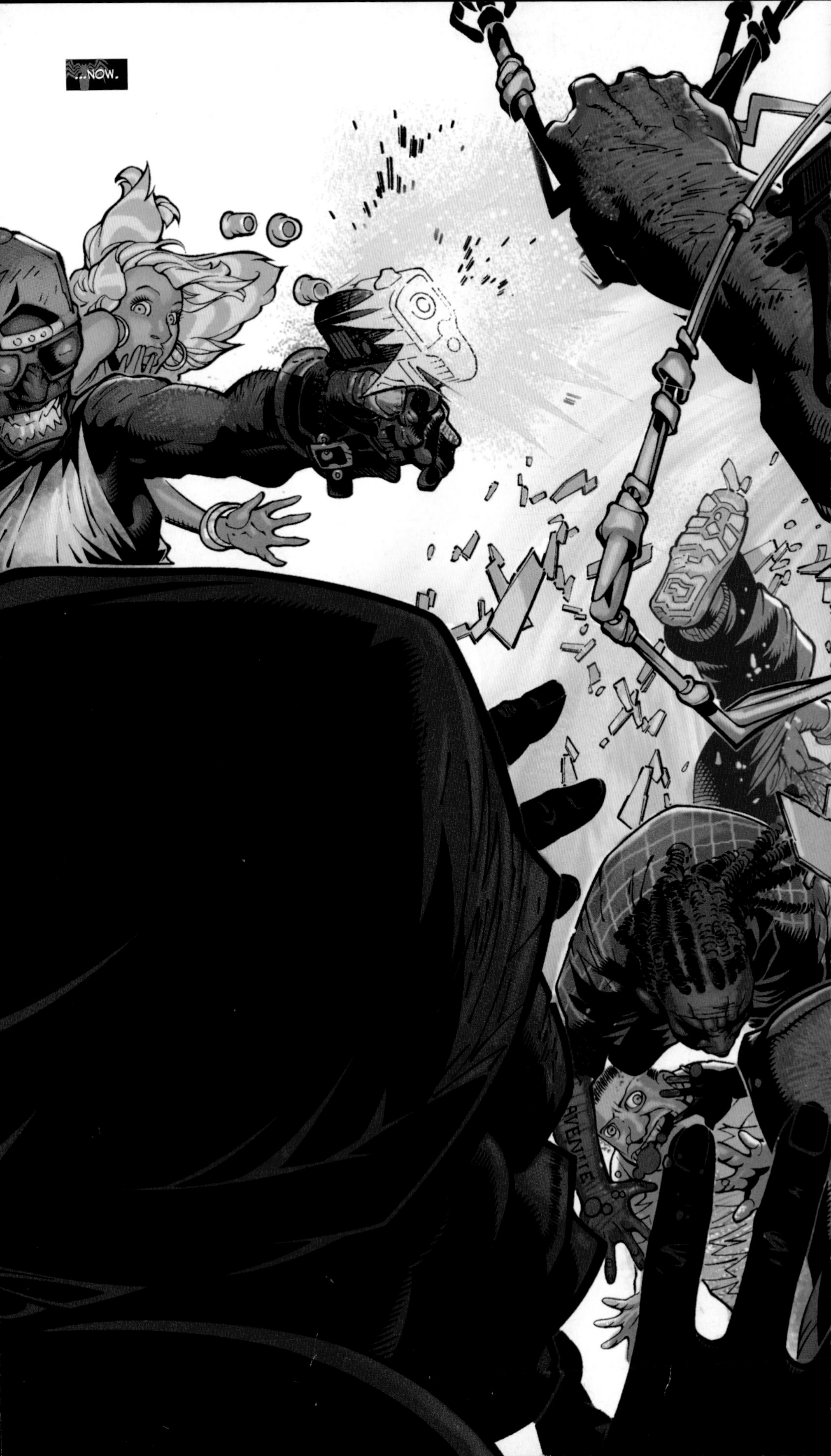
...NOW.

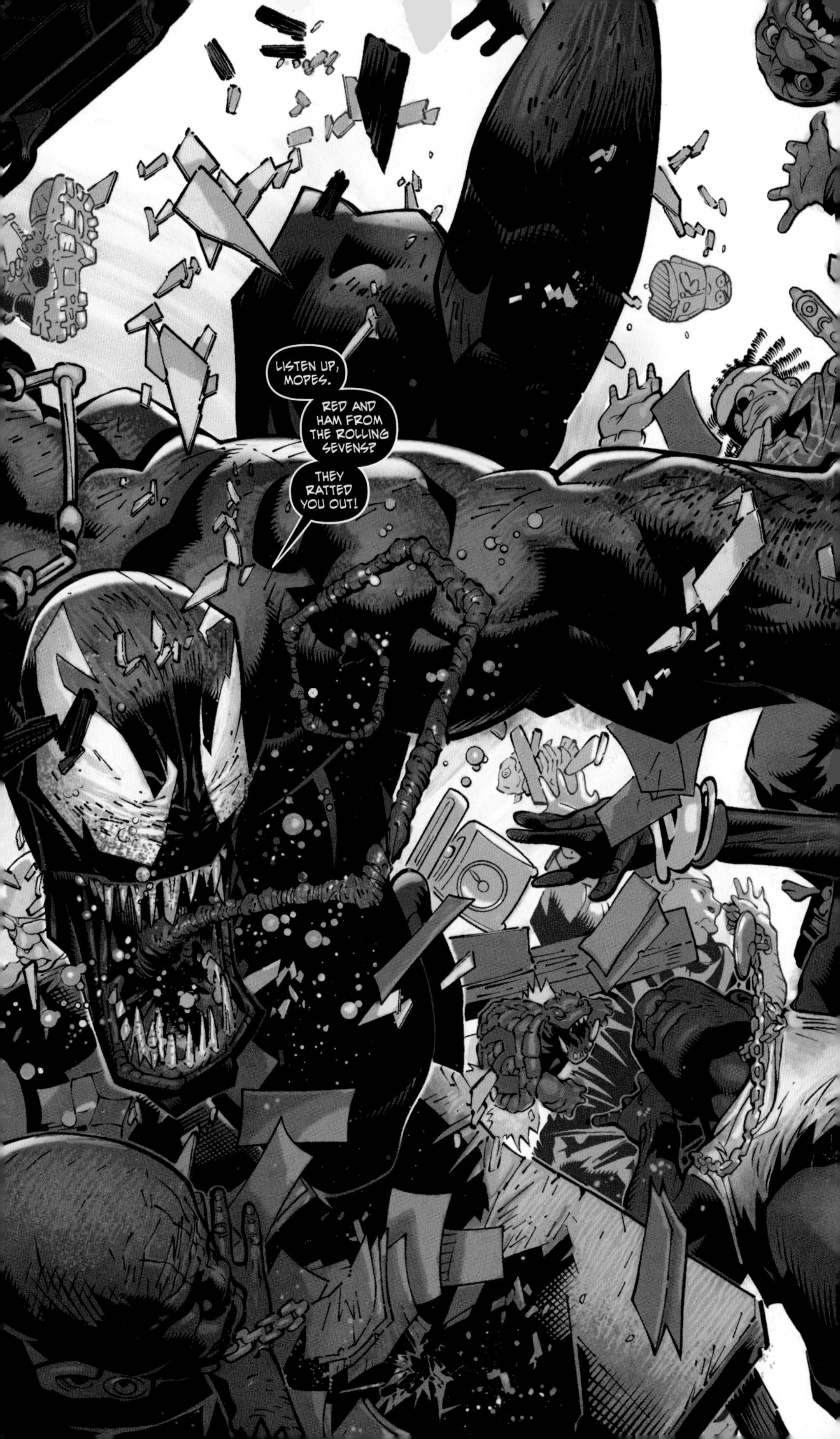
LISTEN UP, MOPES.
RED AND HAM FROM THE ROLLING SEVENS?
THEY RATTED YOU OUT!

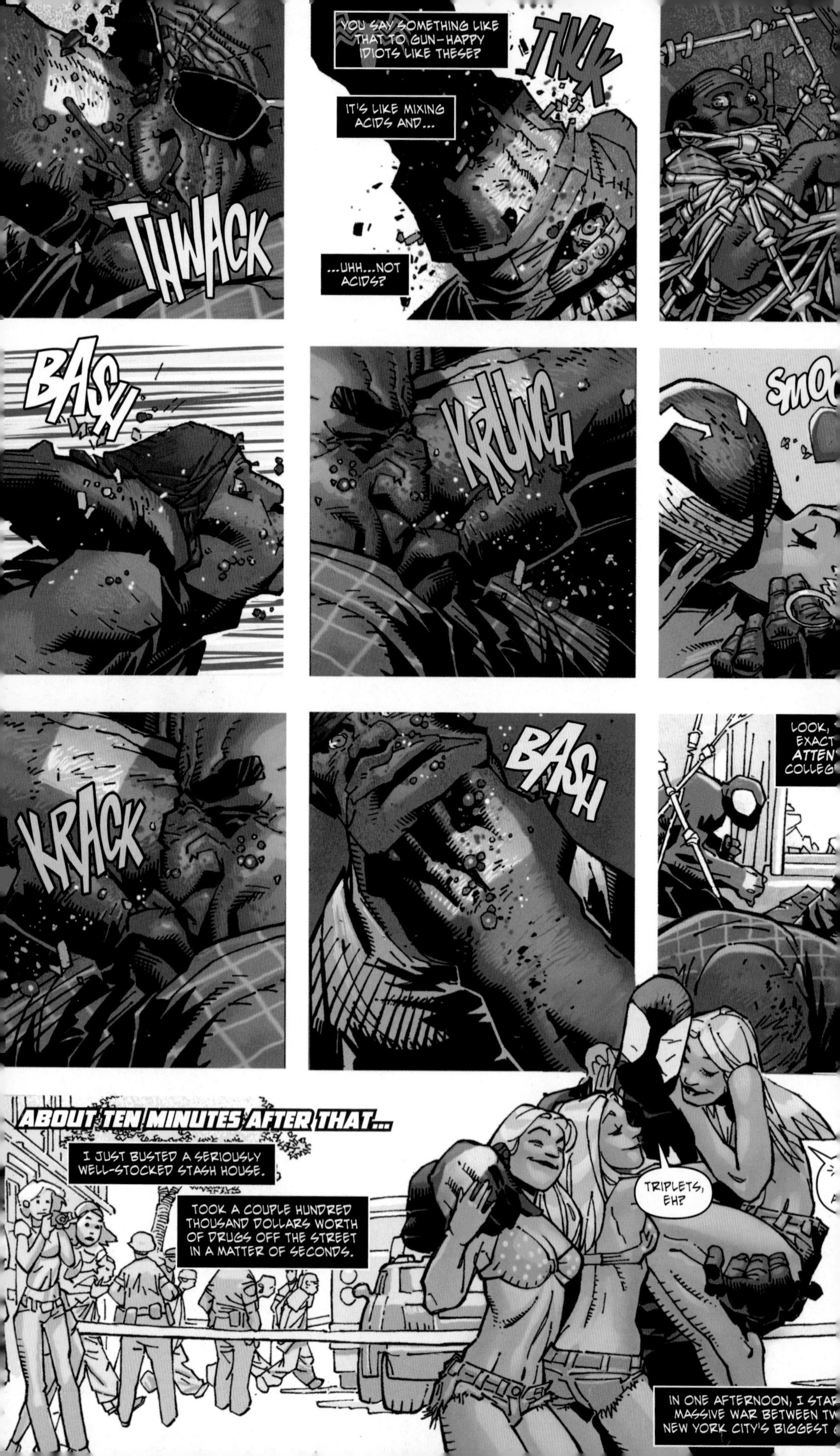
THWACK
YOU SAY SOMETHING LIKE THAT TO GUN-HAPPY IDIOTS LIKE THESE?
THUK
IT'S LIKE MIXING ACIDS AND...
...UHH...NOT ACIDS?
BASH
KRUNCH
KRACK
BASH
ABOUT TEN MINUTES AFTER THAT...
I JUST BUSTED A SERIOUSLY WELL-STOCKED STASH HOUSE.
TOOK A COUPLE HUNDRED THOUSAND DOLLARS WORTH OF DRUGS OFF THE STREET IN A MATTER OF SECONDS.
TRIPLETS, EH?

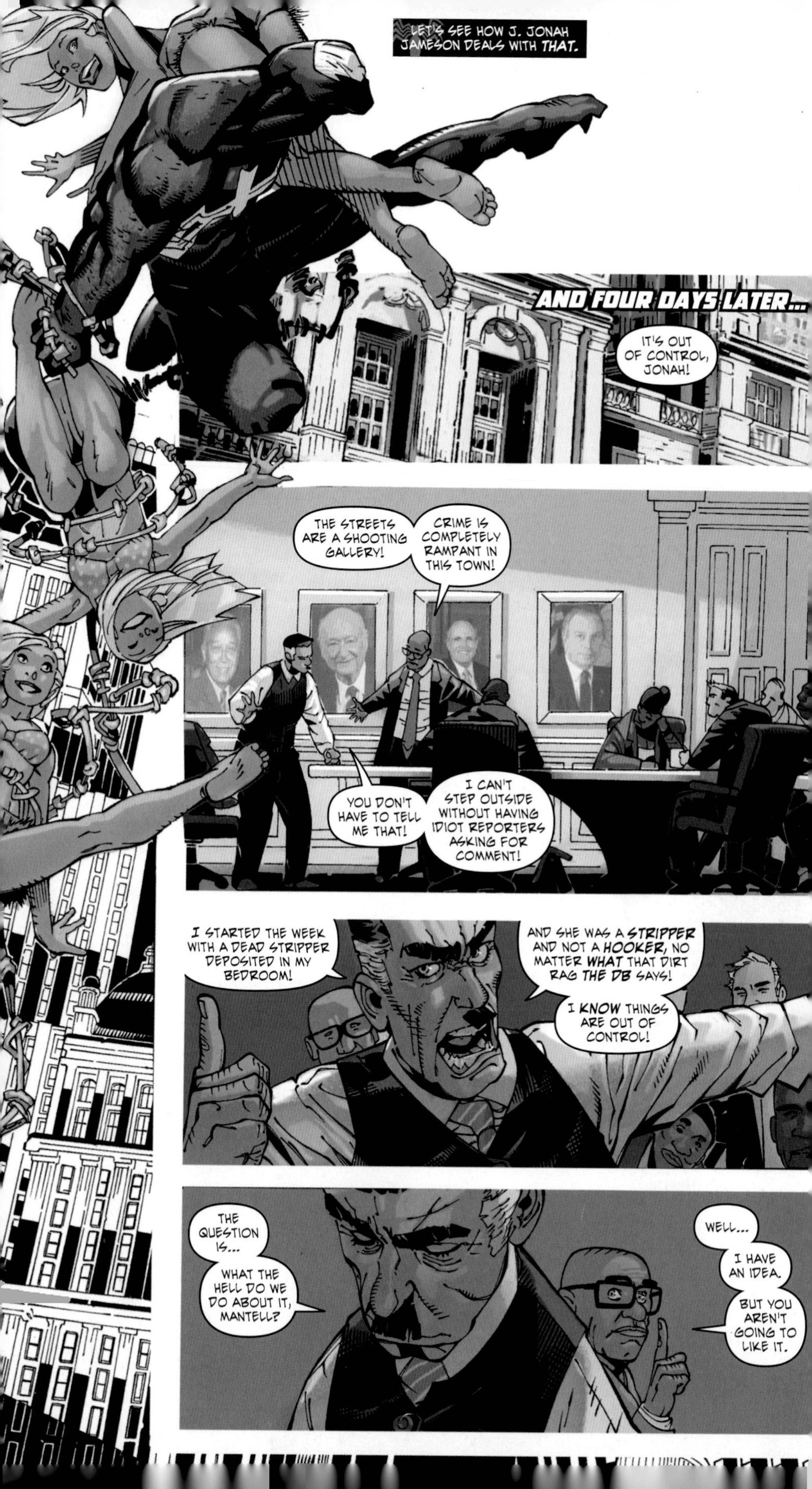
LET'S SEE HOW J. JONAH JAMESON DEALS WITH THAT.
AND FOUR DAYS LATER...
IT'S OUT OF CONTROL, JONAH!
THE STREETS ARE A SHOOTING GALLERY!
CRIME IS COMPLETELY RAMPANT IN THIS TOWN!
YOU DON'T HAVE TO TELL ME THAT!
I CAN'T STEP OUTSIDE WITHOUT HAVING IDIOT REPORTERS ASKING FOR COMMENT!
I STARTED THE WEEK WITH A DEAD STRIPPER DEPOSITED IN MY BEDROOM!
AND SHE WAS A STRIPPER AND NOT A HOOKER, NO MATTER WHAT THAT DIRT RAG THE DB SAYS!
I KNOW THINGS ARE OUT OF CONTROL!
THE QUESTION IS...
WHAT THE HELL DO WE DO ABOUT IT, MANTELL?
WELL...
I HAVE AN IDEA.
BUT YOU AREN'T GOING TO LIKE IT.

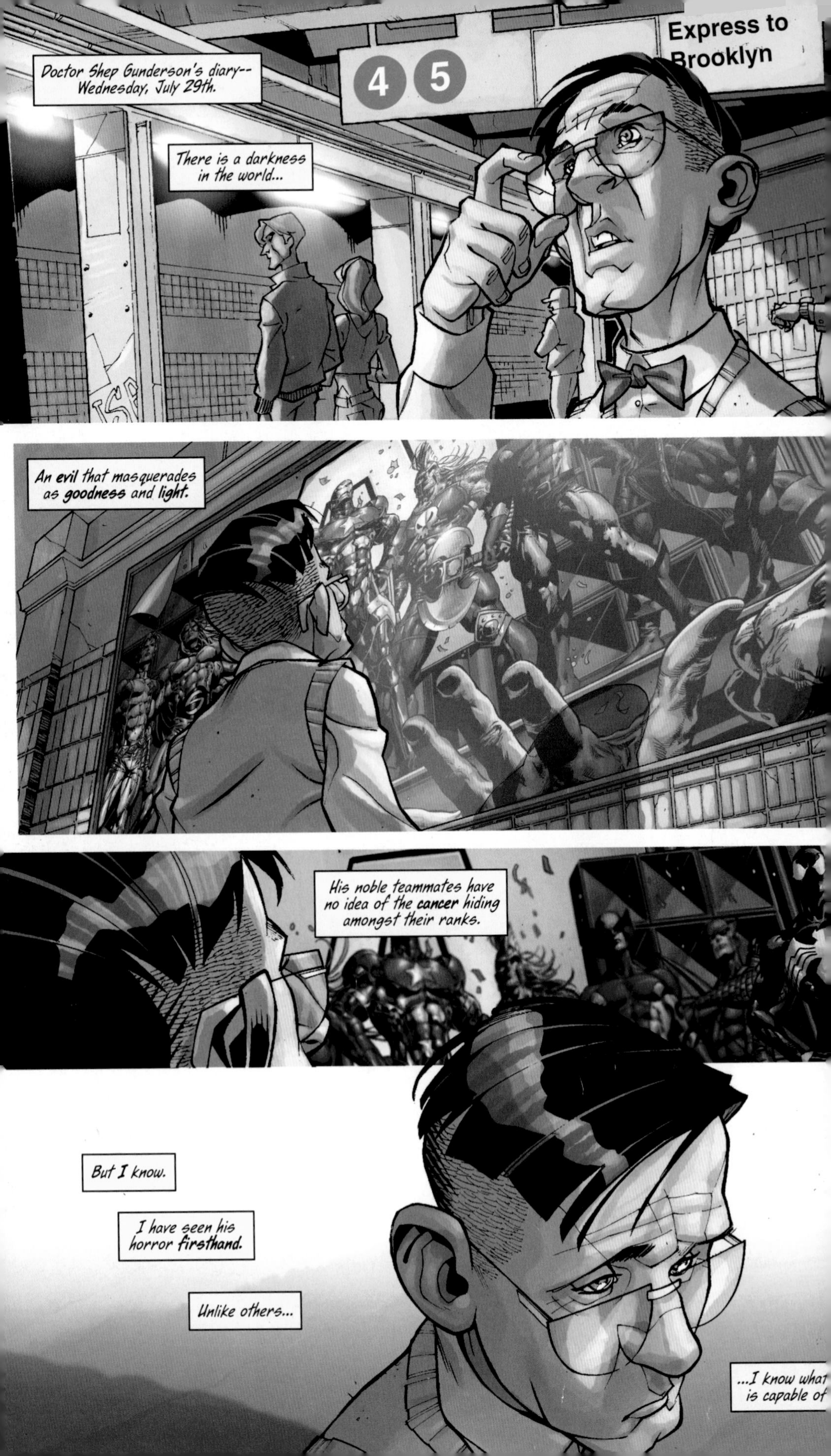

Express to Brooklyn
4
5
Doctor Shep Gunderson's diary-- Wednesday, July 29th.
There is a darkness in the world...
An evil that masquerades as goodness and light.
His noble teammates have no idea of the cancer hiding amongst their ranks.
But I know.
I have seen his horror firsthand.
Unlike others...
...I know what is capable of

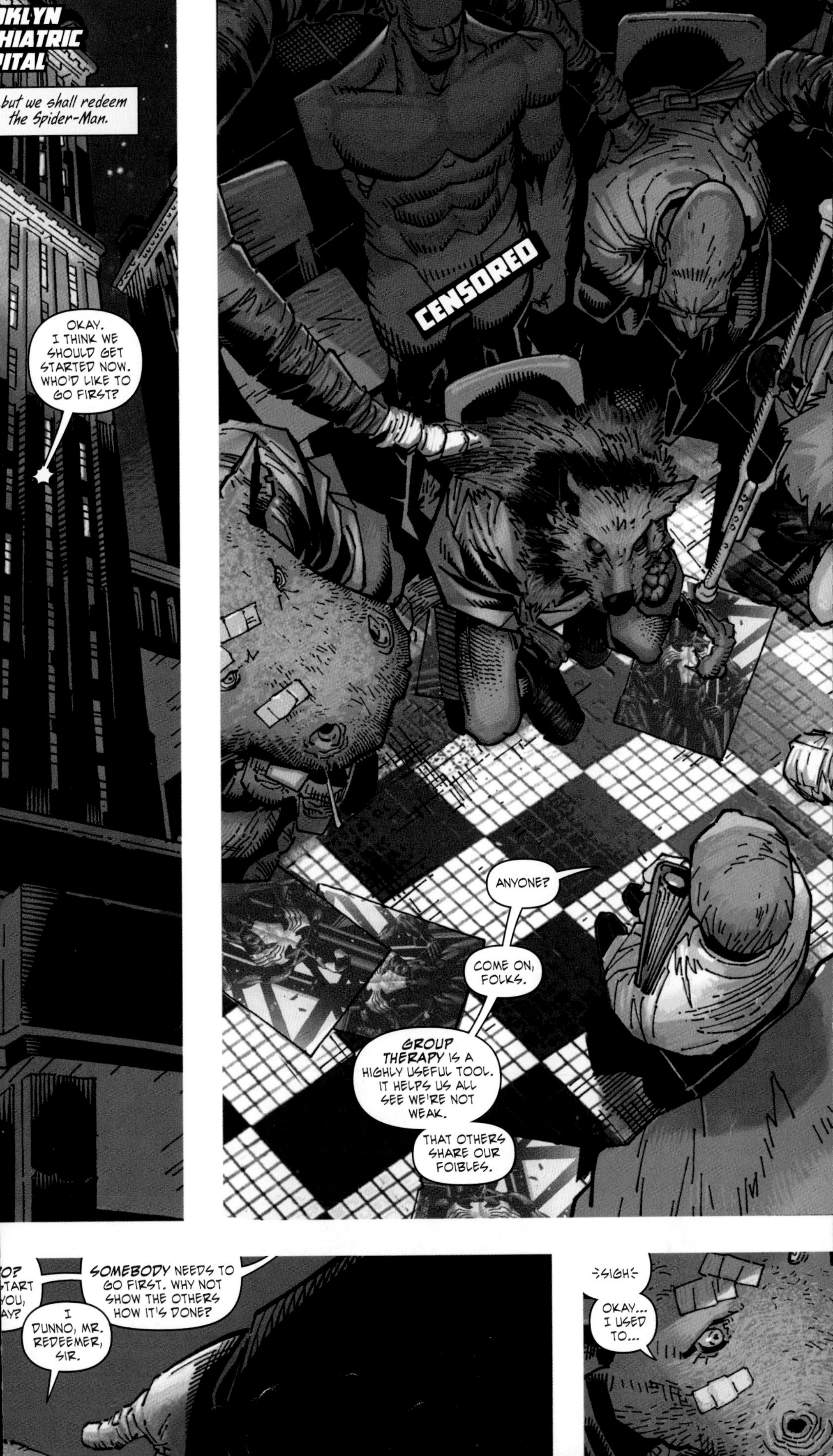

UKLYN
HIATRIC
PITAL
but we shall redeem the Spider-Man.
OKAY. I THINK WE SHOULD GET STARTED NOW. WHO'D LIKE TO GO FIRST?
CENSORED
ANYONE?
COME ON, FOLKS.
GROUP THERAPY IS A HIGHLY USEFUL TOOL. IT HELPS US ALL SEE WE'RE NOT WEAK.
THAT OTHERS SHARE OUR FOIBLES.
SOMEBODY NEEDS TO GO FIRST. WHY NOT SHOW THE OTHERS HOW IT'S DONE?
I DUNNO, MR. REDEEMER, SIR.
=SIGH=
OKAY... I USED TO...

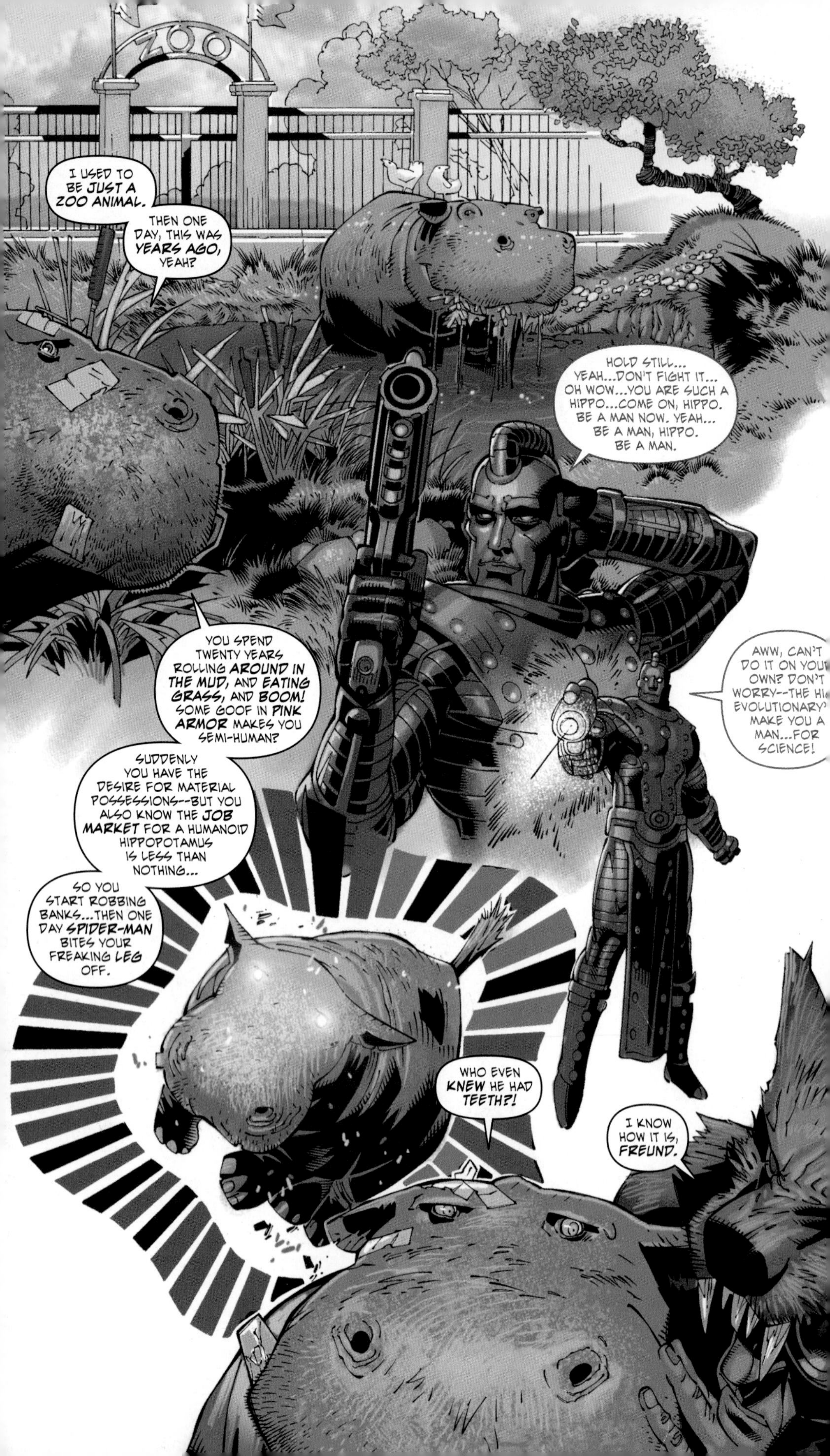

ZOO
I USED TO BE JUST A ZOO ANIMAL.
THEN ONE DAY, THIS WAS YEARS AGO, YEAH?
HOLD STILL... YEAH...DON'T FIGHT IT... OH WOW...YOU ARE SUCH A HIPPO...COME ON, HIPPO. BE A MAN NOW. YEAH... BE A MAN, HIPPO. BE A MAN.
YOU SPEND TWENTY YEARS ROLLING AROUND IN THE MUD, AND EATING GRASS, AND BOOM! SOME GOOF IN PINK ARMOR MAKES YOU SEMI-HUMAN?
AWW, CAN'T DO IT ON YOU OWN? DON'T WORRY--THE HI EVOLUTIONARY MAKE YOU A MAN...FOR SCIENCE!
SUDDENLY YOU HAVE THE DESIRE FOR MATERIAL POSSESSIONS--BUT YOU ALSO KNOW THE JOB MARKET FOR A HUMANOID HIPPOPOTAMUS IS LESS THAN NOTHING...
SO YOU START ROBBING BANKS...THEN ONE DAY SPIDER-MAN BITES YOUR FREAKING LEG OFF.
WHO EVEN KNEW HE HAD TEETH?!
I KNOW HOW IT IS, FREUND.

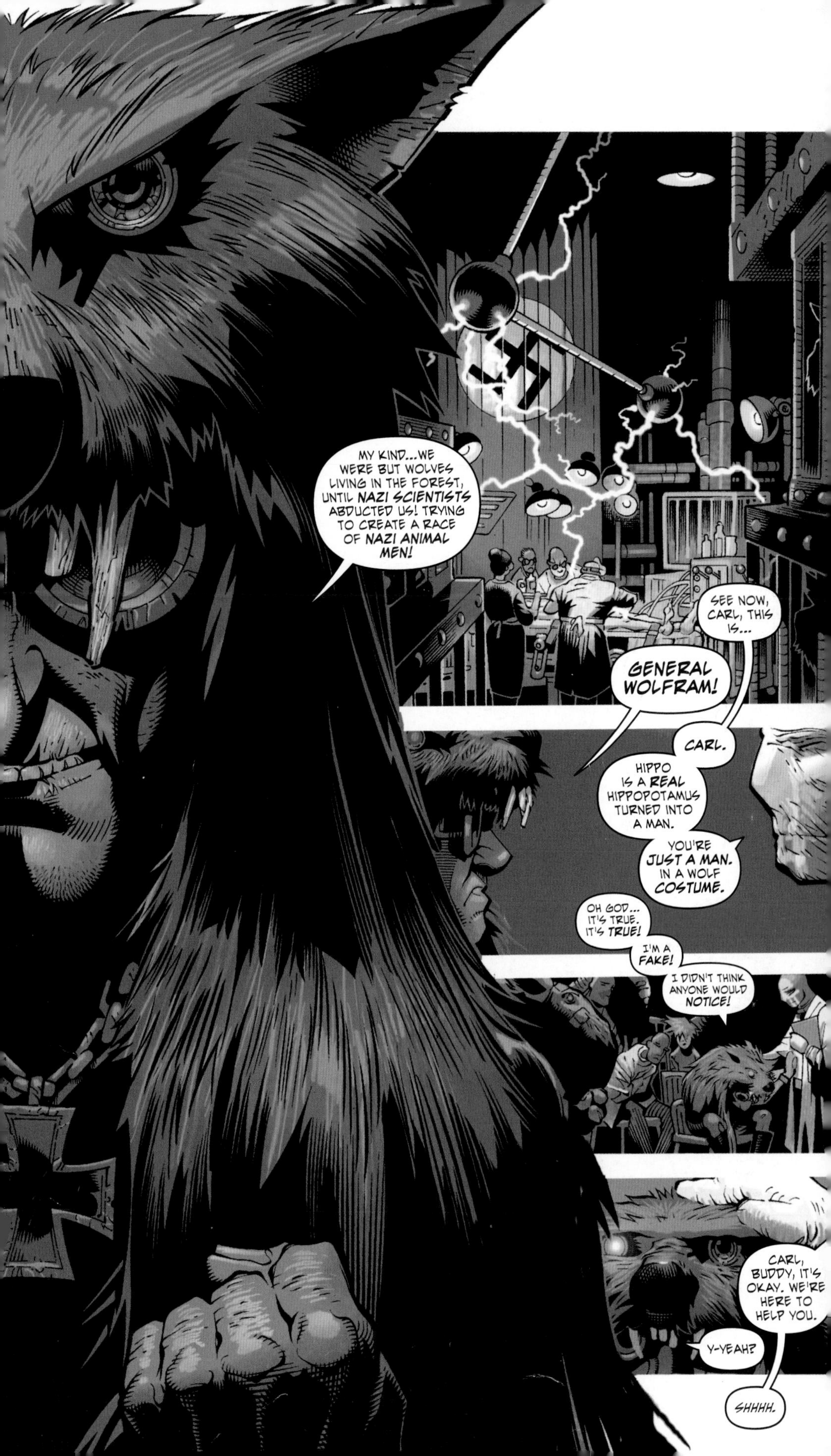
MY KIND...WE WERE BUT WOLVES LIVING IN THE FOREST, UNTIL NAZI SCIENTISTS ABDUCTED US! TRYING TO CREATE A RACE OF NAZI ANIMAL MEN!
SEE NOW, CARL, THIS IS...
GENERAL WOLFRAM!
CARL.
HIPPO IS A REAL HIPPOPOTAMUS TURNED INTO A MAN.
YOU'RE JUST A MAN. IN A WOLF COSTUME.
OH GOD... IT'S TRUE. IT'S TRUE!
I'M A FAKE!
I DIDN'T THINK ANYONE WOULD NOTICE!
CARL, BUDDY, IT'S OKAY. WE'RE HERE TO HELP YOU.
Y-YEAH?
SHHHH.

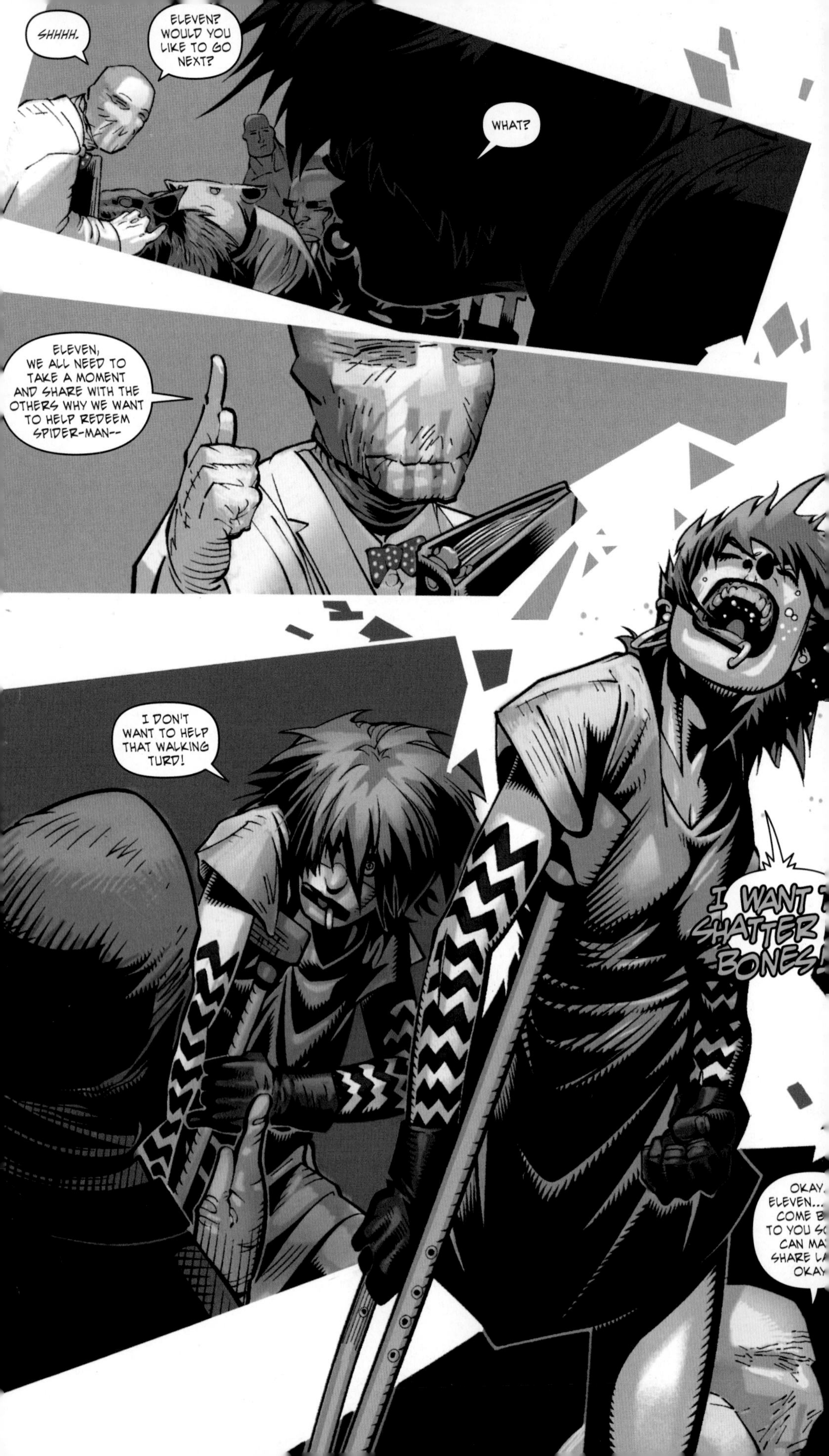

SHHHH.
ELEVEN? WOULD YOU LIKE TO GO NEXT?
WHAT?
ELEVEN, WE ALL NEED TO TAKE A MOMENT AND SHARE WITH THE OTHERS WHY WE WANT TO HELP REDEEM SPIDER-MAN--
I DON'T WANT TO HELP THAT WALKING TURD!

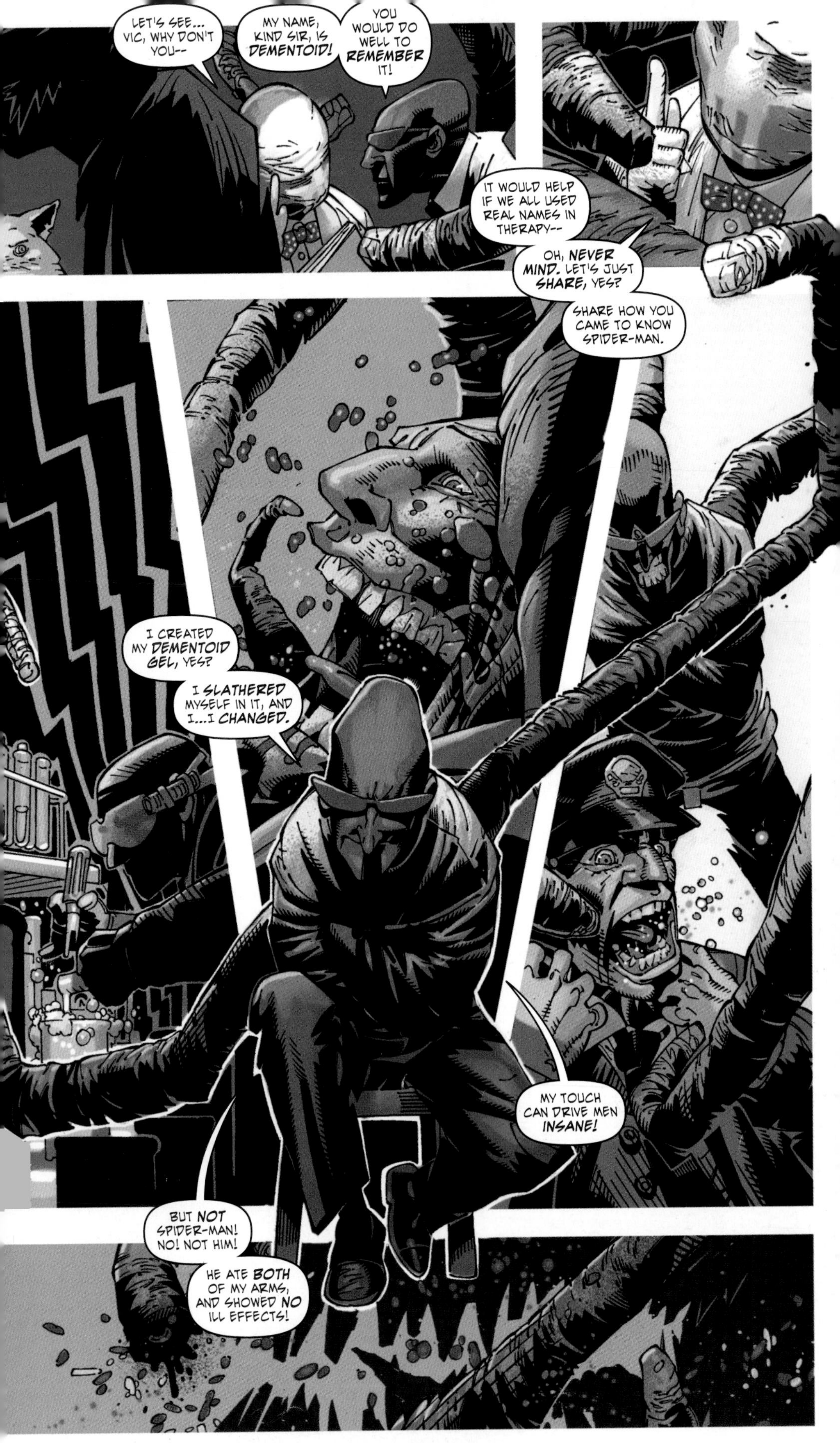
LET'S SEE... VIC, WHY DON'T YOU--
MY NAME, KIND SIR, IS DEMENTOID!
YOU WOULD DO WELL TO REMEMBER IT!
IT WOULD HELP IF WE ALL USED REAL NAMES IN THERAPY--
OH, NEVER MIND. LET'S JUST SHARE, YES?
SHARE HOW YOU CAME TO KNOW SPIDER-MAN.
I CREATED MY DEMENTOID GEL, YES?
I SLATHERED MYSELF IN IT, AND I...I CHANGED.
MY TOUCH CAN DRIVE MEN INSANE!
BUT NOT SPIDER-MAN! NO! NOT HIM!
HE ATE BOTH OF MY ARMS, AND SHOWED NO ILL EFFECTS!

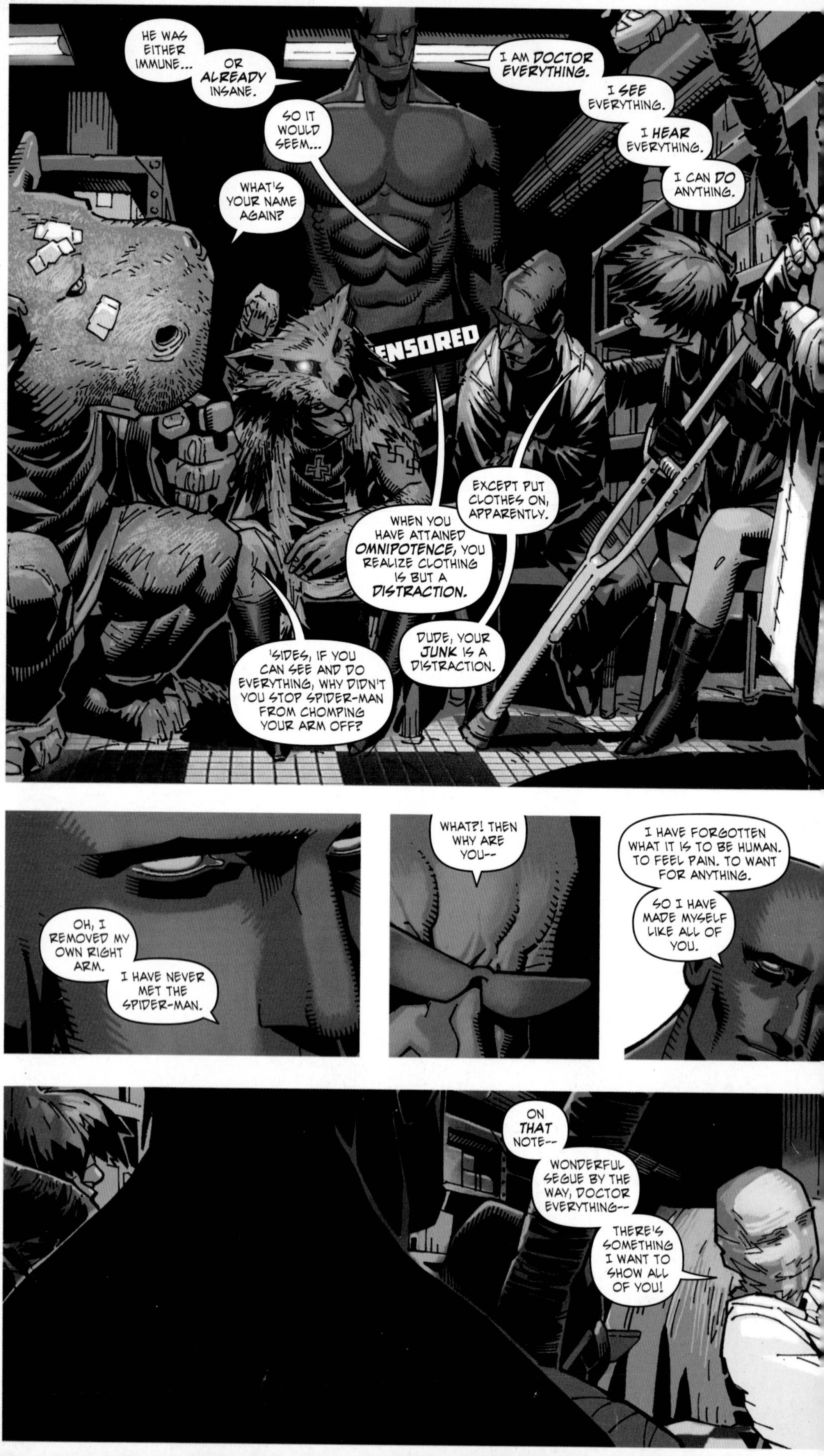
HE WAS EITHER IMMUNE...
OR ALREADY INSANE.
SO IT WOULD SEEM...
WHAT'S YOUR NAME AGAIN?
I AM DOCTOR EVERYTHING.
I SEE EVERYTHING.
I HEAR EVERYTHING.
I CAN DO ANYTHING.
ENSORED
EXCEPT PUT CLOTHES ON, APPARENTLY.
WHEN YOU HAVE ATTAINED OMNIPOTENCE, YOU REALIZE CLOTHING IS BUT A DISTRACTION.
DUDE, YOUR JUNK IS A DISTRACTION.
'SIDES, IF YOU CAN SEE AND DO EVERYTHING, WHY DIDN'T YOU STOP SPIDER-MAN FROM CHOMPING YOUR ARM OFF?
OH, I REMOVED MY OWN RIGHT ARM.
I HAVE NEVER MET THE SPIDER-MAN.
WHAT?! THEN WHY ARE YOU--
I HAVE FORGOTTEN WHAT IT IS TO BE HUMAN. TO FEEL PAIN. TO WANT FOR ANYTHING.
SO I HAVE MADE MYSELF LIKE ALL OF YOU.
ON THAT NOTE--
WONDERFUL SEGUE BY THE WAY, DOCTOR EVERYTHING--
THERE'S SOMETHING I WANT TO SHOW ALL OF YOU!

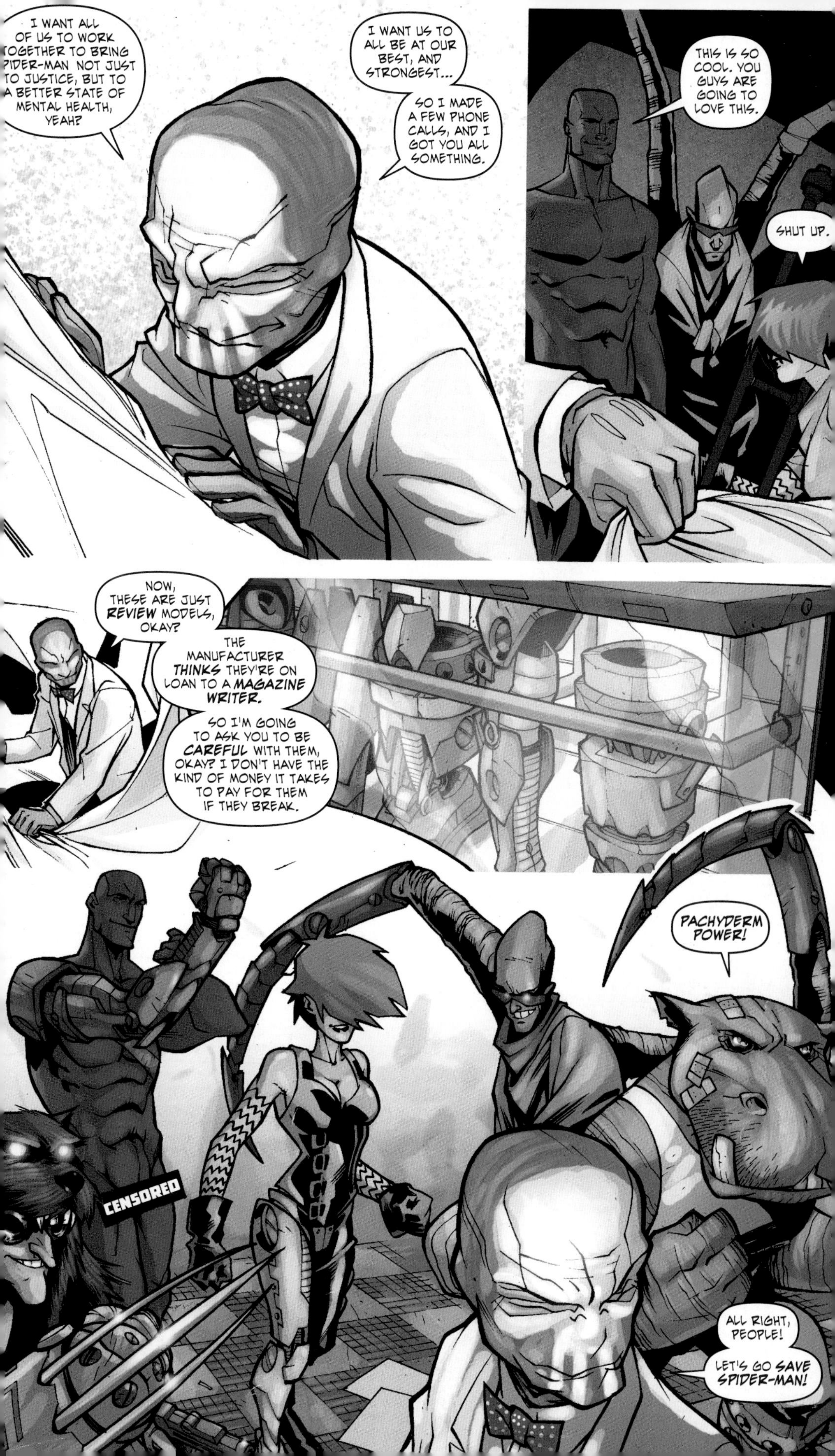

I WANT ALL OF US TO WORK TOGETHER TO BRING SPIDER-MAN NOT JUST TO JUSTICE, BUT TO A BETTER STATE OF MENTAL HEALTH, YEAH?
I WANT US TO ALL BE AT OUR BEST, AND STRONGEST...
SO I MADE A FEW PHONE CALLS, AND I GOT YOU ALL SOMETHING.
THIS IS SO COOL. YOU GUYS ARE GOING TO LOVE THIS.
SHUT UP.
NOW, THESE ARE JUST REVIEW MODELS, OKAY?
THE MANUFACTURER THINKS THEY'RE ON LOAN TO A MAGAZINE WRITER.
SO I'M GOING TO ASK YOU TO BE CAREFUL WITH THEM, OKAY? I DON'T HAVE THE KIND OF MONEY IT TAKES TO PAY FOR THEM IF THEY BREAK.
PACHYDERM POWER!
CENSORED
ALL RIGHT, PEOPLE!
LET'S GO SAVE SPIDER-MAN!

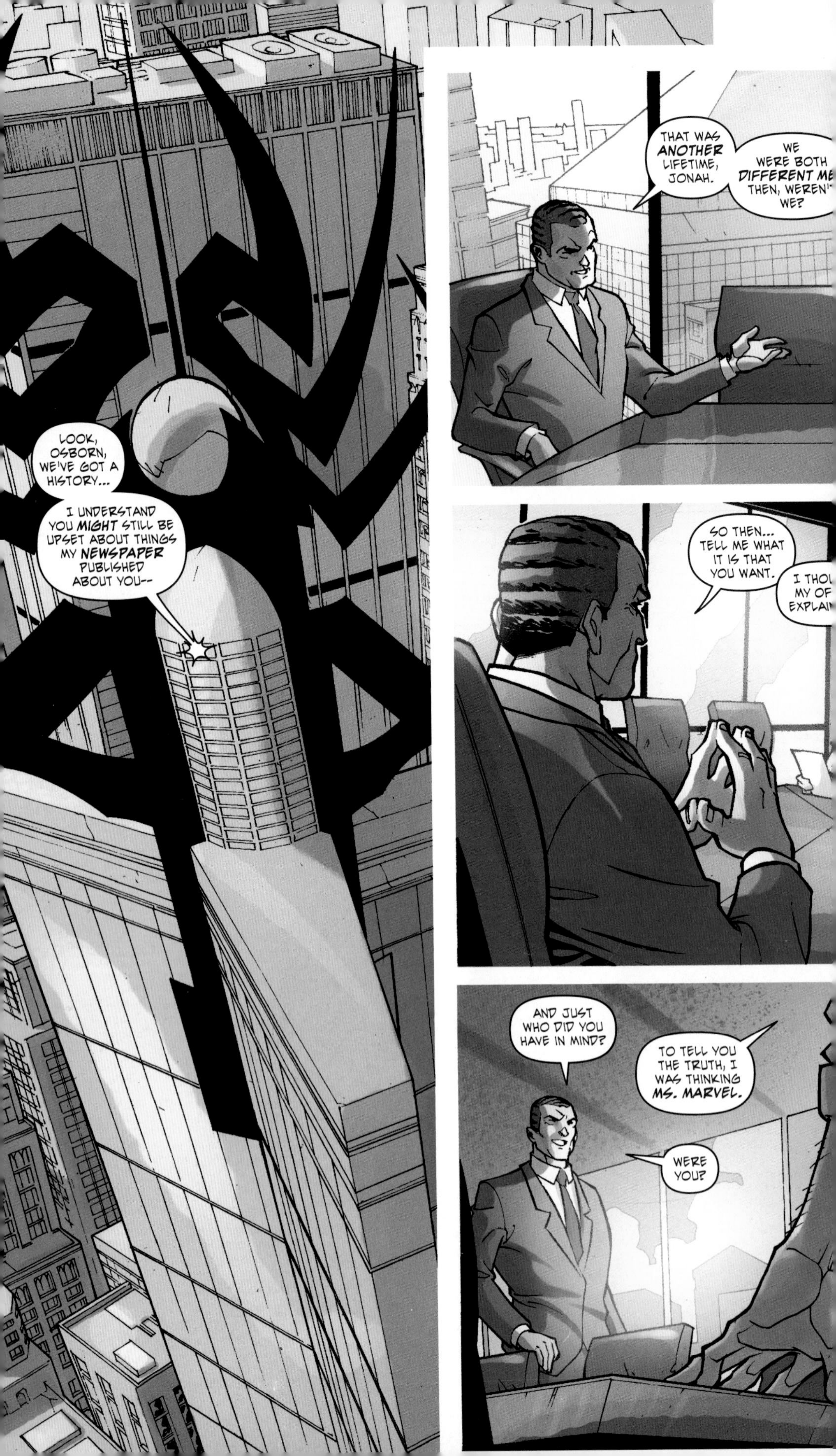
LOOK, OSBORN, WE'VE GOT A HISTORY...
I UNDERSTAND YOU **MIGHT** STILL BE UPSET ABOUT THINGS MY **NEWSPAPER** PUBLISHED ABOUT YOU--
THAT WAS **ANOTHER** LIFETIME, JONAH.
WE WERE BOTH **DIFFERENT ME** THEN, WEREN'T WE?
SO THEN... TELL ME WHAT IT IS THAT YOU WANT.
I THOU MY OF EXPLAI
AND JUST WHO DID YOU HAVE IN MIND?
TO TELL YOU THE TRUTH, I WAS THINKING **MS. MARVEL.**
WERE YOU?

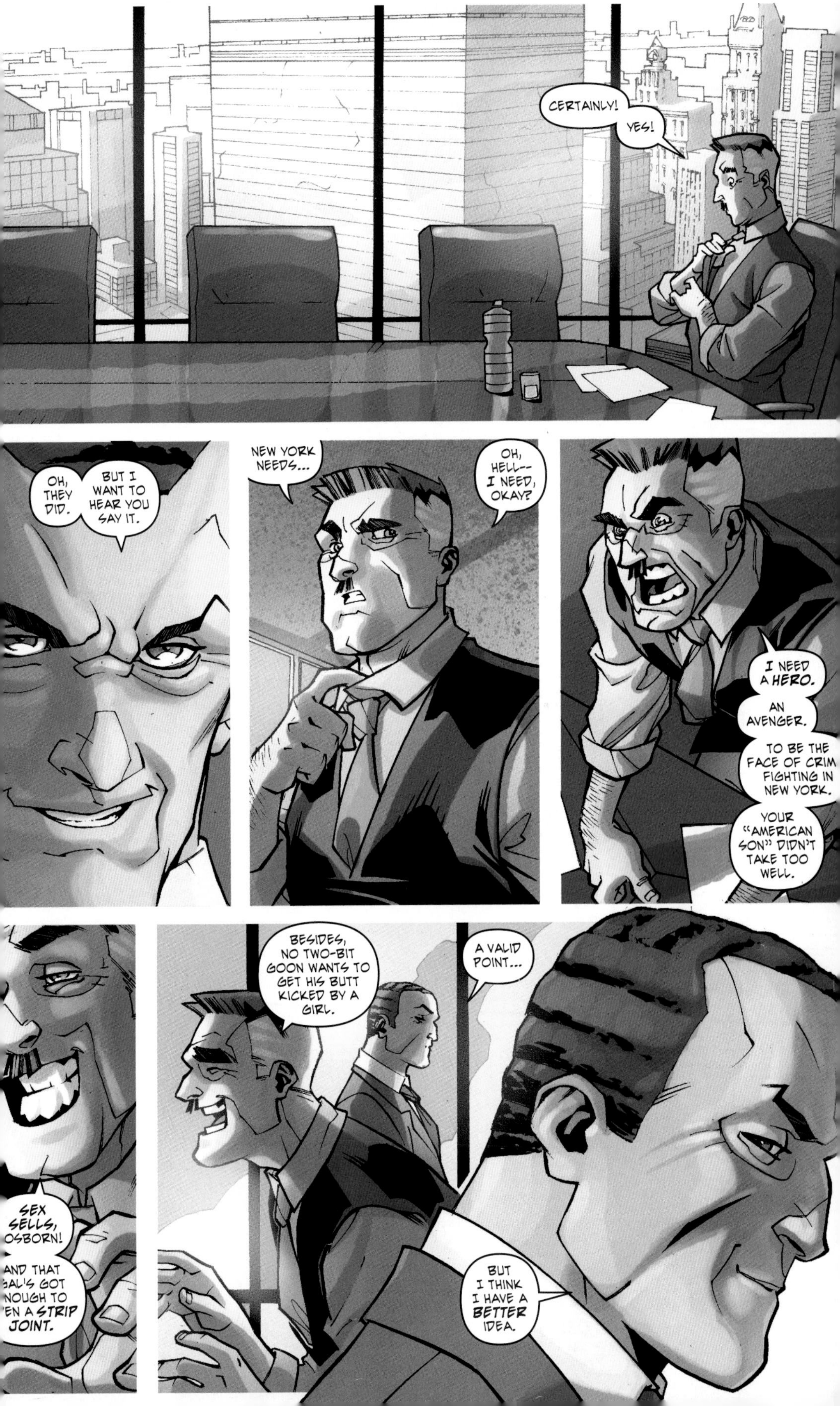
CERTAINLY!
YES!
OH, THEY DID.
BUT I WANT TO HEAR YOU SAY IT.
NEW YORK NEEDS...
OH, HELL-- I NEED, OKAY?
I NEED A HERO.
AN AVENGER.
TO BE THE FACE OF CRIM FIGHTING IN NEW YORK.
YOUR "AMERICAN SON" DIDN'T TAKE TOO WELL.
SEX SELLS, OSBORN!
AND THAT GAL'S GOT NOUGH TO EN A STRIP JOINT.
BESIDES, NO TWO-BIT GOON WANTS TO GET HIS BUTT KICKED BY A GIRL.
A VALID POINT...
BUT I THINK I HAVE A BETTER IDEA.

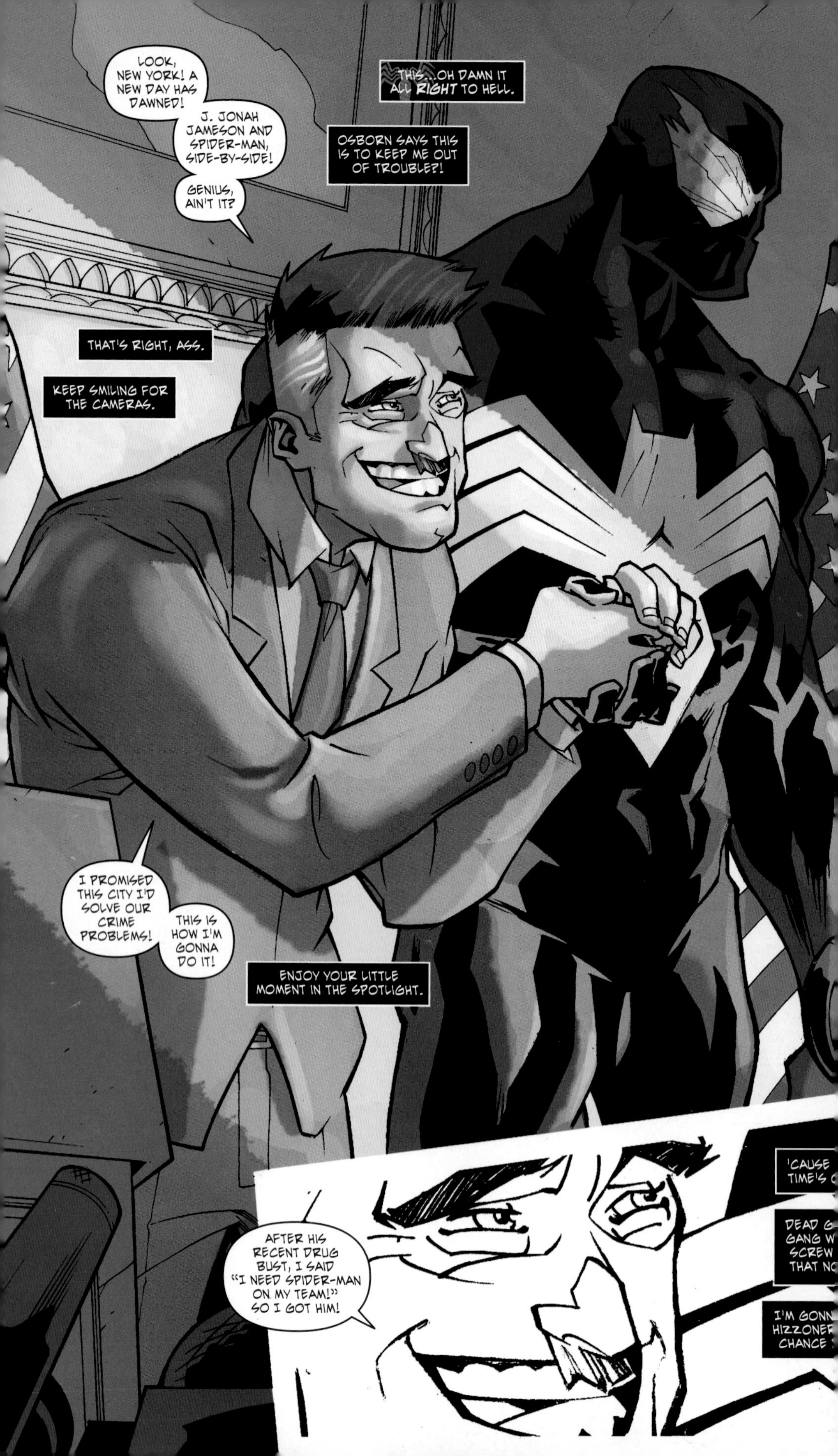

LOOK, NEW YORK! A NEW DAY HAS DAWNED!
J. JONAH JAMESON AND SPIDER-MAN, SIDE-BY-SIDE!
GENIUS, AIN'T IT?
THIS...OH DAMN IT ALL RIGHT TO HELL.
OSBORN SAYS THIS IS TO KEEP ME OUT OF TROUBLE?!
THAT'S RIGHT, ASS.
KEEP SMILING FOR THE CAMERAS.
I PROMISED THIS CITY I'D SOLVE OUR CRIME PROBLEMS!
THIS IS HOW I'M GONNA DO IT!
ENJOY YOUR LITTLE MOMENT IN THE SPOTLIGHT.
AFTER HIS RECENT DRUG BUST, I SAID "I NEED SPIDER-MAN ON MY TEAM!" SO I GOT HIM!

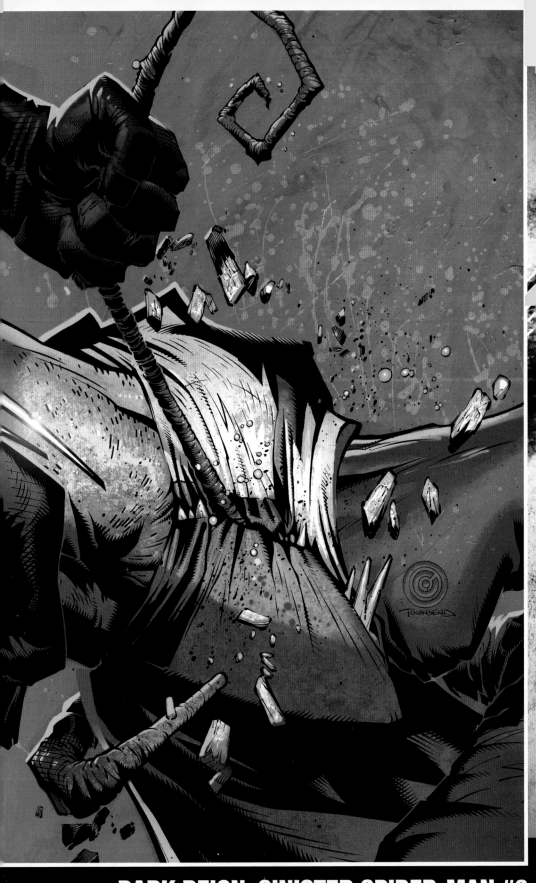

DARK REIGN: SINISTER SPIDER-MAN #3

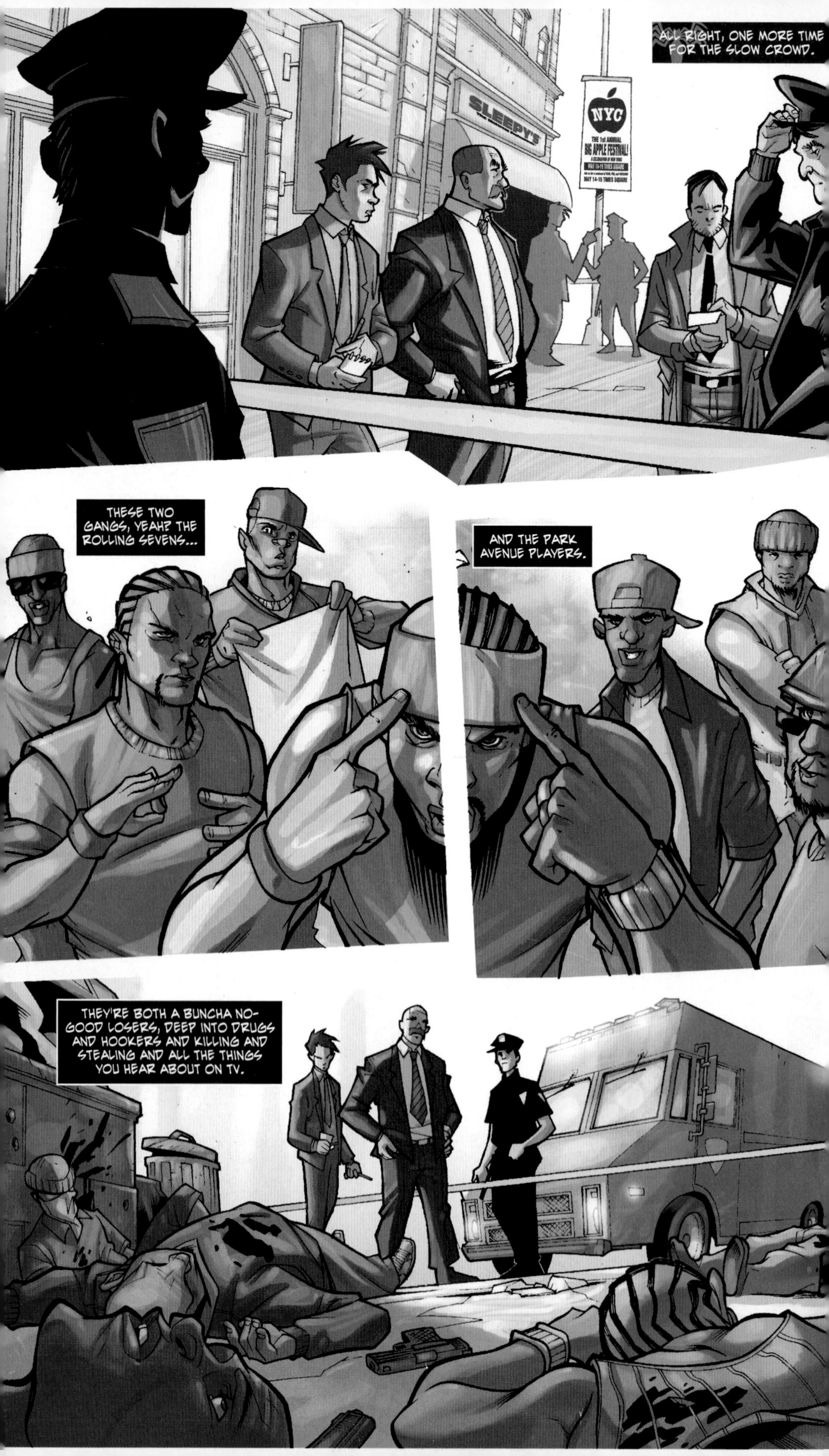
ALL RIGHT, ONE MORE TIME FOR THE SLOW CROWD.
SLEEPY'S
NYC
THE 1st ANNUAL BIG APPLE FESTIVAL!
MAY 14-15 TIMES SQUARE
THESE TWO GANGS, YEAH? THE ROLLING SEVENS...
AND THE PARK AVENUE PLAYERS.
THEY'RE BOTH A BUNCHA NO-GOOD LOSERS, DEEP INTO DRUGS AND HOOKERS AND KILLING AND STEALING AND ALL THE THINGS YOU HEAR ABOUT ON TV.

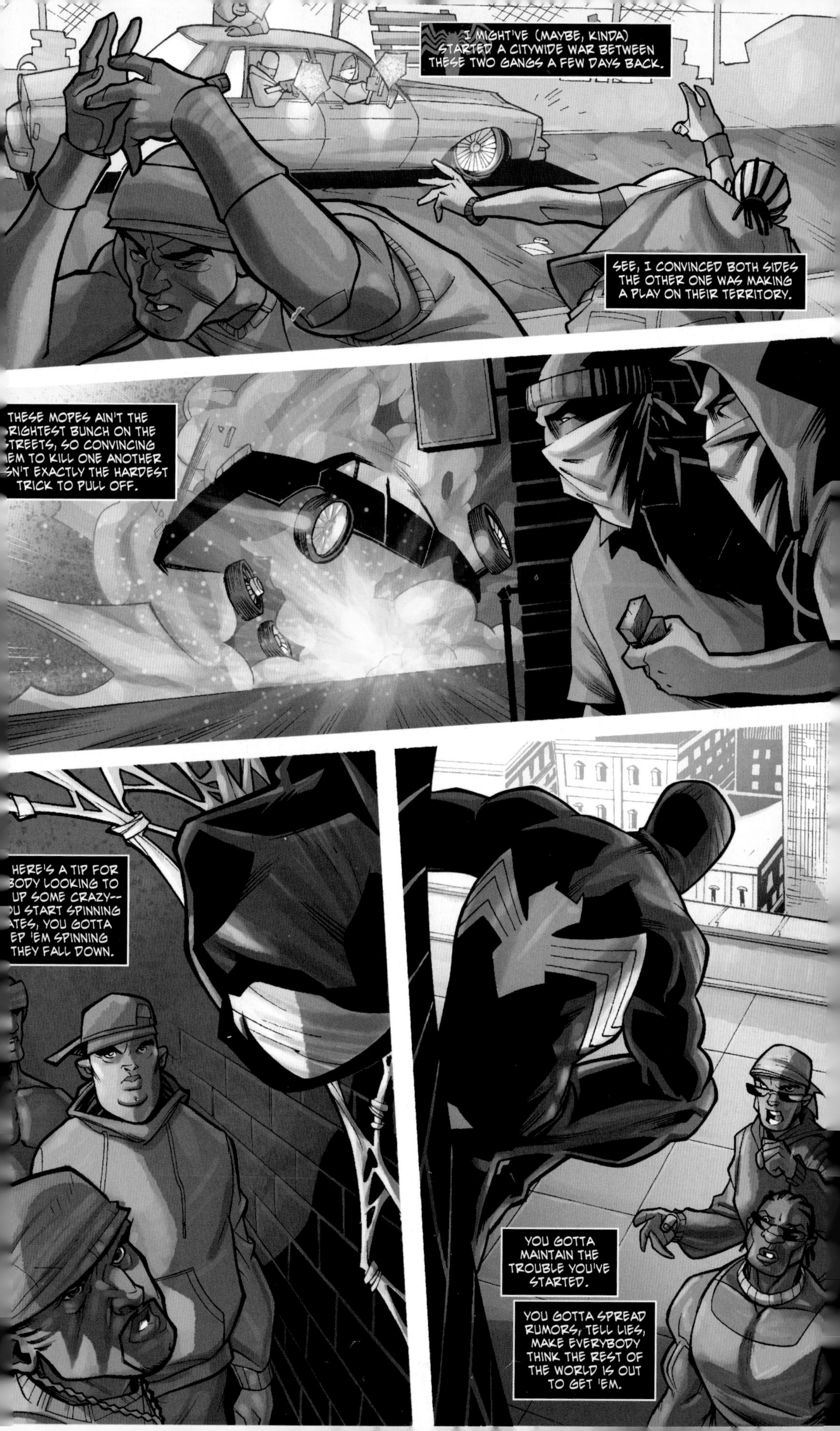
I MIGHT'VE (MAYBE, KINDA) STARTED A CITYWIDE WAR BETWEEN THESE TWO GANGS A FEW DAYS BACK.
SEE, I CONVINCED BOTH SIDES THE OTHER ONE WAS MAKING A PLAY ON THEIR TERRITORY.
THESE MOPES AIN'T THE RIGHTEST BUNCH ON THE TREETS, SO CONVINCING EM TO KILL ONE ANOTHER SN'T EXACTLY THE HARDEST TRICK TO PULL OFF.
HERE'S A TIP FOR BODY LOOKING TO UP SOME CRAZY-- OU START SPINNING ATES, YOU GOTTA EP 'EM SPINNING THEY FALL DOWN.
YOU GOTTA MAINTAIN THE TROUBLE YOU'VE STARTED.
YOU GOTTA SPREAD RUMORS, TELL LIES, MAKE EVERYBODY THINK THE REST OF THE WORLD IS OUT TO GET 'EM.

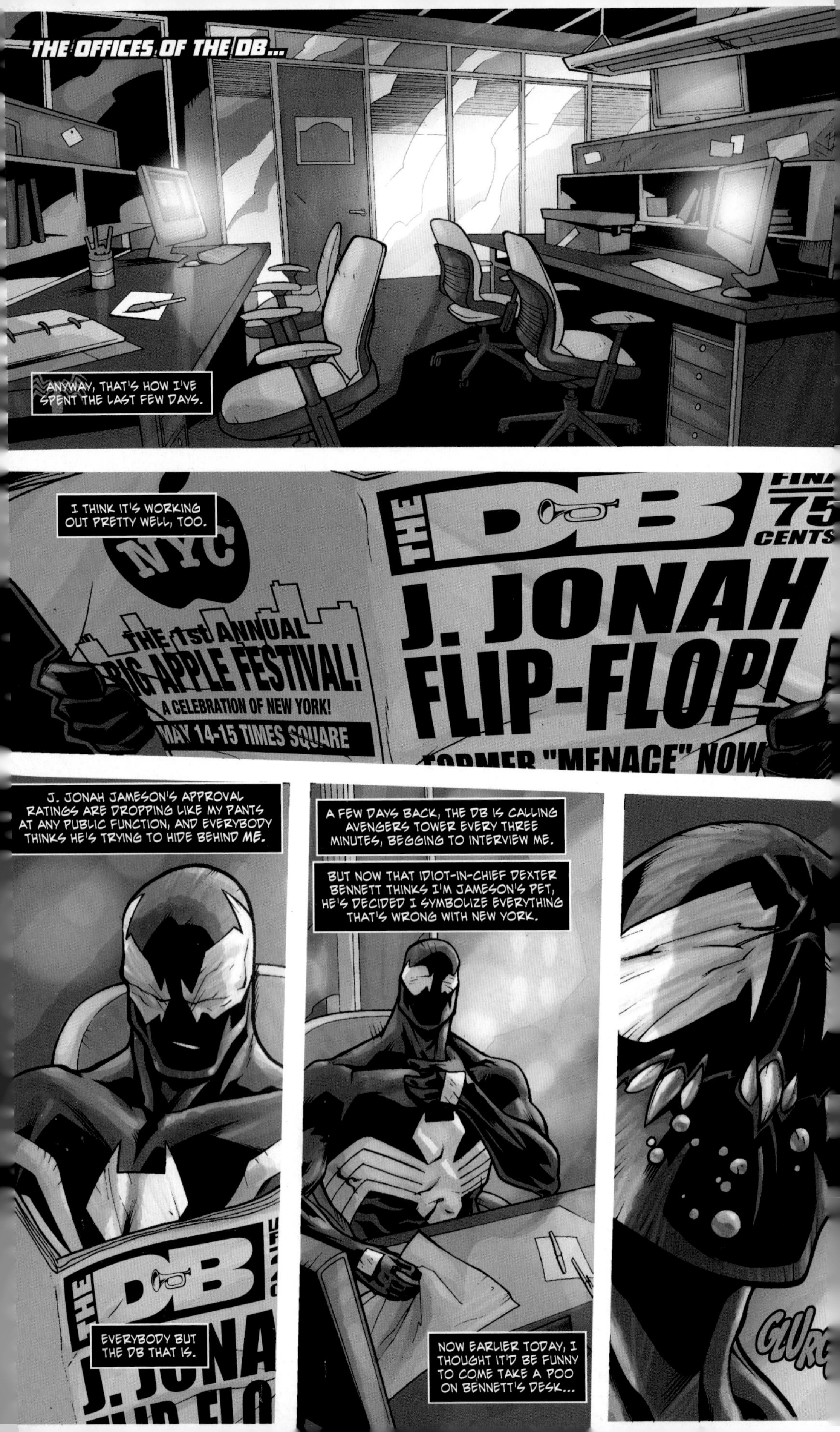
THE OFFICES OF THE DB...
ANYWAY, THAT'S HOW I'VE SPENT THE LAST FEW DAYS.
I THINK IT'S WORKING OUT PRETTY WELL, TOO.
NYC
THE 1st ANNUAL BIG APPLE FESTIVAL!
A CELEBRATION OF NEW YORK!
MAY 14-15 TIMES SQUARE
THE DB
75 CENTS
J. JONAH FLIP-FLOP!
J. JONAH JAMESON'S APPROVAL RATINGS ARE DROPPING LIKE MY PANTS AT ANY PUBLIC FUNCTION, AND EVERYBODY THINKS HE'S TRYING TO HIDE BEHIND ME.
EVERYBODY BUT THE DB THAT IS.
A FEW DAYS BACK, THE DB IS CALLING AVENGERS TOWER EVERY THREE MINUTES, BEGGING TO INTERVIEW ME.
BUT NOW THAT IDIOT-IN-CHIEF DEXTER BENNETT THINKS I'M JAMESON'S PET, HE'S DECIDED I SYMBOLIZE EVERYTHING THAT'S WRONG WITH NEW YORK.
NOW EARLIER TODAY, I THOUGHT IT'D BE FUNNY TO COME TAKE A POO ON BENNETT'S DESK...

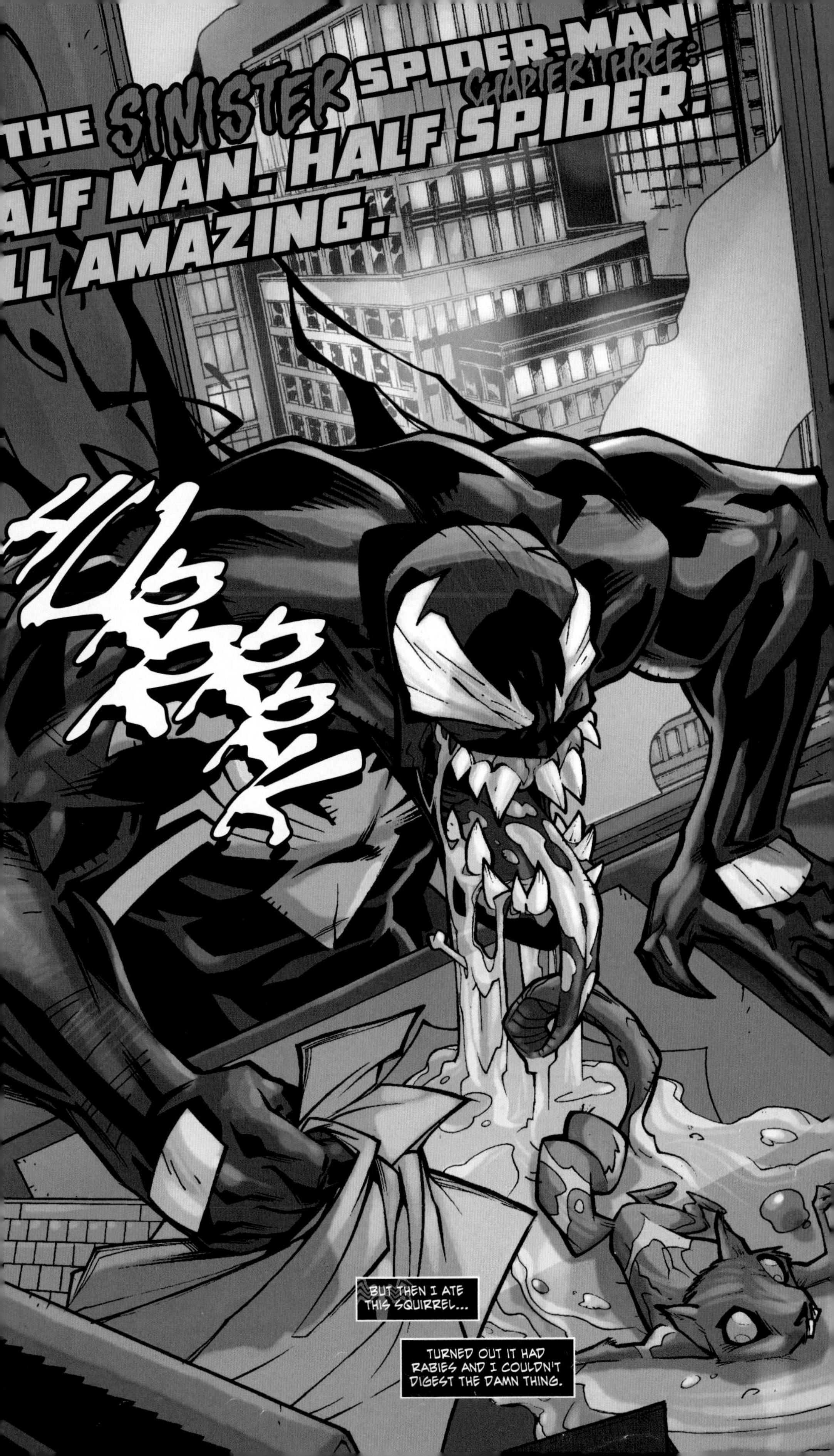
THE SINISTER SPIDER-MAN
CHAPTER THREE:
HALF MAN. HALF SPIDER.
ALL AMAZING.
HURRRK
BUT THEN I ATE THIS SQUIRREL...
TURNED OUT IT HAD RABIES AND I COULDN'T DIGEST THE DAMN THING.

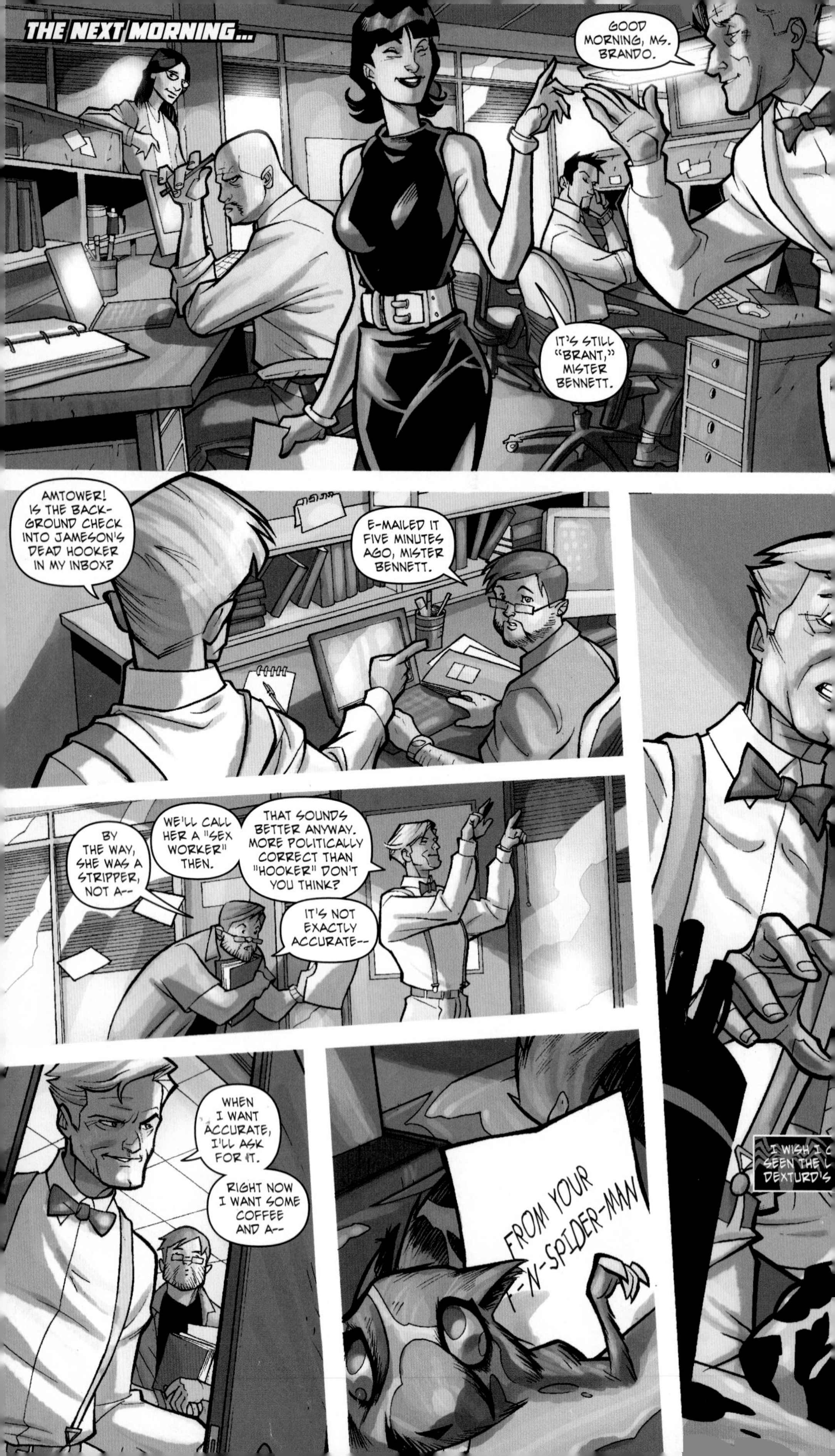
THE NEXT MORNING...
GOOD MORNING, MS. BRANDO.
IT'S STILL "BRANT," MISTER BENNETT.
AMTOWER! IS THE BACK-GROUND CHECK INTO JAMESON'S DEAD HOOKER IN MY INBOX?
E-MAILED IT FIVE MINUTES AGO, MISTER BENNETT.
BY THE WAY, SHE WAS A STRIPPER, NOT A--
WE'LL CALL HER A "SEX WORKER" THEN.
THAT SOUNDS BETTER ANYWAY. MORE POLITICALLY CORRECT THAN "HOOKER" DON'T YOU THINK?
IT'S NOT EXACTLY ACCURATE--
WHEN I WANT ACCURATE, I'LL ASK FOR IT.
RIGHT NOW I WANT SOME COFFEE AND A--
FROM YOUR F-N-SPIDER-MAN
I WISH I C
SEEN THE L
DEXTURD'S

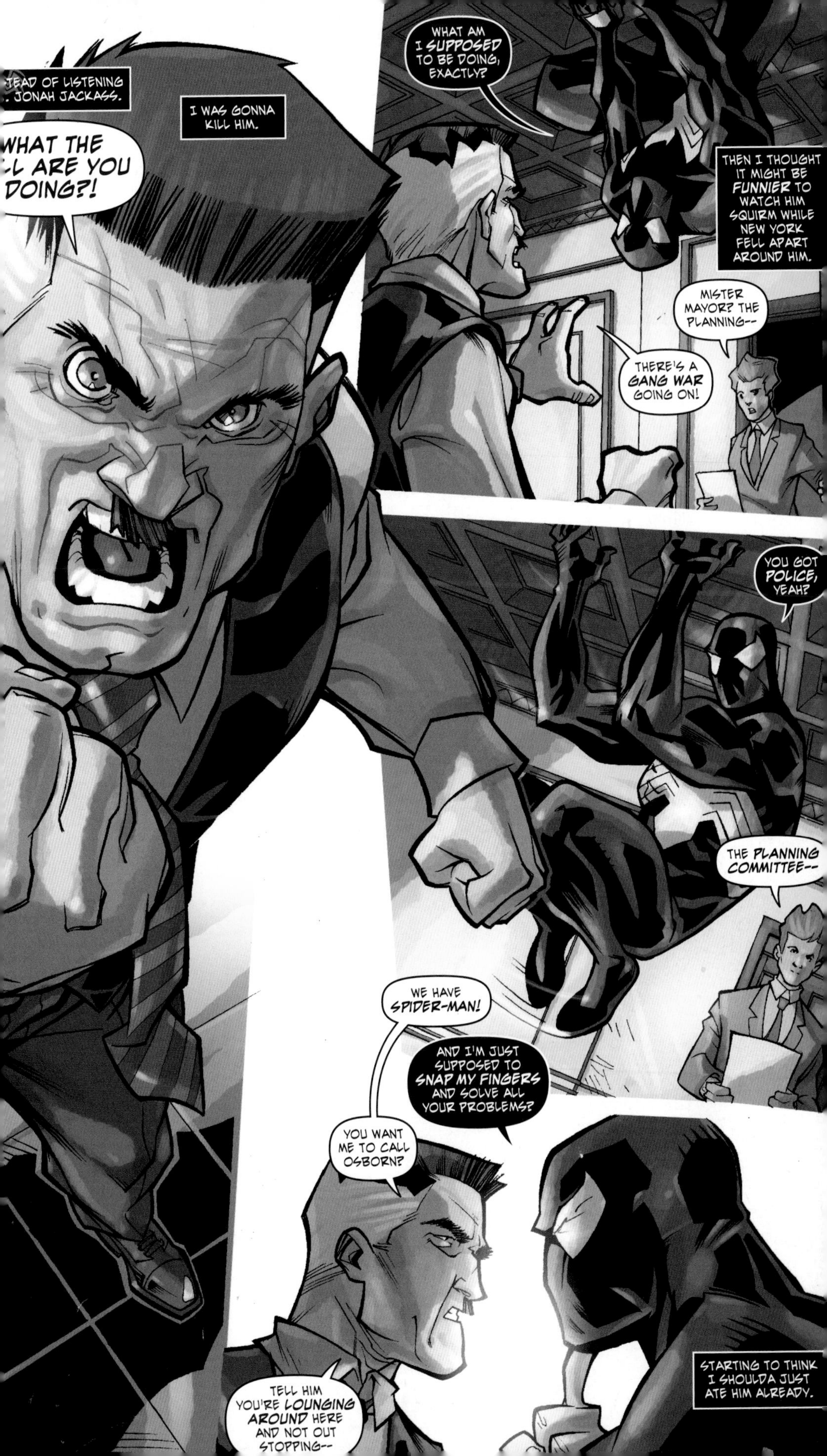

TEAD OF LISTENING
. JONAH JACKASS.
I WAS GONNA KILL HIM.
WHAT THE -L ARE YOU DOING?!
WHAT AM I SUPPOSED TO BE DOING, EXACTLY?
THEN I THOUGHT IT MIGHT BE FUNNIER TO WATCH HIM SQUIRM WHILE NEW YORK FELL APART AROUND HIM.
MISTER MAYOR? THE PLANNING--
THERE'S A GANG WAR GOING ON!
YOU GOT POLICE, YEAH?
THE PLANNING COMMITTEE--
WE HAVE SPIDER-MAN!
AND I'M JUST SUPPOSED TO SNAP MY FINGERS AND SOLVE ALL YOUR PROBLEMS?
YOU WANT ME TO CALL OSBORN?
TELL HIM YOU'RE LOUNGING AROUND HERE AND NOT OUT STOPPING--
STARTING TO THINK I SHOULDA JUST ATE HIM ALREADY.

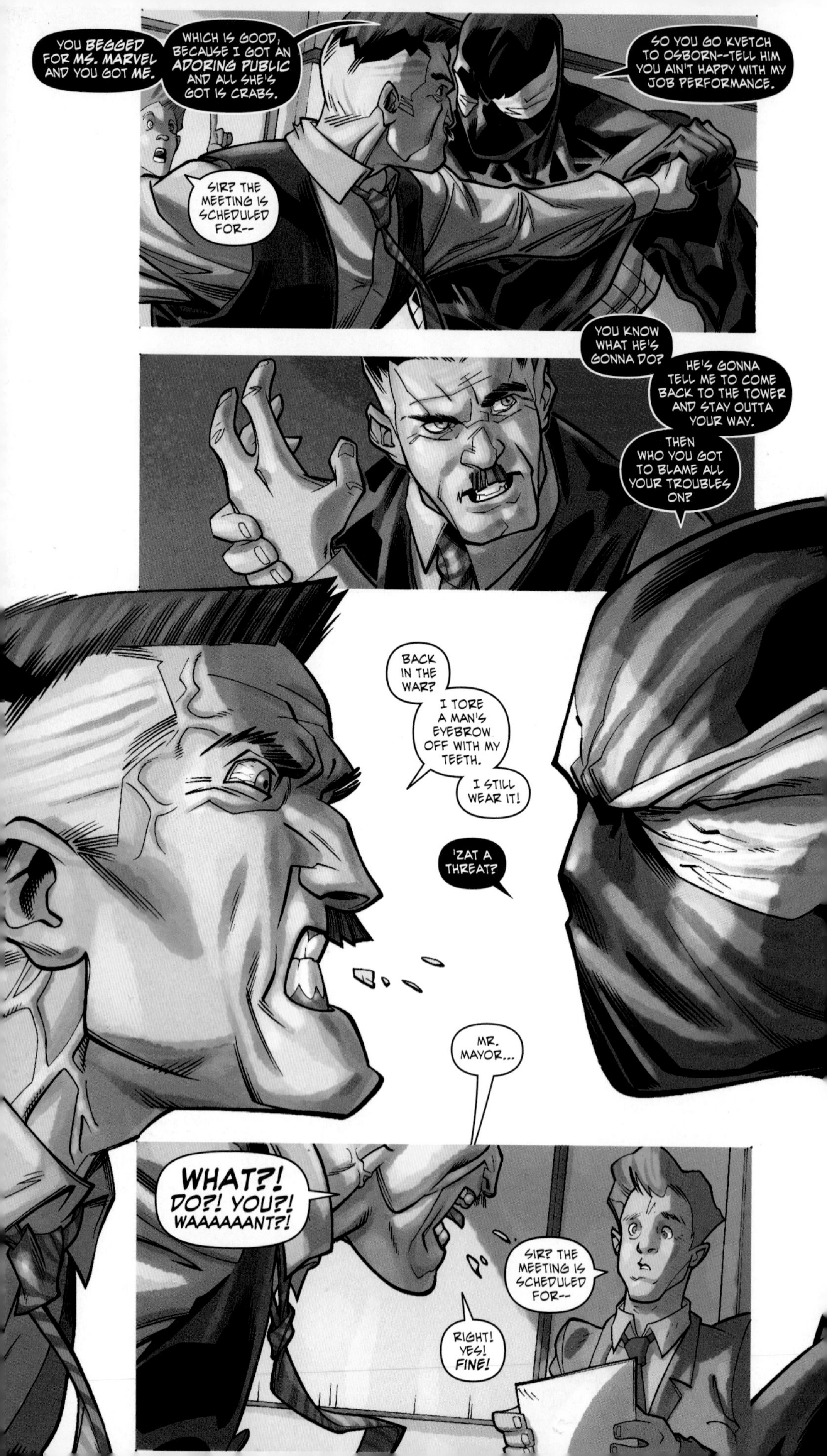
YOU BEGGED FOR MS. MARVEL AND YOU GOT ME.
WHICH IS GOOD, BECAUSE I GOT AN ADORING PUBLIC AND ALL SHE'S GOT IS CRABS.
SO YOU GO KVETCH TO OSBORN--TELL HIM YOU AIN'T HAPPY WITH MY JOB PERFORMANCE.
SIR? THE MEETING IS SCHEDULED FOR--
YOU KNOW WHAT HE'S GONNA DO?
HE'S GONNA TELL ME TO COME BACK TO THE TOWER AND STAY OUTTA YOUR WAY.
THEN WHO YOU GOT TO BLAME ALL YOUR TROUBLES ON?
BACK IN THE WAR?
I TORE A MAN'S EYEBROW OFF WITH MY TEETH.
I STILL WEAR IT!
'ZAT A THREAT?
MR. MAYOR...
WHAT?! DO?! YOU?! WAAAAAANT?!
SIR? THE MEETING IS SCHEDULED FOR--
RIGHT! YES! FINE!

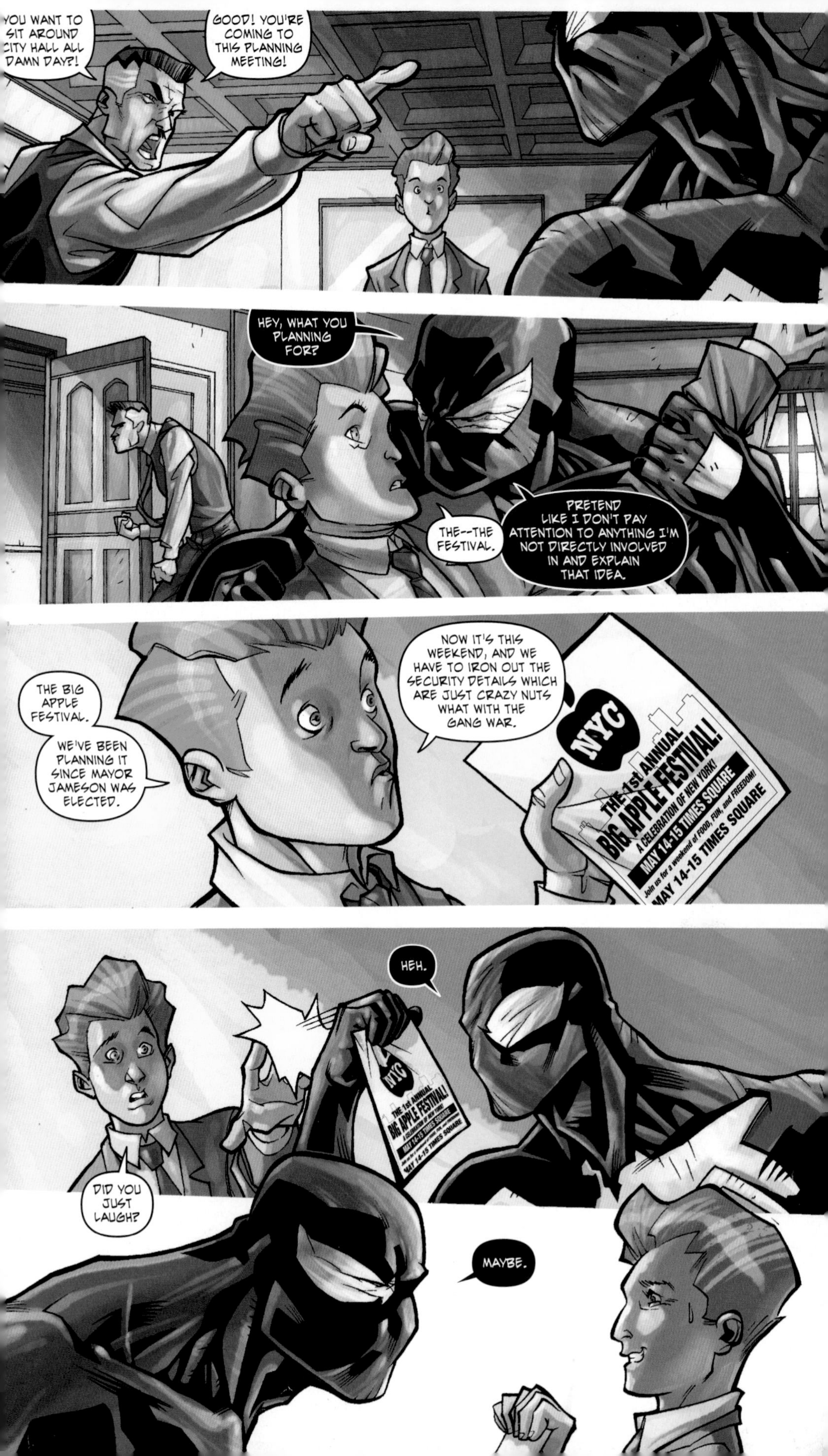
YOU WANT TO SIT AROUND CITY HALL ALL DAMN DAY?!
GOOD! YOU'RE COMING TO THIS PLANNING MEETING!
HEY, WHAT YOU PLANNING FOR?
THE--THE FESTIVAL.
PRETEND LIKE I DON'T PAY ATTENTION TO ANYTHING I'M NOT DIRECTLY INVOLVED IN AND EXPLAIN THAT IDEA.
THE BIG APPLE FESTIVAL.
WE'VE BEEN PLANNING IT SINCE MAYOR JAMESON WAS ELECTED.
NOW IT'S THIS WEEKEND, AND WE HAVE TO IRON OUT THE SECURITY DETAILS WHICH ARE JUST CRAZY NUTS WHAT WITH THE GANG WAR.
NYC
THE 1st ANNUAL BIG APPLE FESTIVAL!
A CELEBRATION OF NEW YORK!
MAY 14-15 TIMES SQUARE
Join us for a weekend of FOOD, FUN, and FREEDOM!
MAY 14-15 TIMES SQUARE
HEH.
DID YOU JUST LAUGH?
MAYBE.

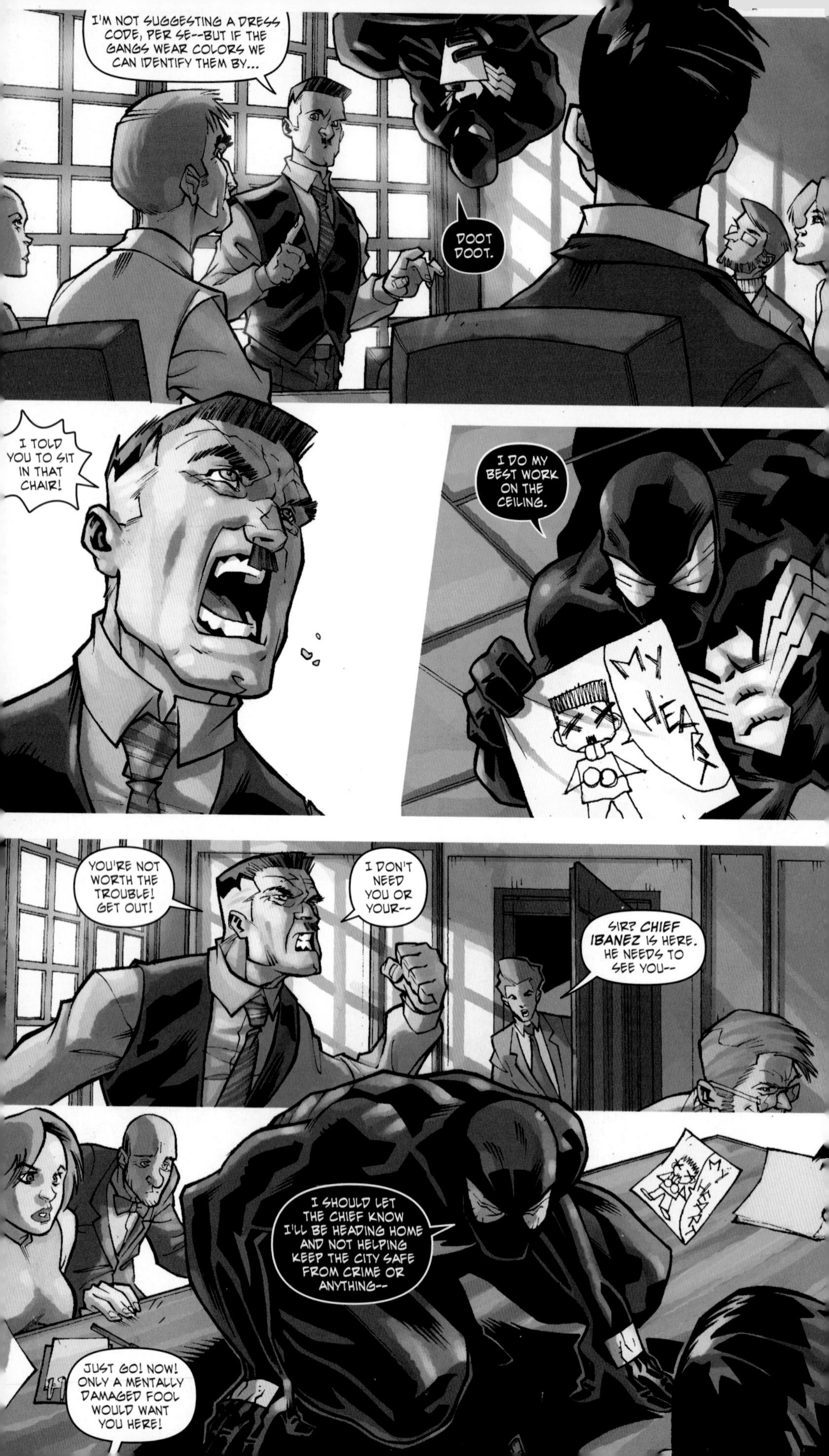
I'M NOT SUGGESTING A DRESS CODE, PER SE--BUT IF THE GANGS WEAR COLORS WE CAN IDENTIFY THEM BY...
DOOT DOOT.
I TOLD YOU TO SIT IN THAT CHAIR!
I DO MY BEST WORK ON THE CEILING.
MY HEART
YOU'RE NOT WORTH THE TROUBLE! GET OUT!
I DON'T NEED YOU OR YOUR--
SIR? CHIEF IBANEZ IS HERE. HE NEEDS TO SEE YOU--
I SHOULD LET THE CHIEF KNOW I'LL BE HEADING HOME AND NOT HELPING KEEP THE CITY SAFE FROM CRIME OR ANYTHING--
MY HEART
JUST GO! NOW! ONLY A MENTALLY DAMAGED FOOL WOULD WANT YOU HERE!

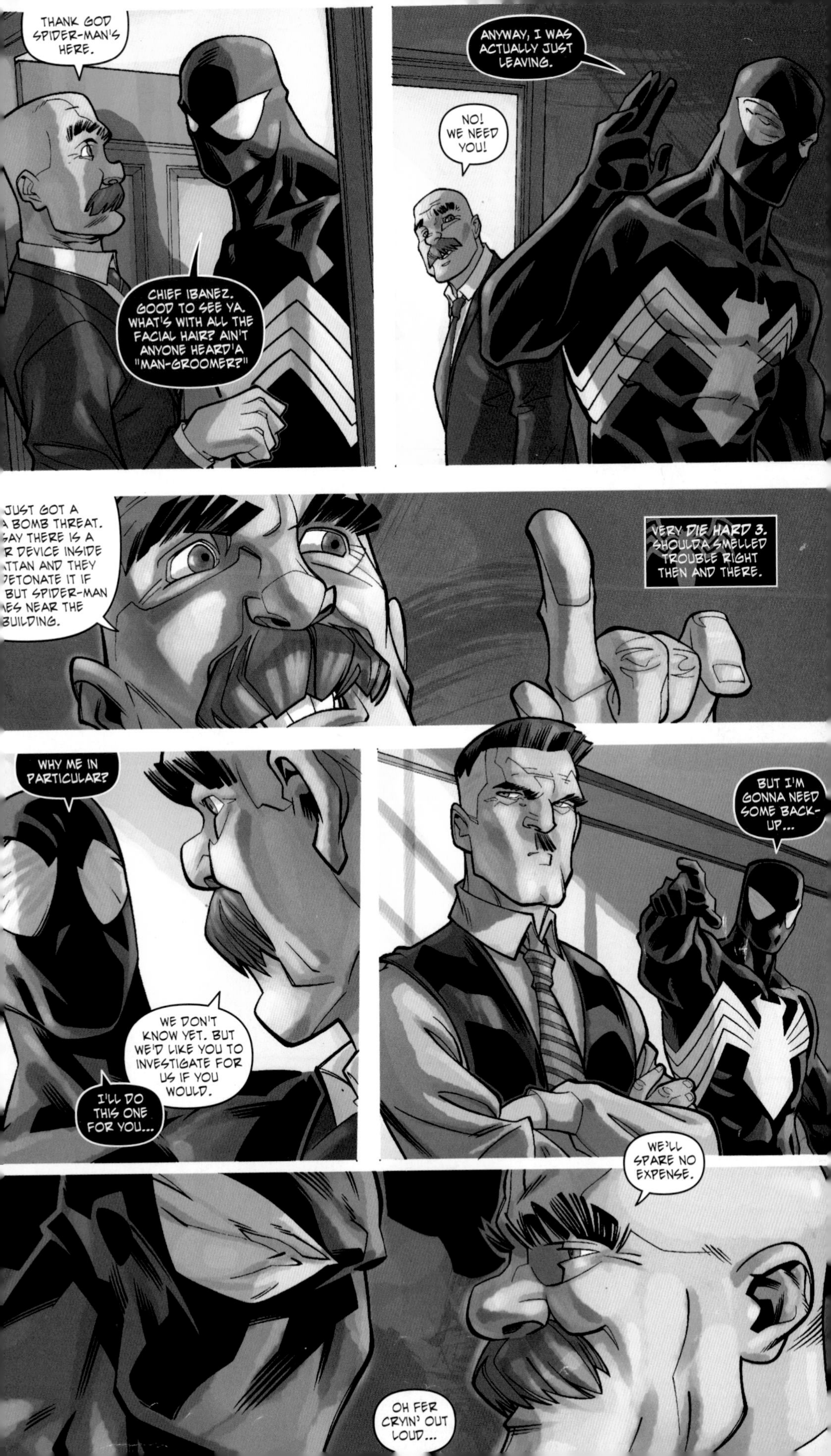
THANK GOD SPIDER-MAN'S HERE.
CHIEF IBANEZ. GOOD TO SEE YA. WHAT'S WITH ALL THE FACIAL HAIR? AIN'T ANYONE HEARD'A "MAN-GROOMER?"
ANYWAY, I WAS ACTUALLY JUST LEAVING.
NO! WE NEED YOU!
JUST GOT A A BOMB THREAT. SAY THERE IS A R DEVICE INSIDE TTAN AND THEY ETONATE IT IF BUT SPIDER-MAN ES NEAR THE BUILDING.
VERY *DIE HARD 3.* SHOULDA SMELLED TROUBLE RIGHT THEN AND THERE.
WHY ME IN PARTICULAR?
WE DON'T KNOW YET. BUT WE'D LIKE YOU TO INVESTIGATE FOR US IF YOU WOULD.
I'LL DO THIS ONE FOR YOU...
BUT I'M GONNA NEED SOME BACK-UP...
WE'LL SPARE NO EXPENSE.
OH FER CRYIN' OUT LOUD...

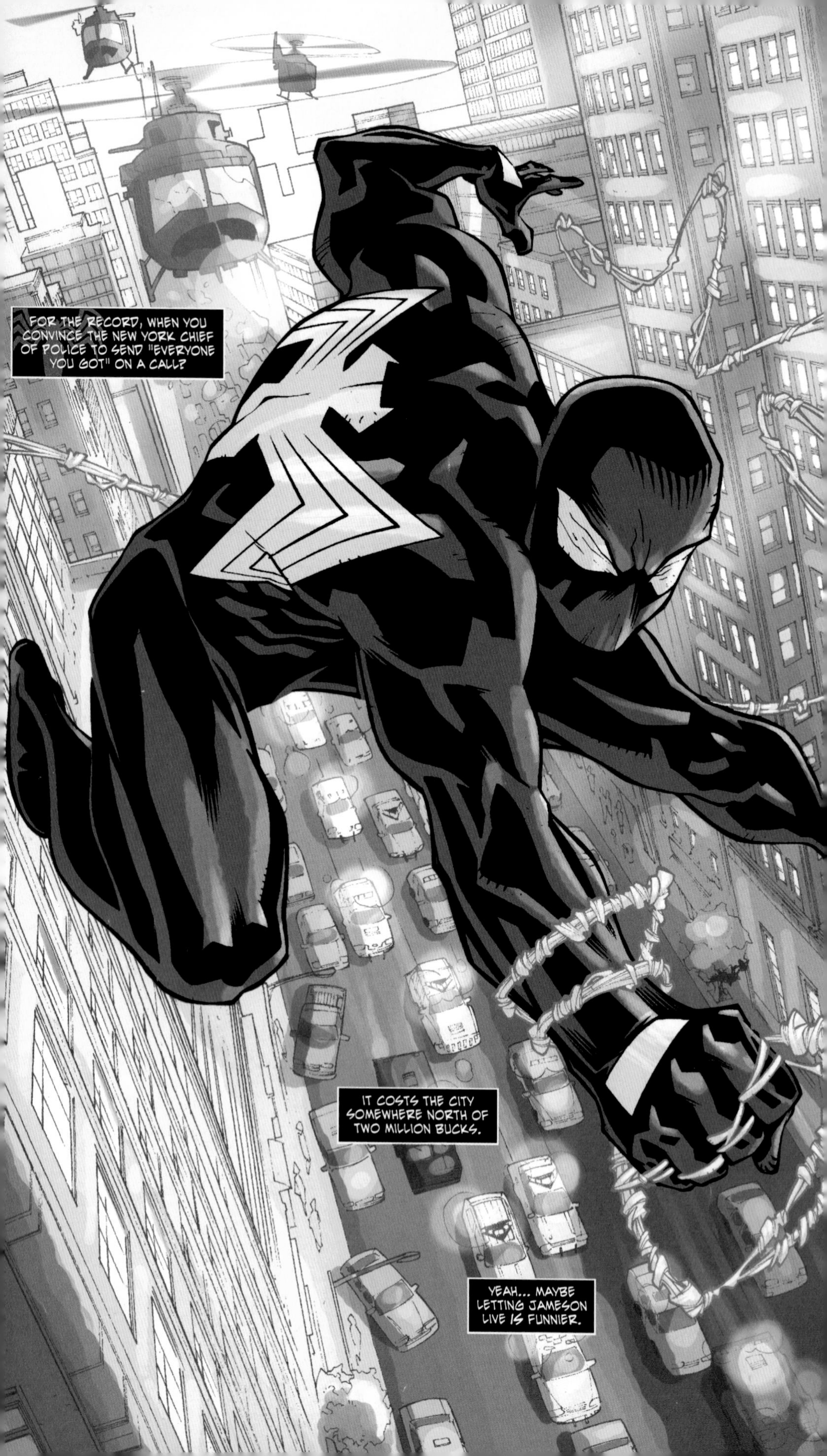
FOR THE RECORD, WHEN YOU CONVINCE THE NEW YORK CHIEF OF POLICE TO SEND "EVERYONE YOU GOT" ON A CALL?
IT COSTS THE CITY SOMEWHERE NORTH OF TWO MILLION BUCKS.
YEAH... MAYBE LETTING JAMESON LIVE IS FUNNIER.

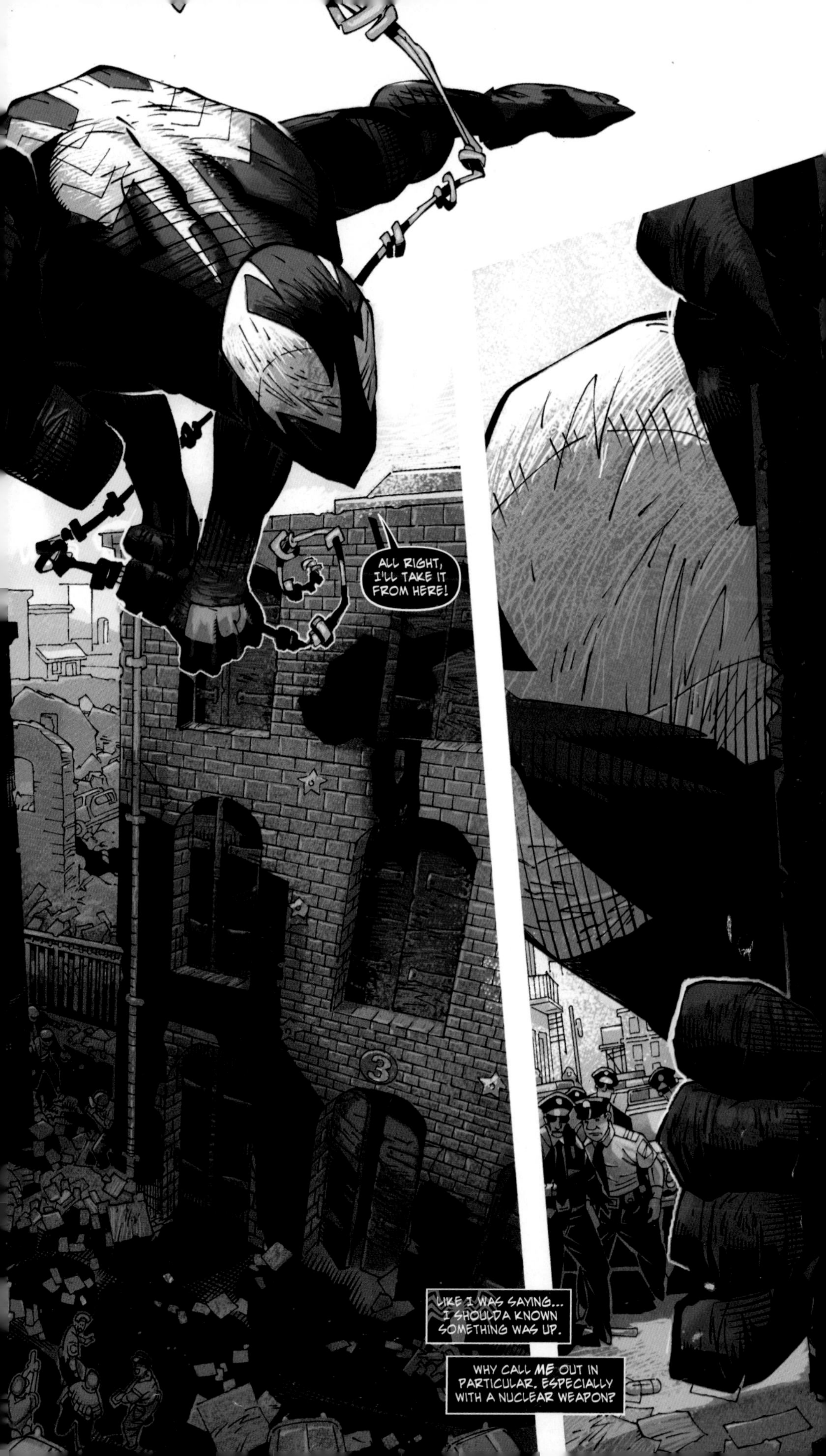
ALL RIGHT, I'LL TAKE IT FROM HERE!
LIKE I WAS SAYING... I SHOULDA KNOWN SOMETHING WAS UP.
WHY CALL ME OUT IN PARTICULAR. ESPECIALLY WITH A NUCLEAR WEAPON?

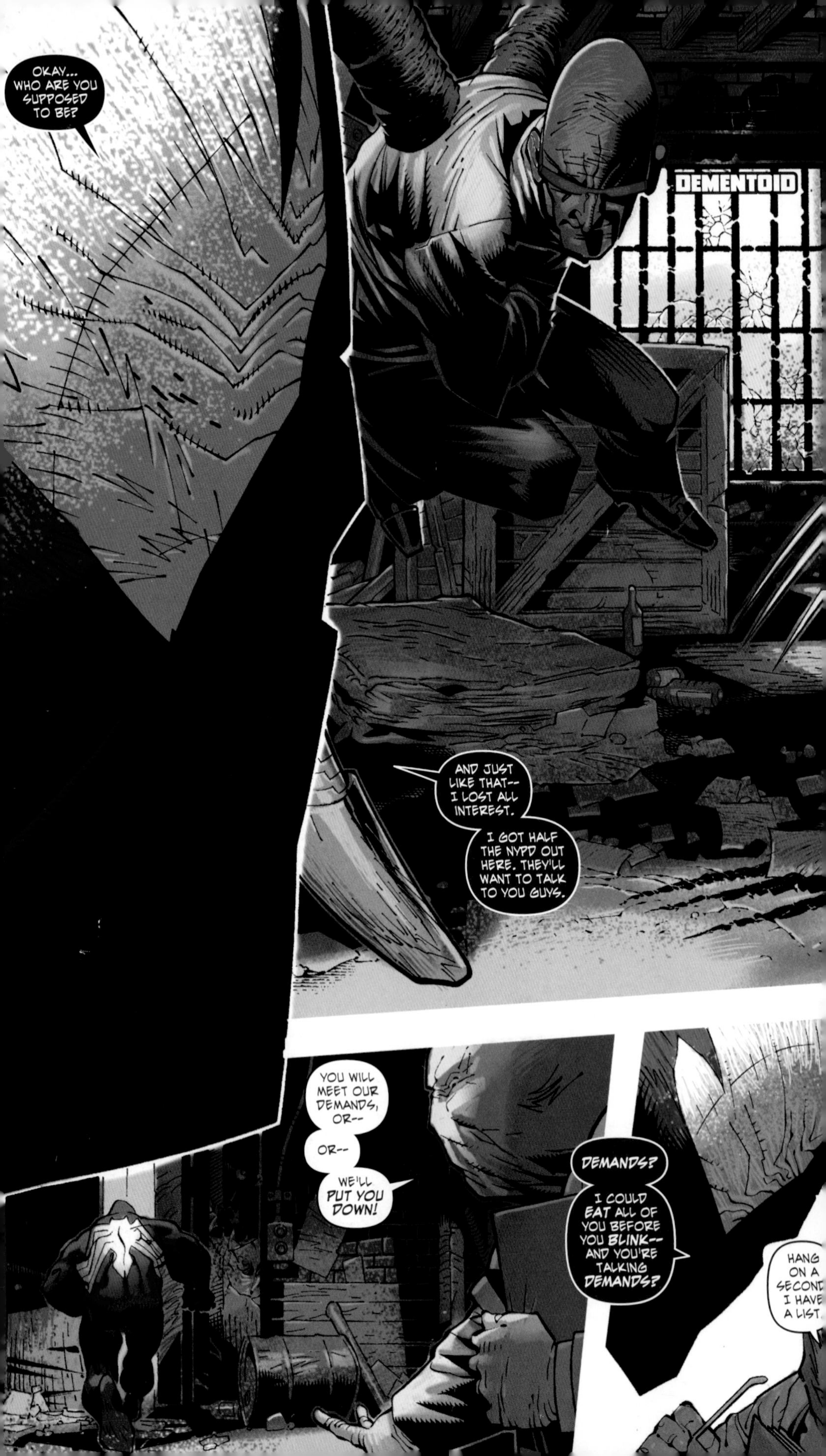
OKAY... WHO ARE YOU SUPPOSED TO BE?
DEMENTOID
AND JUST LIKE THAT-- I LOST ALL INTEREST.
I GOT HALF THE NYPD OUT HERE. THEY'LL WANT TO TALK TO YOU GUYS.
YOU WILL MEET OUR DEMANDS, OR--
OR--
WE'LL PUT YOU DOWN!
DEMANDS?
I COULD EAT ALL OF YOU BEFORE YOU BLINK-- AND YOU'RE TALKING DEMANDS?
HANG ON A SECOND I HAVE A LIST

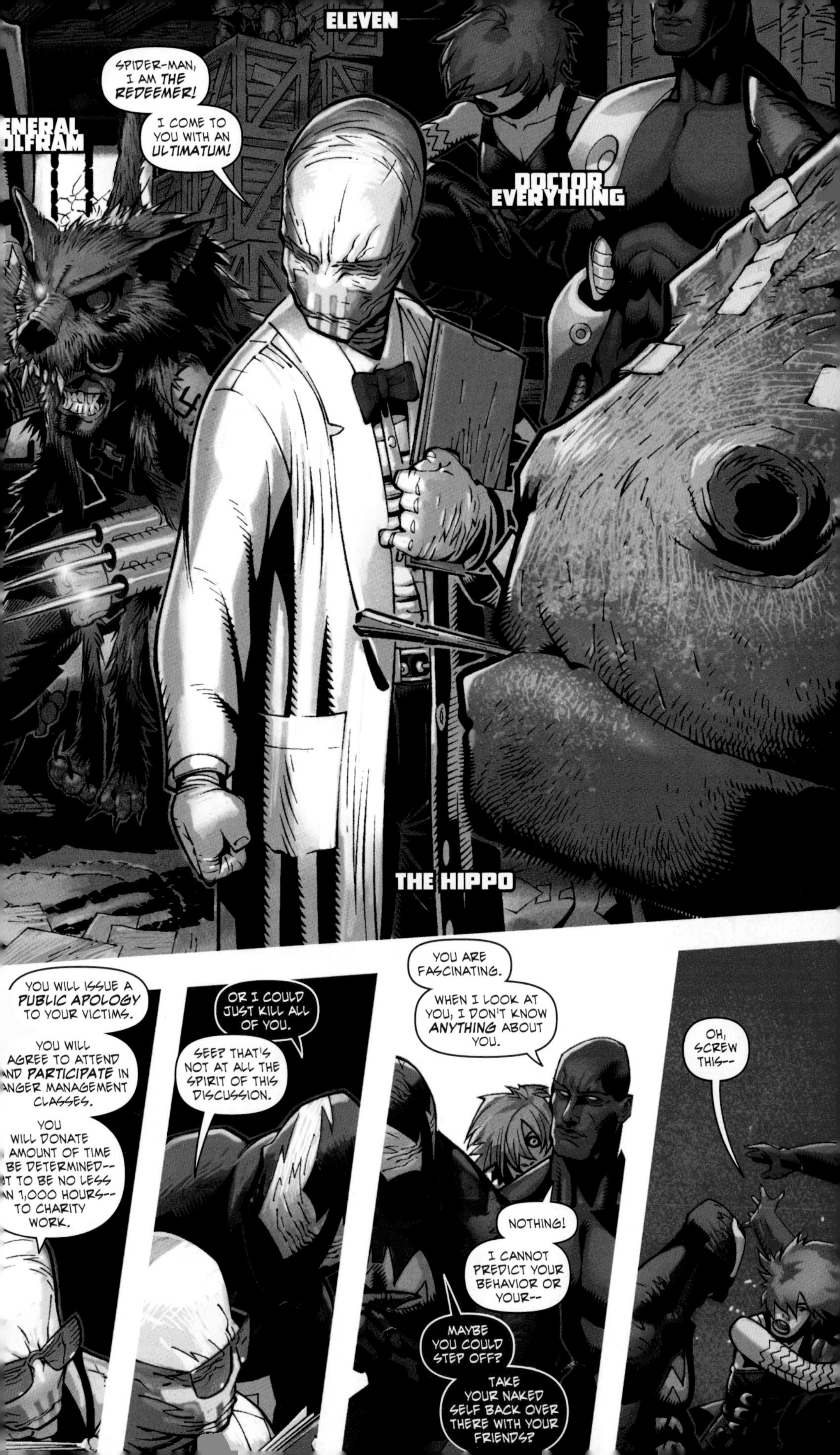

ELEVEN
SPIDER-MAN, I AM THE REDEEMER!
I COME TO YOU WITH AN ULTIMATUM!
ENERAL
OLFRAM
DOCTOR EVERYTHING
THE HIPPO
YOU WILL ISSUE A PUBLIC APOLOGY TO YOUR VICTIMS.
YOU WILL AGREE TO ATTEND ND PARTICIPATE IN NGER MANAGEMENT CLASSES.
YOU WILL DONATE AMOUNT OF TIME BE DETERMINED-- T TO BE NO LESS N 1,000 HOURS-- TO CHARITY WORK.
OR I COULD JUST KILL ALL OF YOU.
SEE? THAT'S NOT AT ALL THE SPIRIT OF THIS DISCUSSION.
YOU ARE FASCINATING.
WHEN I LOOK AT YOU, I DON'T KNOW ANYTHING ABOUT YOU.
NOTHING!
I CANNOT PREDICT YOUR BEHAVIOR OR YOUR--
MAYBE YOU COULD STEP OFF?
TAKE YOUR NAKED SELF BACK OVER THERE WITH YOUR FRIENDS?
OH, SCREW THIS--

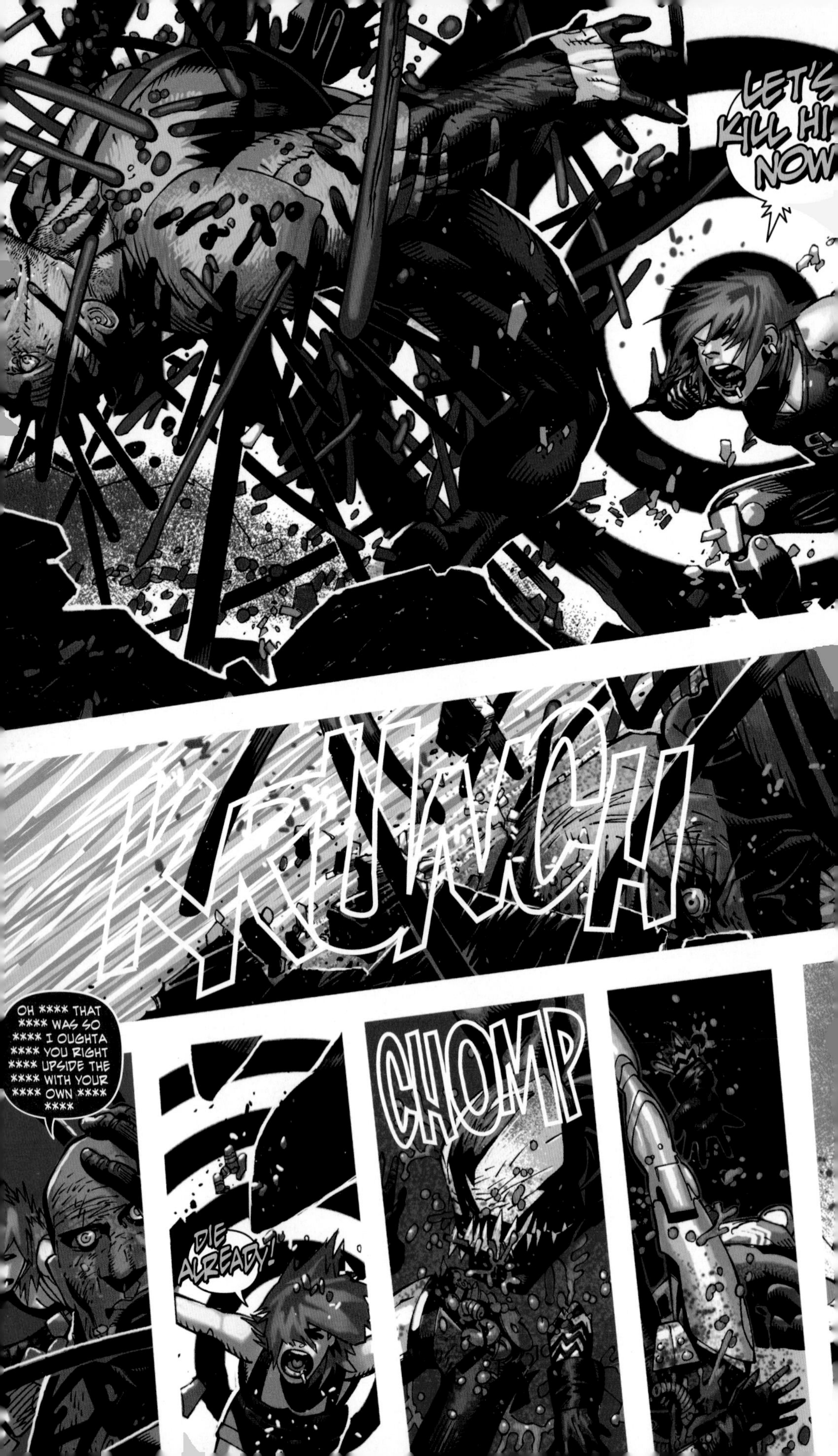
LET'S KILL HI NOW
KRUNCH!
OH **** THAT **** WAS SO **** I OUGHTA **** YOU RIGHT **** UPSIDE THE **** WITH YOUR **** OWN **** ****
DIE ALREADY!
CHOMP

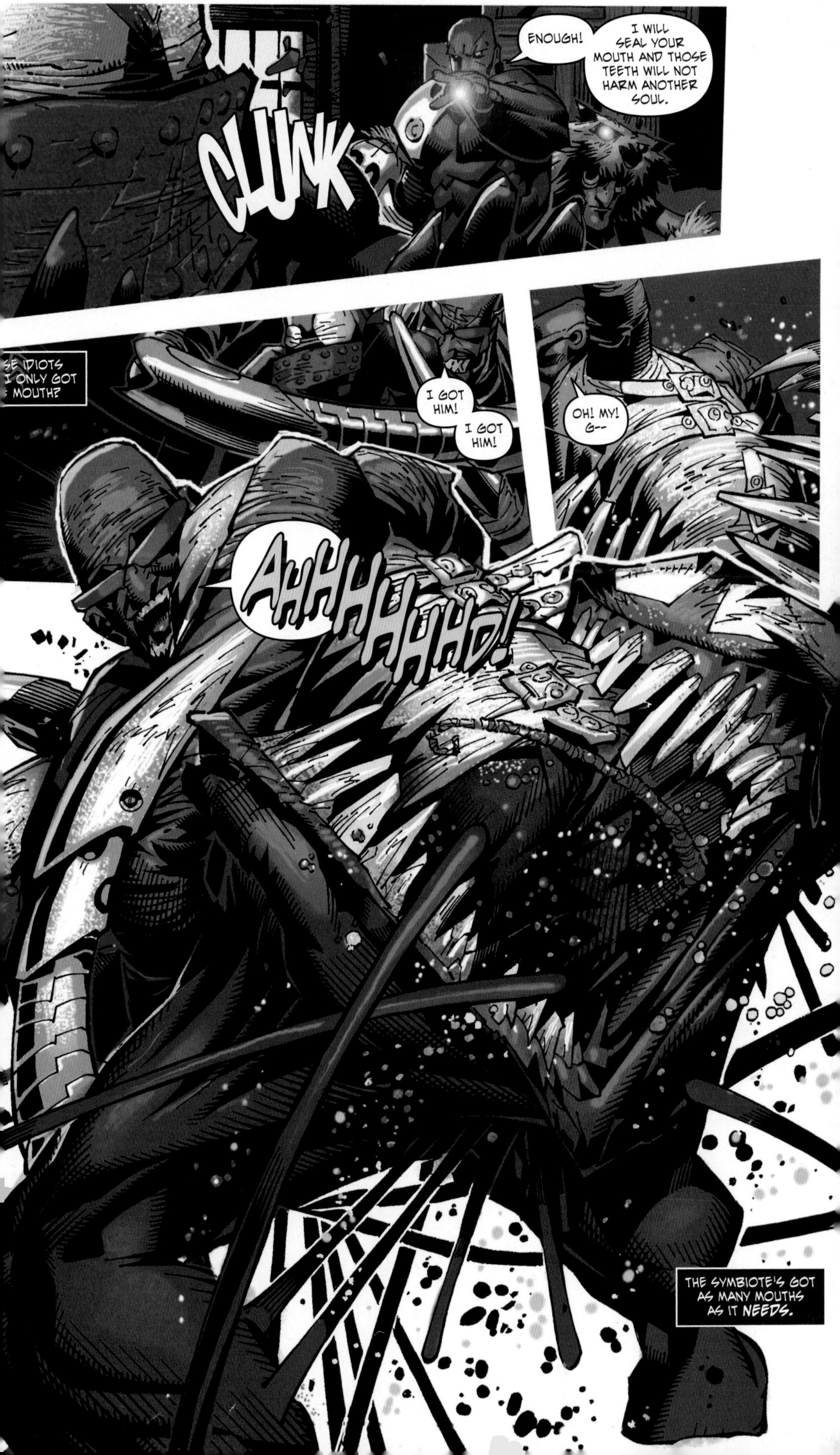
CLUNK
ENOUGH!
I WILL SEAL YOUR MOUTH AND THOSE TEETH WILL NOT HARM ANOTHER SOUL.
SE IDIOTS I ONLY GOT MOUTH?
I GOT HIM!
I GOT HIM!
OH! MY! G--
AHHHHHHD!
THE SYMBIOTE'S GOT AS MANY MOUTHS AS IT NEEDS.

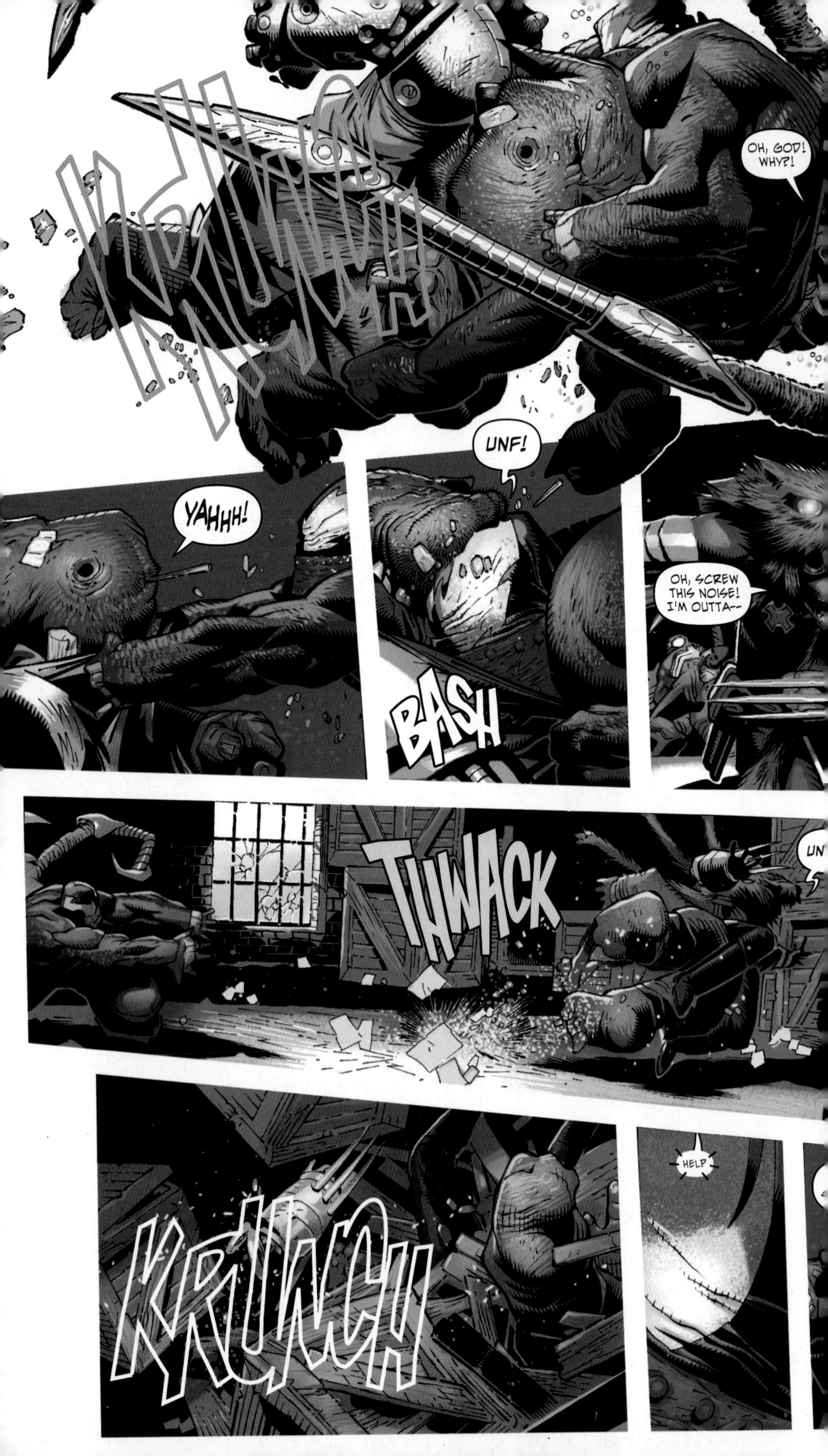
KRUNCH
OH, GOD! WHY?!
YAHHH!
UNF!
BASH
OH, SCREW THIS NOISE! I'M OUTTA--
THWACK
KRUNCH
HELP

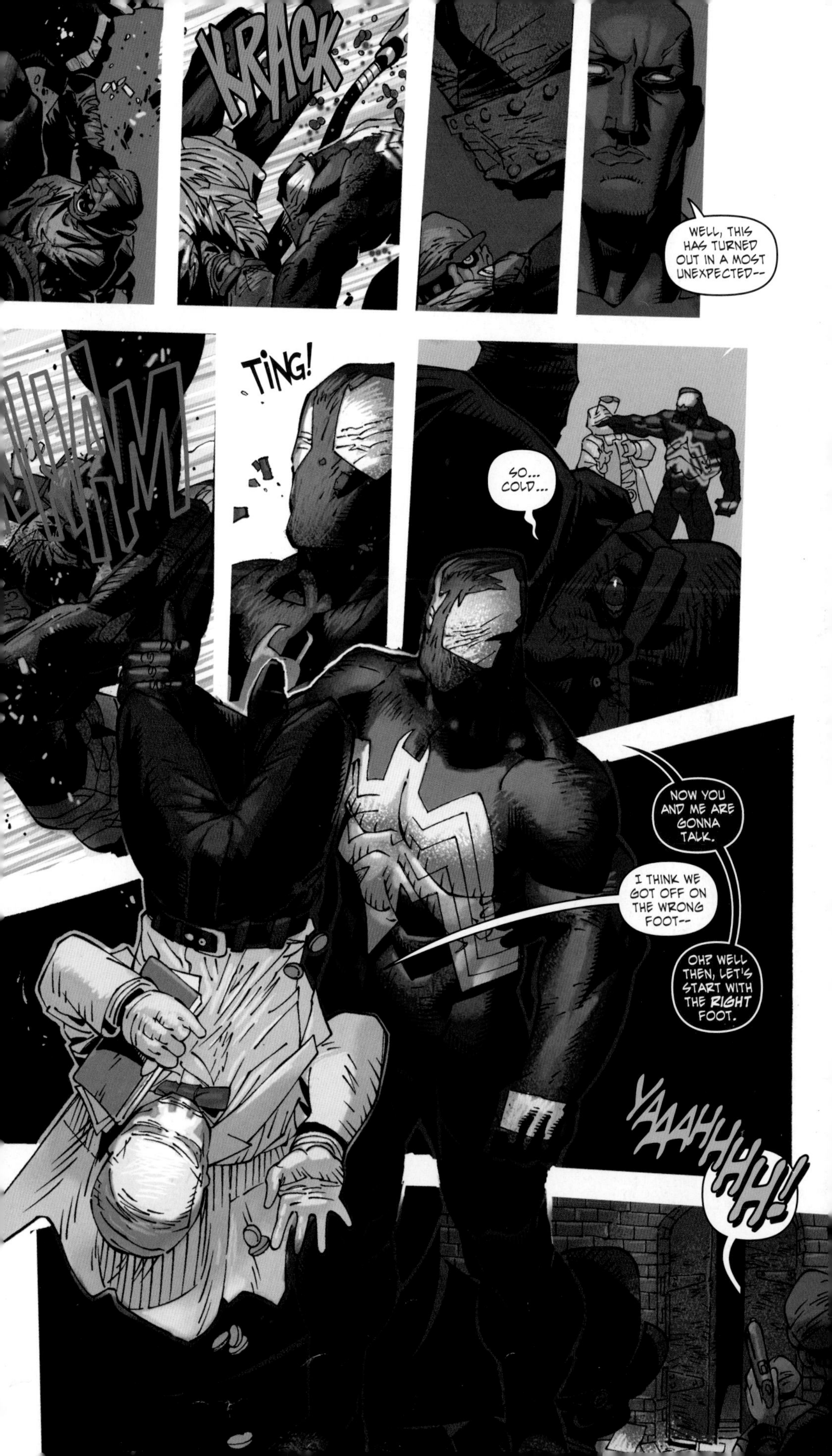
KRACK
WELL, THIS HAS TURNED OUT IN A MOST UNEXPECTED--
TING!
SO... COLD...
NOW YOU AND ME ARE GONNA TALK.
I THINK WE GOT OFF ON THE WRONG FOOT--
OH? WELL THEN, LET'S START WITH THE RIGHT FOOT.
YAAAHHHH!!

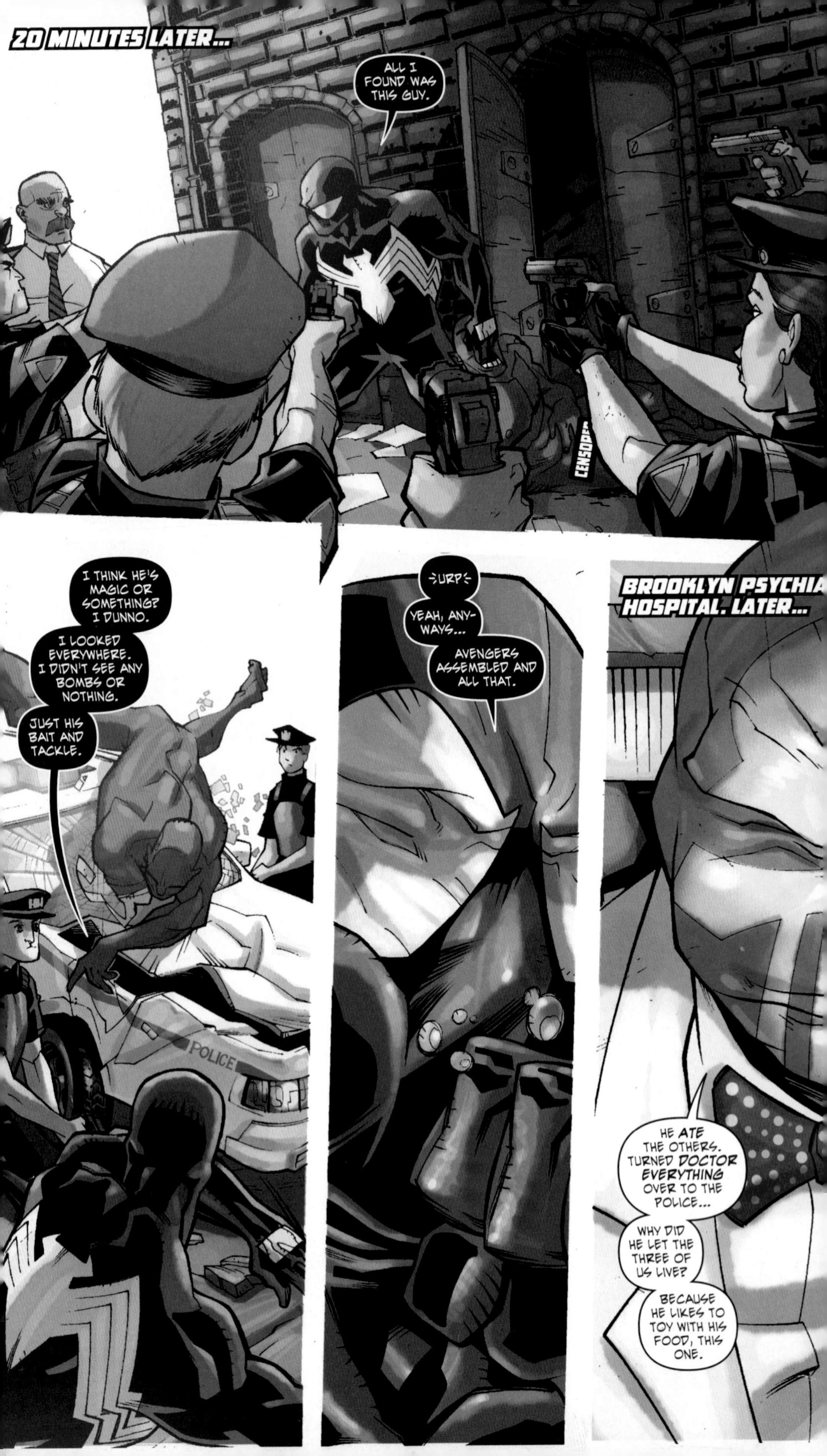
20 MINUTES LATER...
ALL I FOUND WAS THIS GUY.
CENSORED
I THINK HE'S MAGIC OR SOMETHING? I DUNNO.
I LOOKED EVERYWHERE. I DIDN'T SEE ANY BOMBS OR NOTHING.
JUST HIS BAIT AND TACKLE.
POLICE
URP
YEAH, ANY-WAYS...
AVENGERS ASSEMBLED AND ALL THAT.
BROOKLYN PSYCHIA
HOSPITAL. LATER...
HE ATE THE OTHERS. TURNED DOCTOR EVERYTHING OVER TO THE POLICE...
WHY DID HE LET THE THREE OF US LIVE?
BECAUSE HE LIKES TO TOY WITH HIS FOOD, THIS ONE.

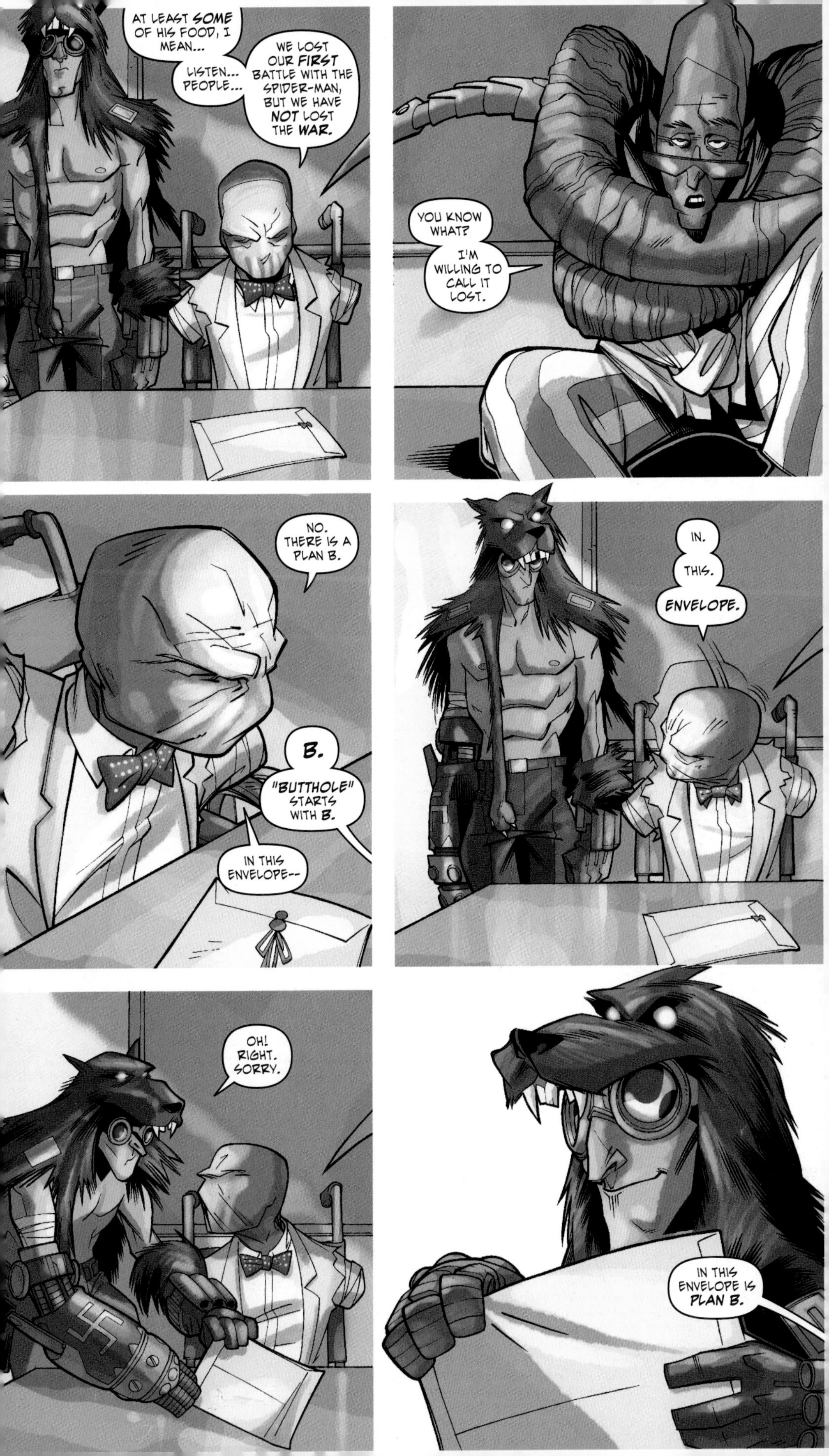
AT LEAST SOME OF HIS FOOD, I MEAN...
LISTEN... PEOPLE...
WE LOST OUR FIRST BATTLE WITH THE SPIDER-MAN, BUT WE HAVE NOT LOST THE WAR.
YOU KNOW WHAT?
I'M WILLING TO CALL IT LOST.
NO. THERE IS A PLAN B.
B.
"BUTTHOLE" STARTS WITH B.
IN THIS ENVELOPE--
IN.
THIS.
ENVELOPE.
OH! RIGHT. SORRY.
IN THIS ENVELOPE IS PLAN B.

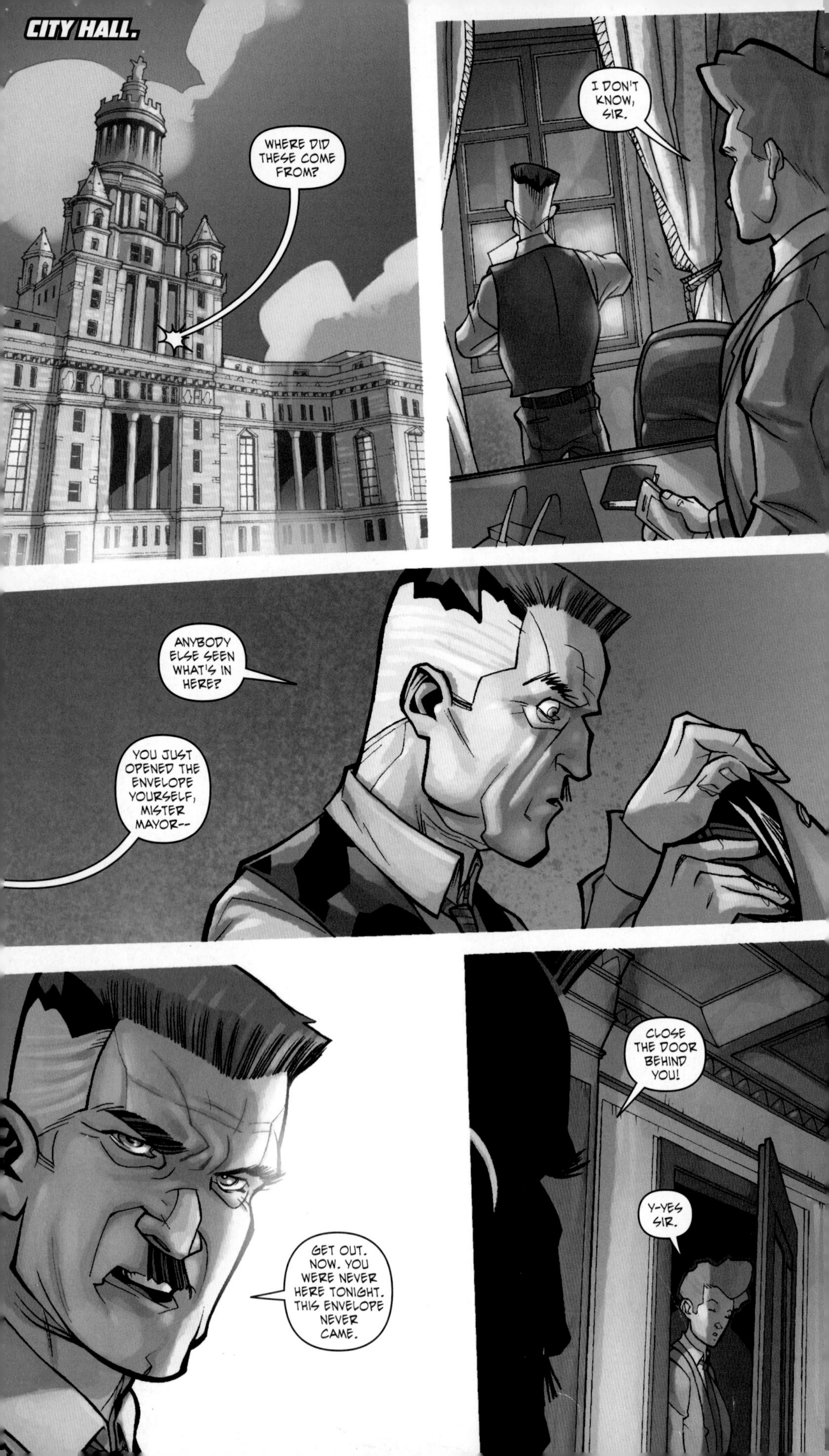
CITY HALL.
WHERE DID THESE COME FROM?
I DON'T KNOW, SIR.
ANYBODY ELSE SEEN WHAT'S IN HERE?
YOU JUST OPENED THE ENVELOPE YOURSELF, MISTER MAYOR--
GET OUT. NOW. YOU WERE NEVER HERE TONIGHT. THIS ENVELOPE NEVER CAME.
CLOSE THE DOOR BEHIND YOU!
Y-YES SIR.

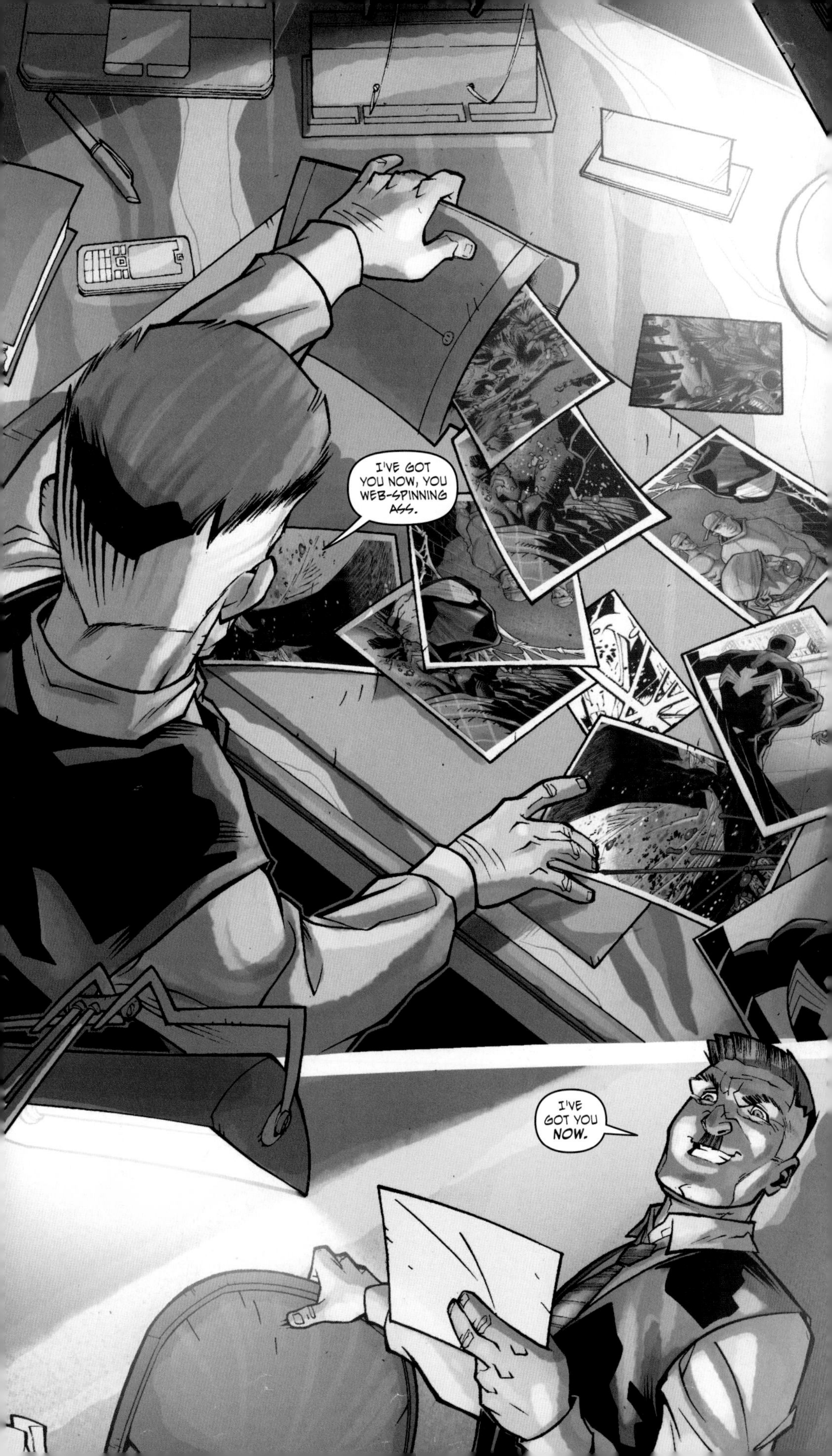
I'VE GOT YOU NOW, YOU WEB-SPINNING ASS.
I'VE GOT YOU NOW.

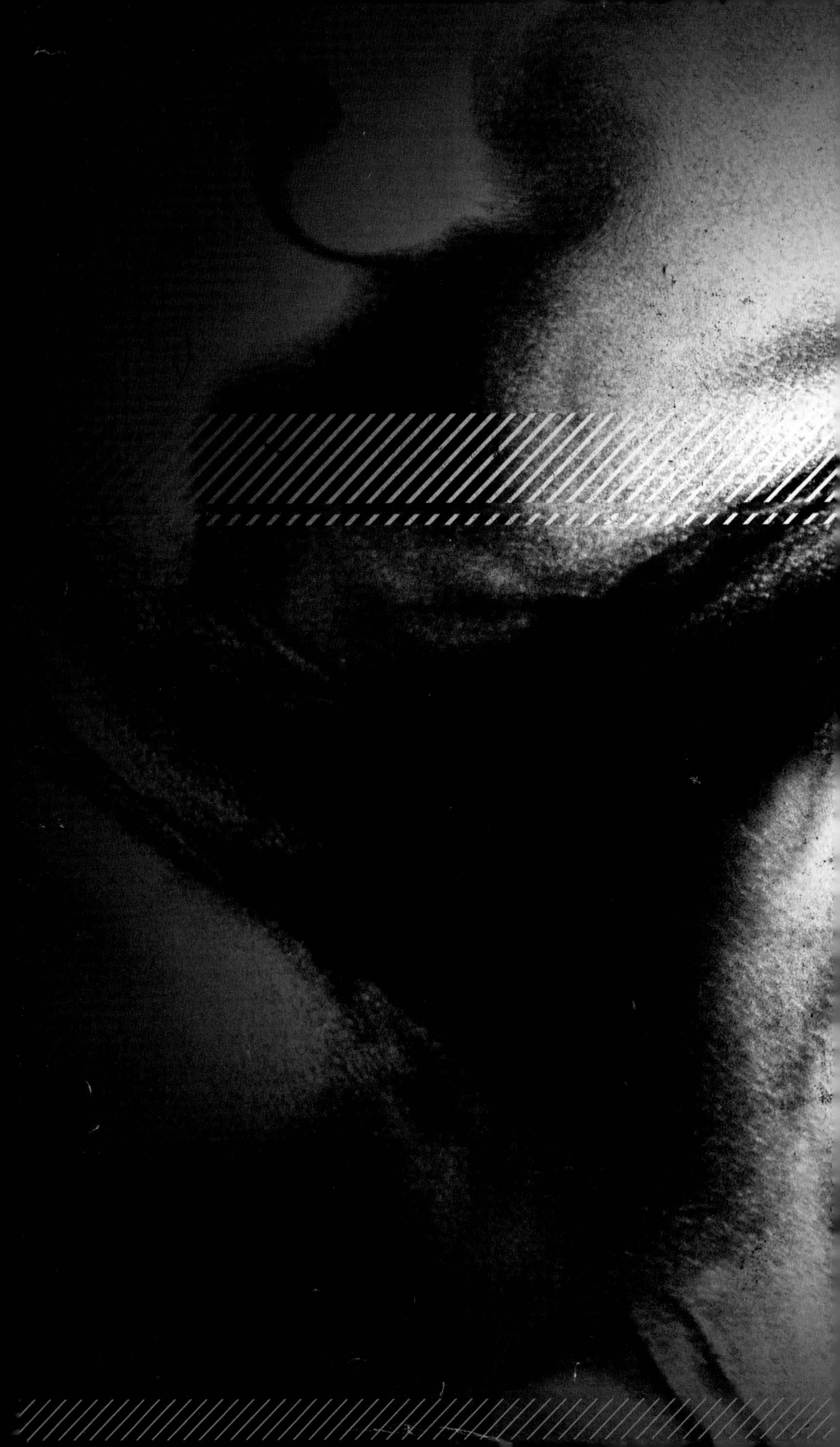

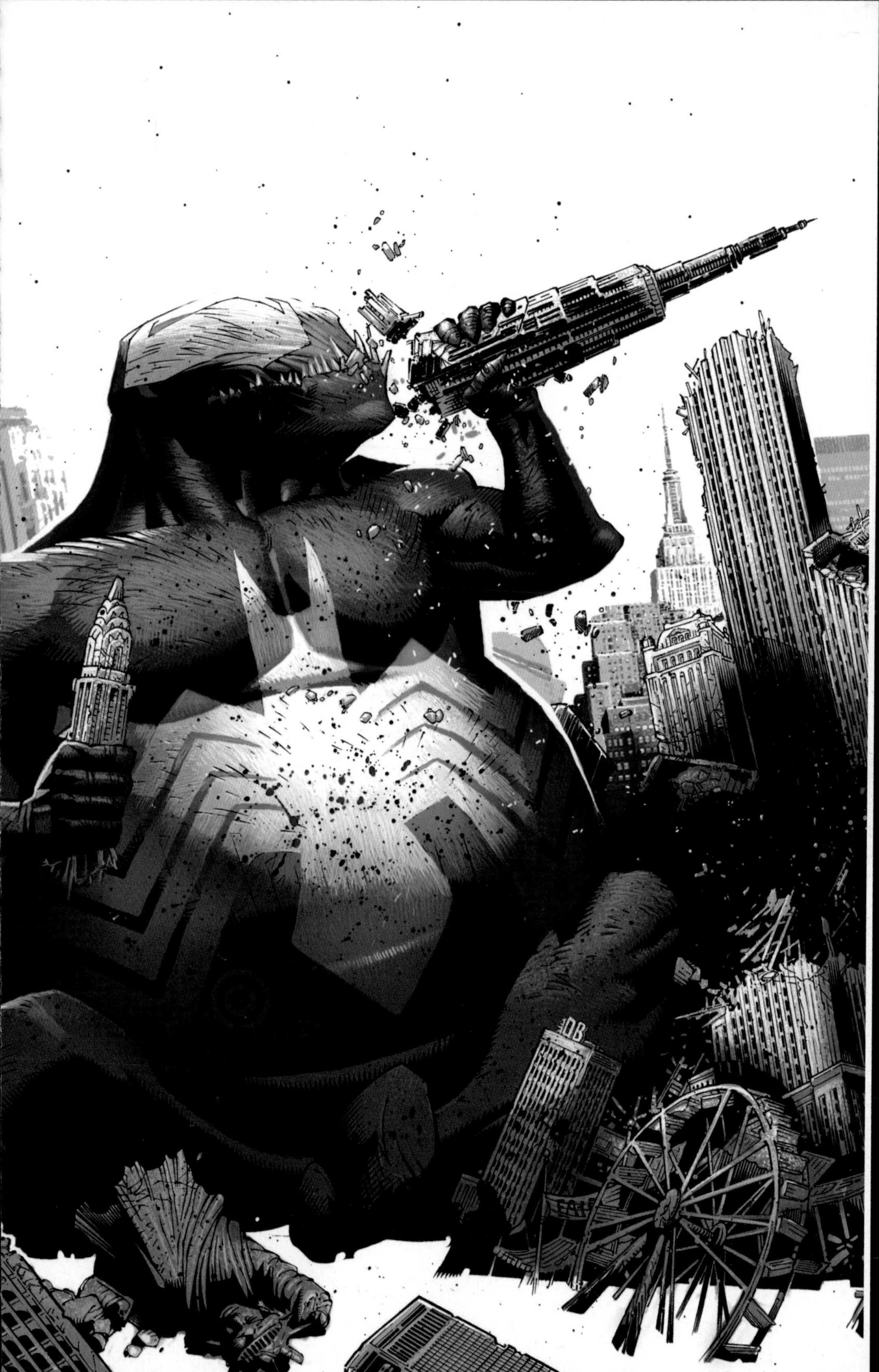

DARK REIGN: SINISTER SPIDER-MAN #4

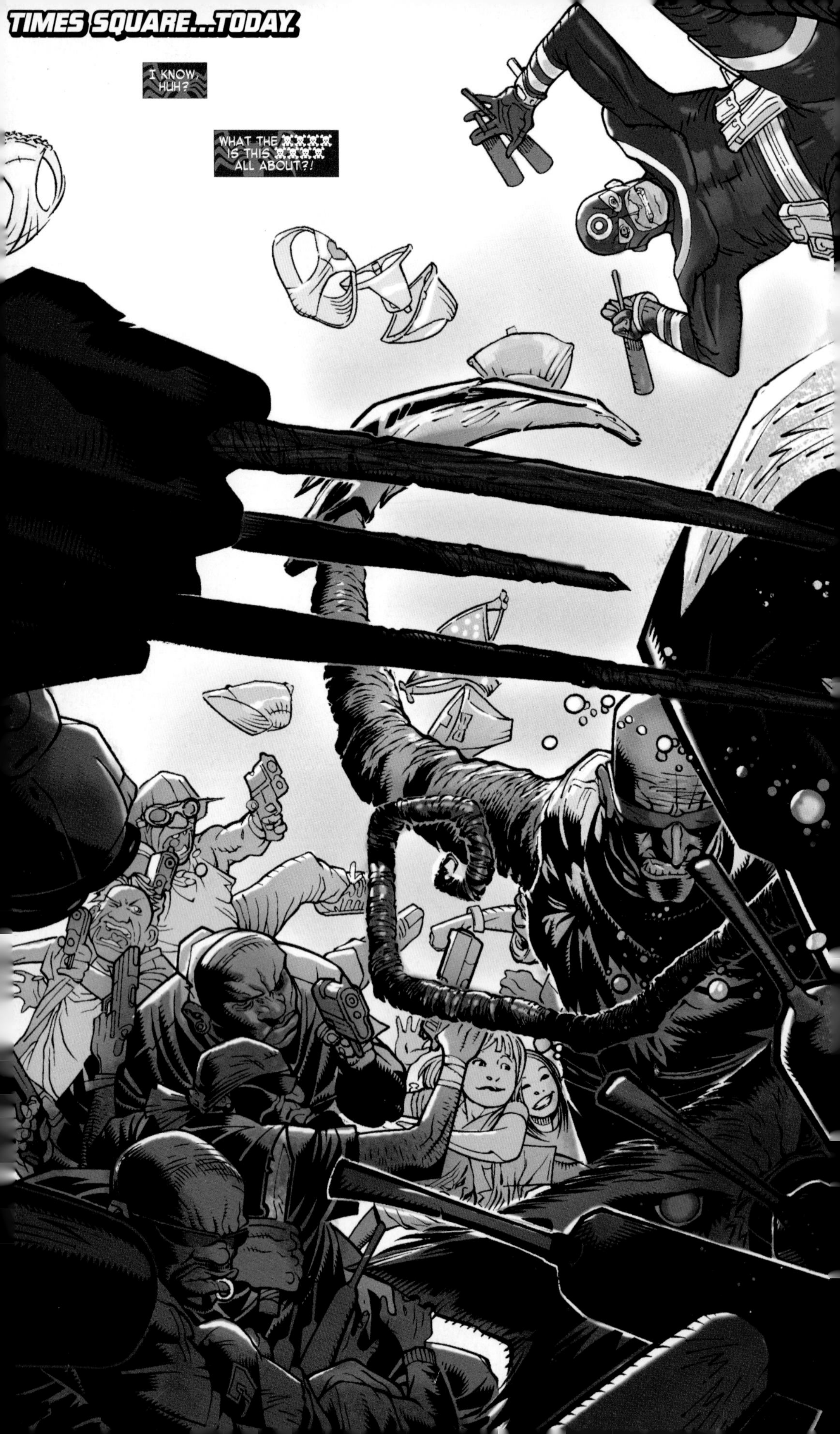
TIMES SQUARE...TODAY.
I KNOW, HUH?
WHAT THE ☠☠☠☠ IS THIS ☠☠☠☠ ALL ABOUT?!

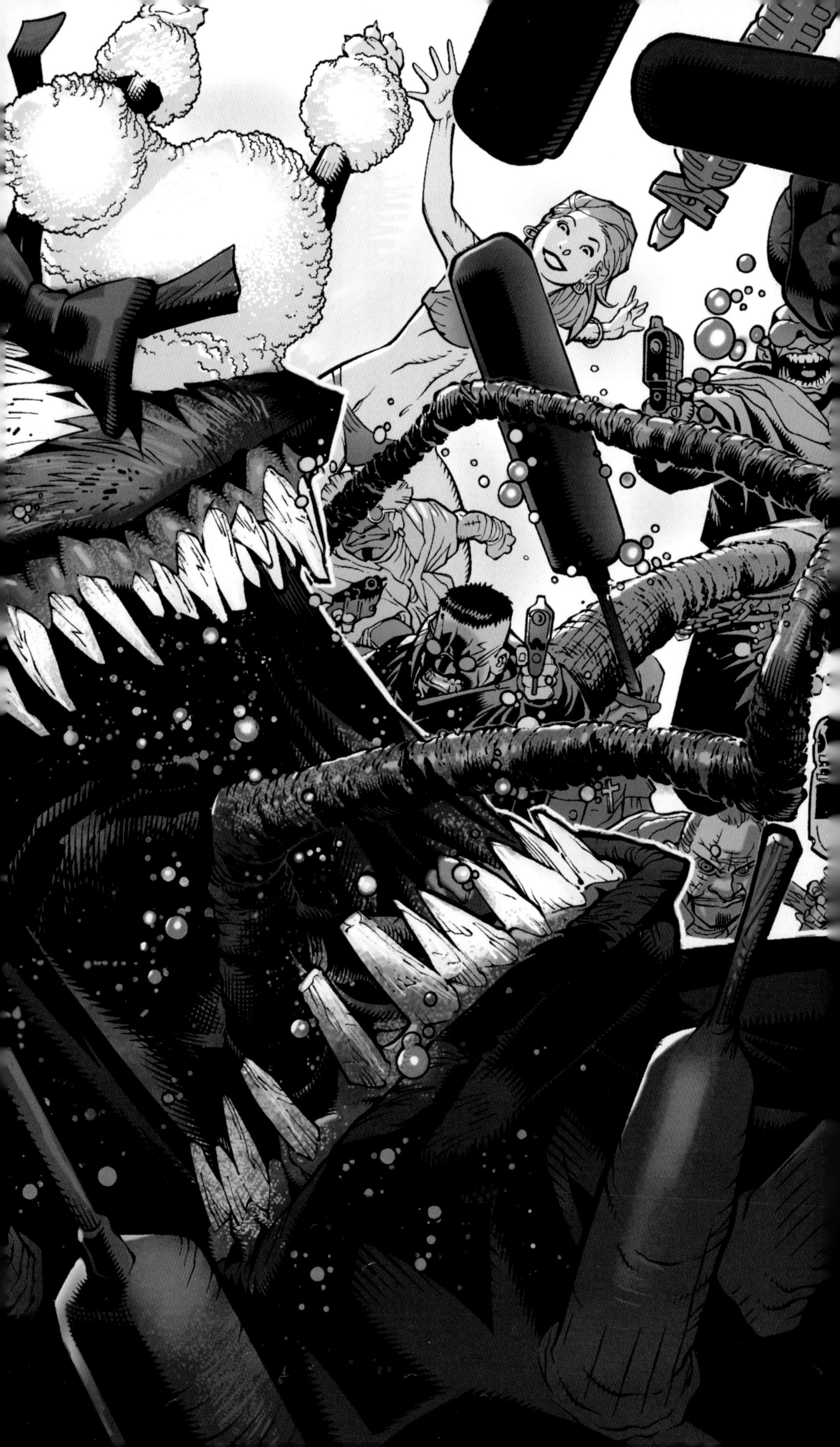

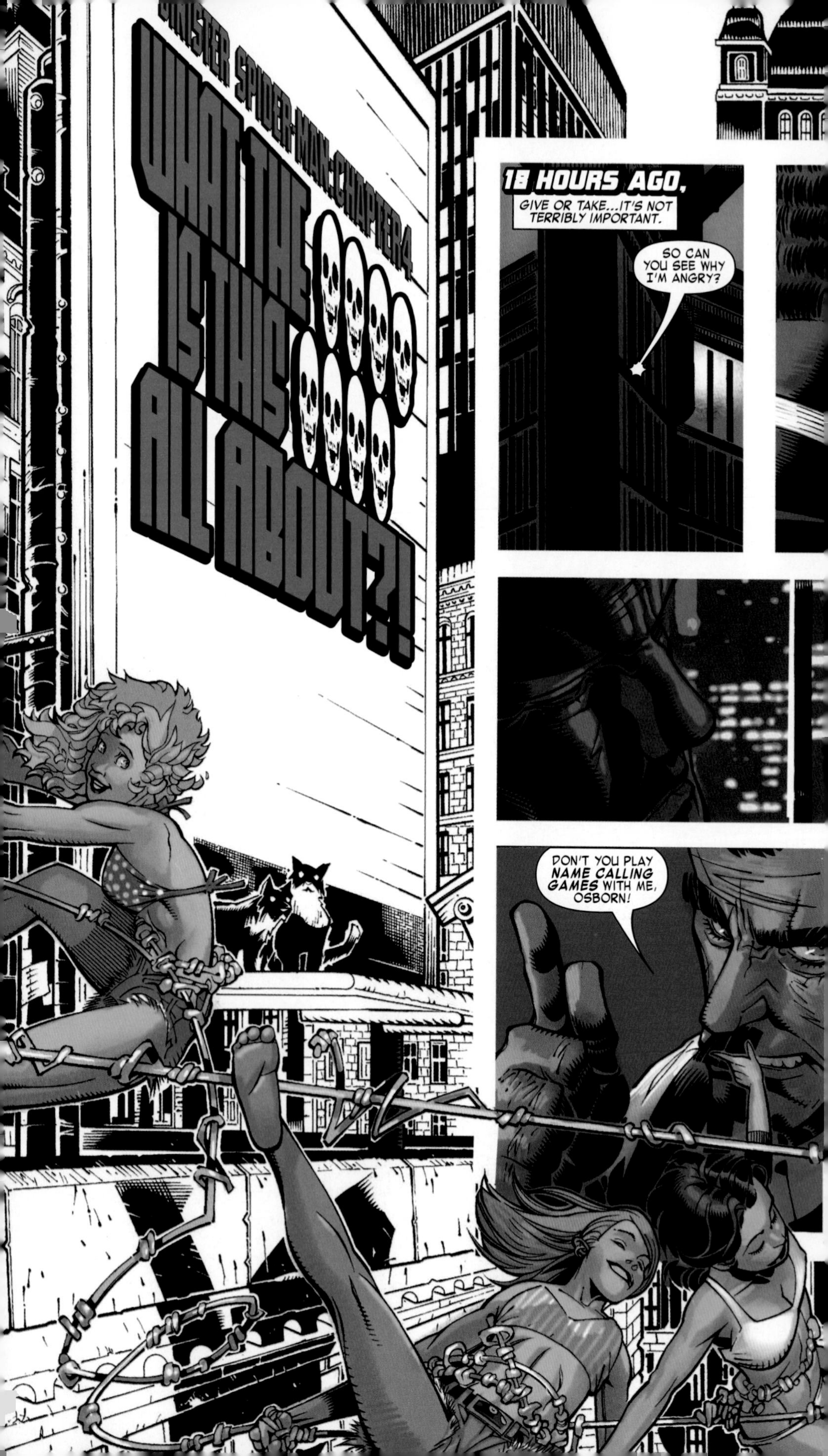

SINISTER SPIDER-MAN: CHAPTER 4
WHAT THE IS THIS ALL ABOUT?!
18 HOURS AGO,
GIVE OR TAKE...IT'S NOT TERRIBLY IMPORTANT.
SO CAN YOU SEE WHY I'M ANGRY?
DON'T YOU PLAY NAME CALLING GAMES WITH ME, OSBORN!

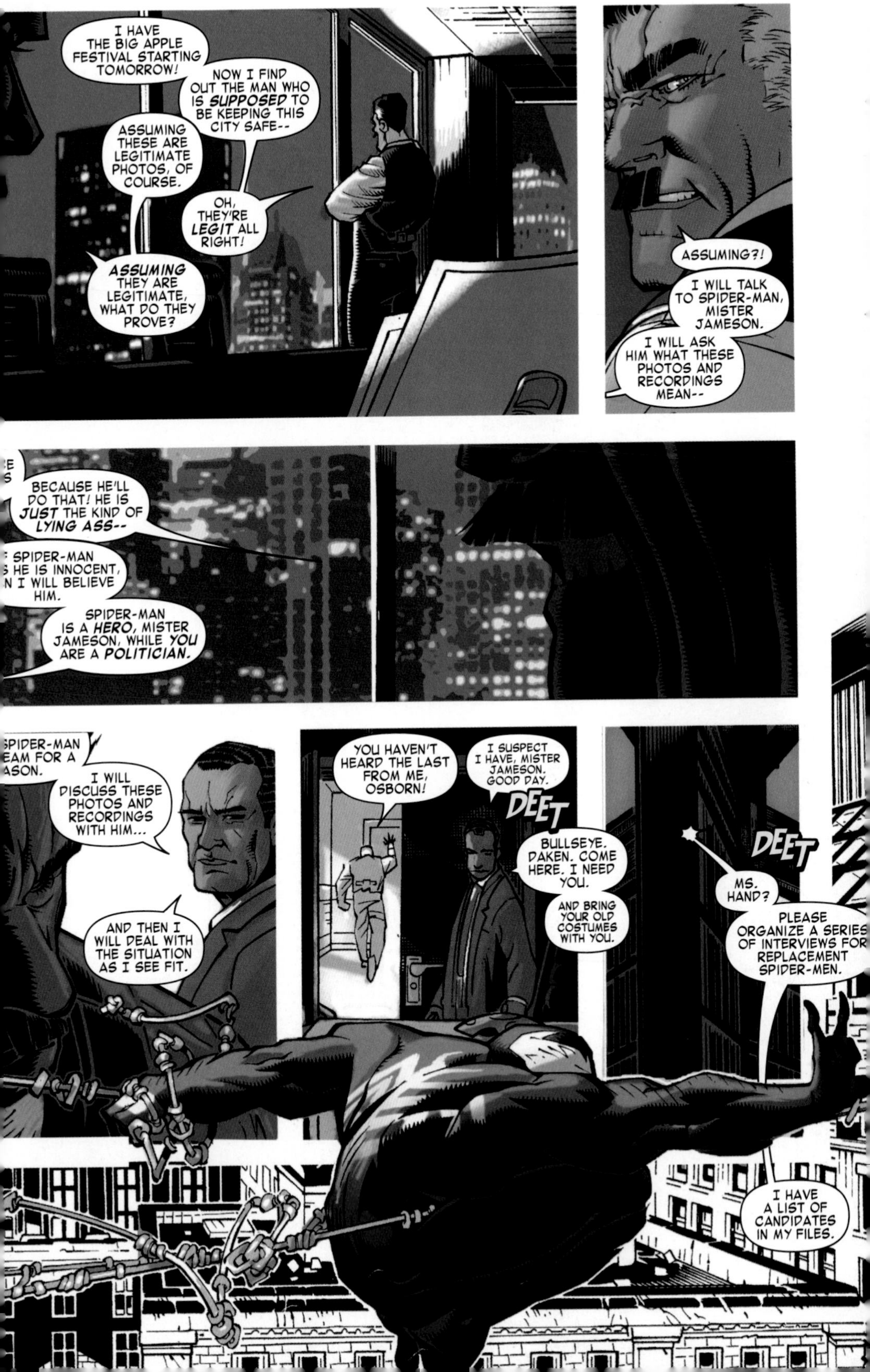
I HAVE THE BIG APPLE FESTIVAL STARTING TOMORROW!
NOW I FIND OUT THE MAN WHO IS SUPPOSED TO BE KEEPING THIS CITY SAFE--
ASSUMING THESE ARE LEGITIMATE PHOTOS, OF COURSE.
OH, THEY'RE LEGIT ALL RIGHT!
ASSUMING THEY ARE LEGITIMATE, WHAT DO THEY PROVE?
ASSUMING?!
I WILL TALK TO SPIDER-MAN, MISTER JAMESON.
I WILL ASK HIM WHAT THESE PHOTOS AND RECORDINGS MEAN--
BECAUSE HE'LL DO THAT! HE IS JUST THE KIND OF LYING ASS--
SPIDER-MAN HE IS INNOCENT, I WILL BELIEVE HIM.
SPIDER-MAN IS A HERO, MISTER JAMESON, WHILE YOU ARE A POLITICIAN.
SPIDER-MAN EAM FOR A ASON.
I WILL DISCUSS THESE PHOTOS AND RECORDINGS WITH HIM...
AND THEN I WILL DEAL WITH THE SITUATION AS I SEE FIT.
YOU HAVEN'T HEARD THE LAST FROM ME, OSBORN!
I SUSPECT I HAVE, MISTER JAMESON. GOOD DAY.
DEET
BULLSEYE. DAKEN. COME HERE. I NEED YOU.
AND BRING YOUR OLD COSTUMES WITH YOU.
DEET
MS. HAND?
PLEASE ORGANIZE A SERIES OF INTERVIEWS FOR REPLACEMENT SPIDER-MEN.
I HAVE A LIST OF CANDIDATES IN MY FILES.

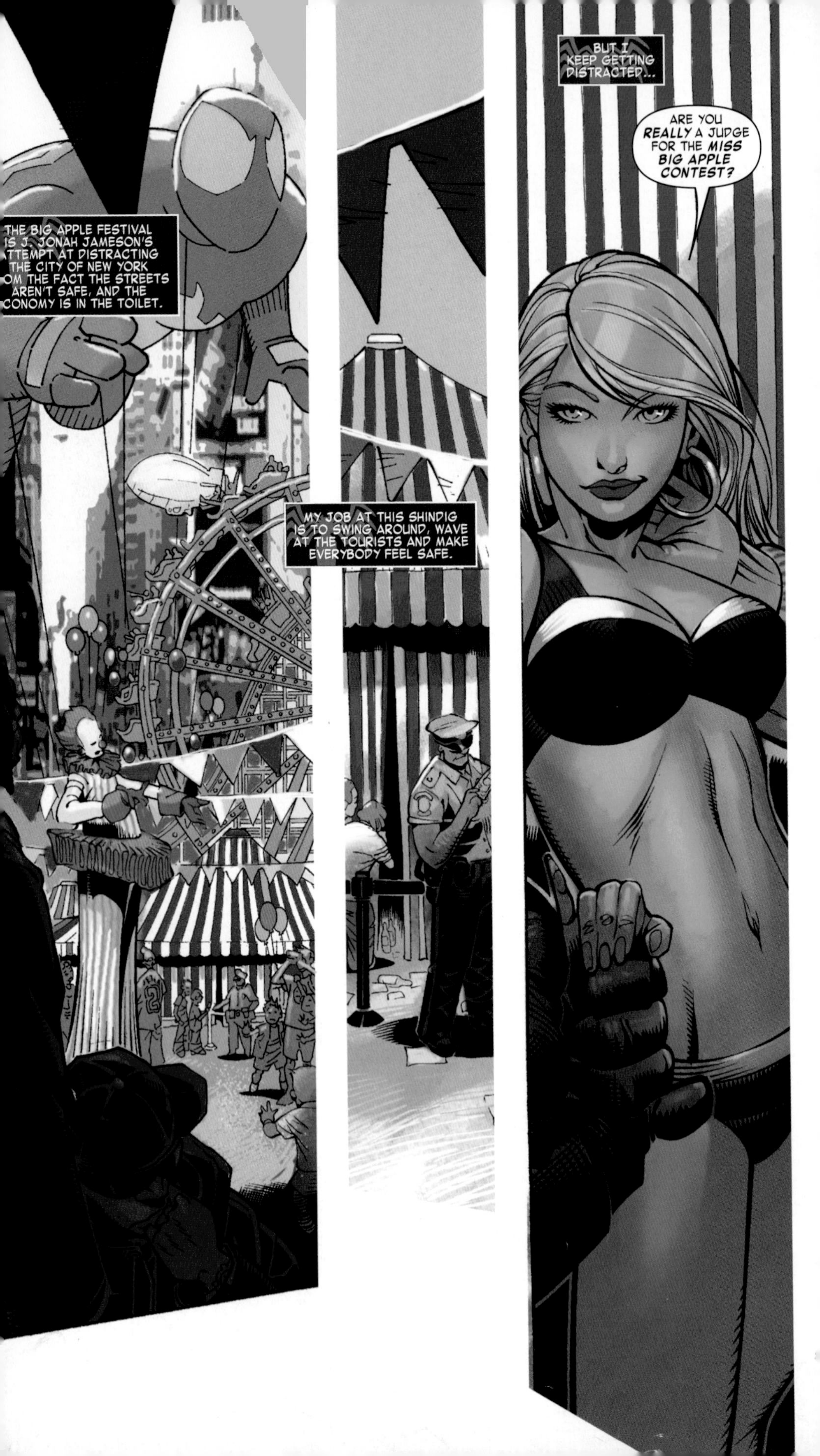
THE BIG APPLE FESTIVAL IS J. JONAH JAMESON'S TTEMPT AT DISTRACTING THE CITY OF NEW YORK OM THE FACT THE STREETS AREN'T SAFE, AND THE CONOMY IS IN THE TOILET.
MY JOB AT THIS SHINDIG IS TO SWING AROUND, WAVE AT THE TOURISTS AND MAKE EVERYBODY FEEL SAFE.
BUT I KEEP GETTING DISTRACTED...
ARE YOU REALLY A JUDGE FOR THE MISS BIG APPLE CONTEST?

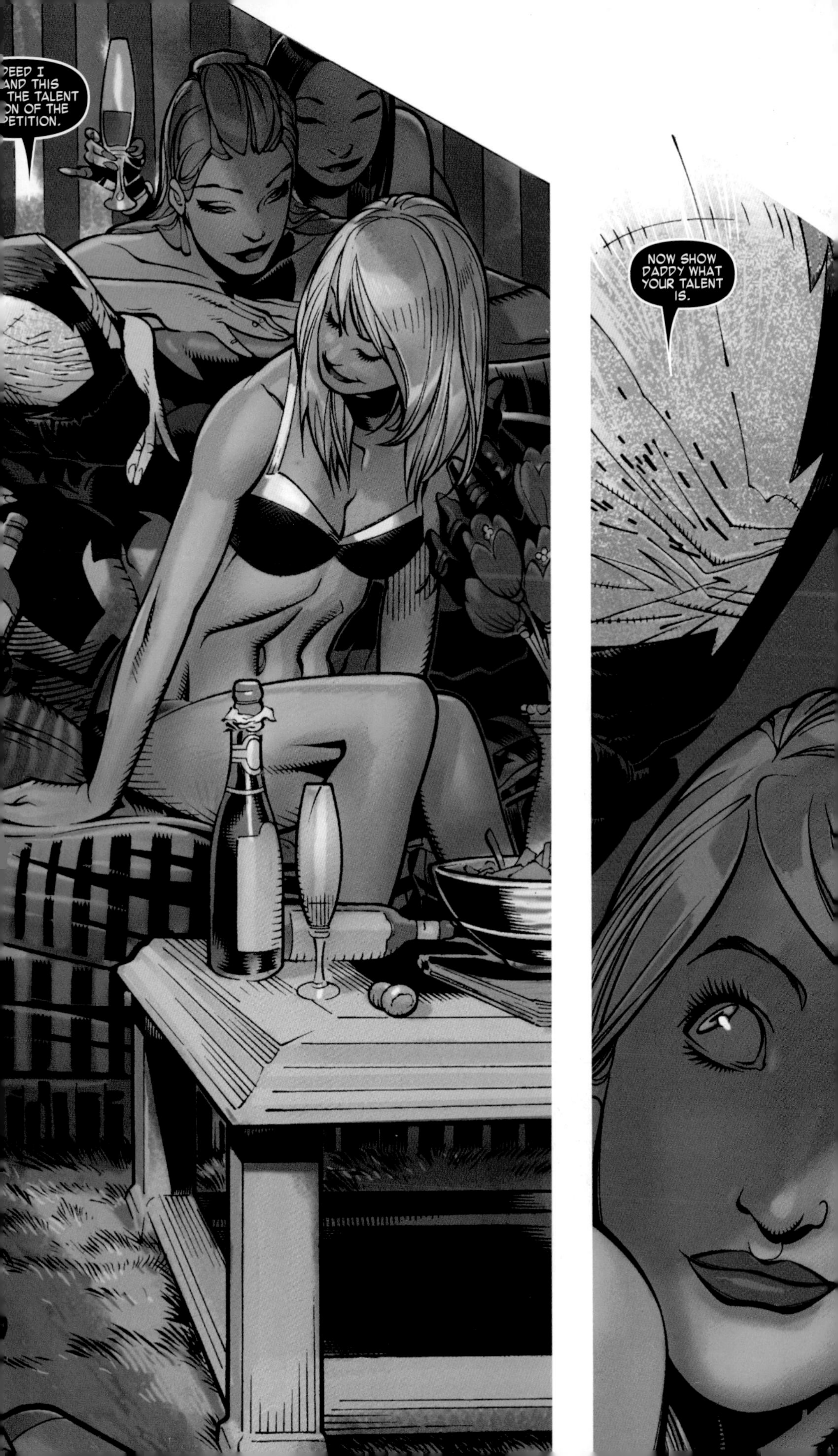
EED I
AND THIS
THE TALENT
ON OF THE
ETITION.
NOW SHOW DADDY WHAT YOUR TALENT IS.

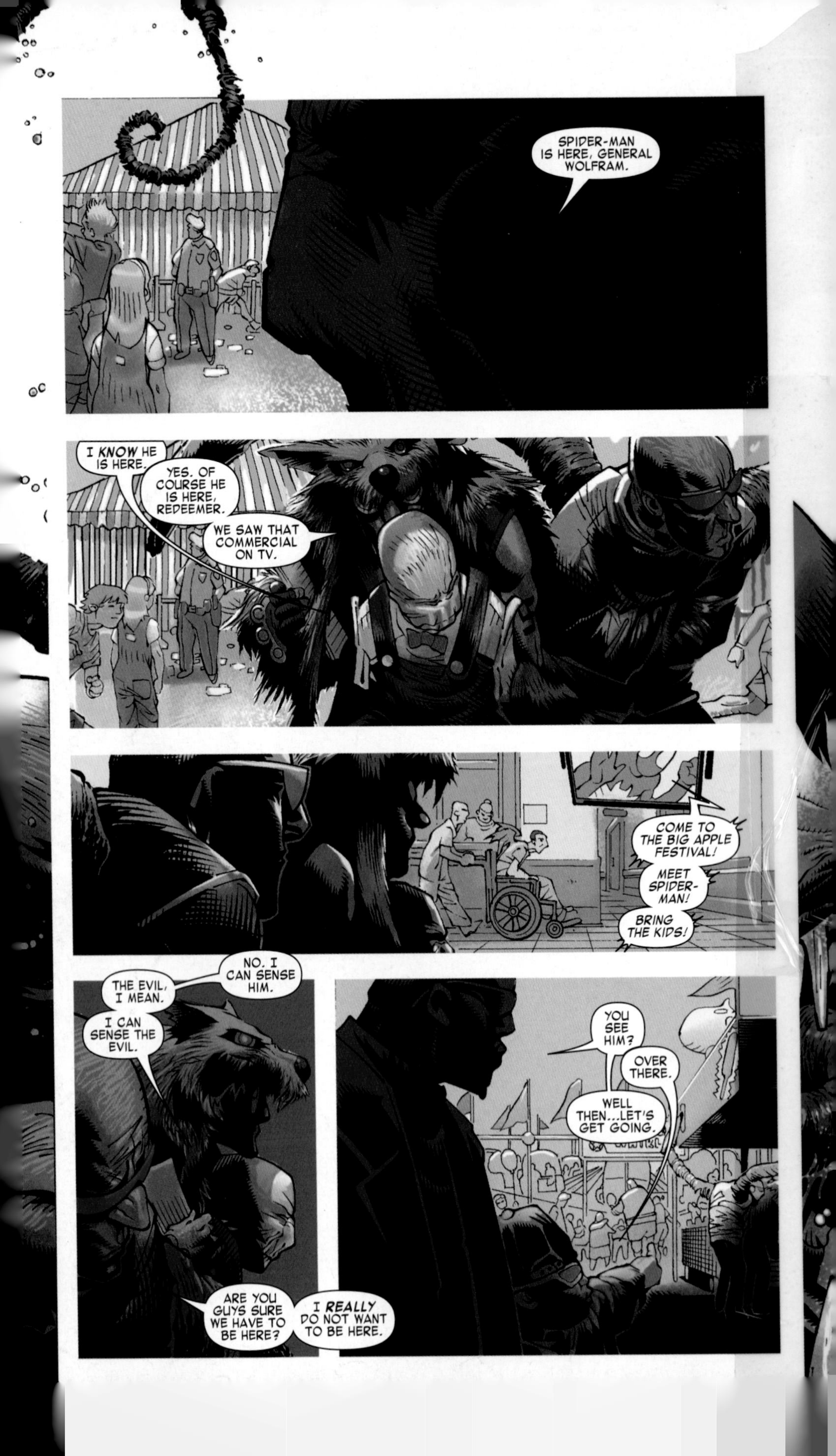
SPIDER-MAN IS HERE, GENERAL WOLFRAM.
I KNOW HE IS HERE.
YES. OF COURSE HE IS HERE, REDEEMER.
WE SAW THAT COMMERCIAL ON TV.
COME TO THE BIG APPLE FESTIVAL!
MEET SPIDER-MAN!
BRING THE KIDS!
NO. I CAN SENSE HIM.
THE EVIL, I MEAN.
I CAN SENSE THE EVIL.
ARE YOU GUYS SURE WE HAVE TO BE HERE?
I REALLY DO NOT WANT TO BE HERE.
YOU SEE HIM?
OVER THERE.
WELL THEN...LET'S GET GOING.

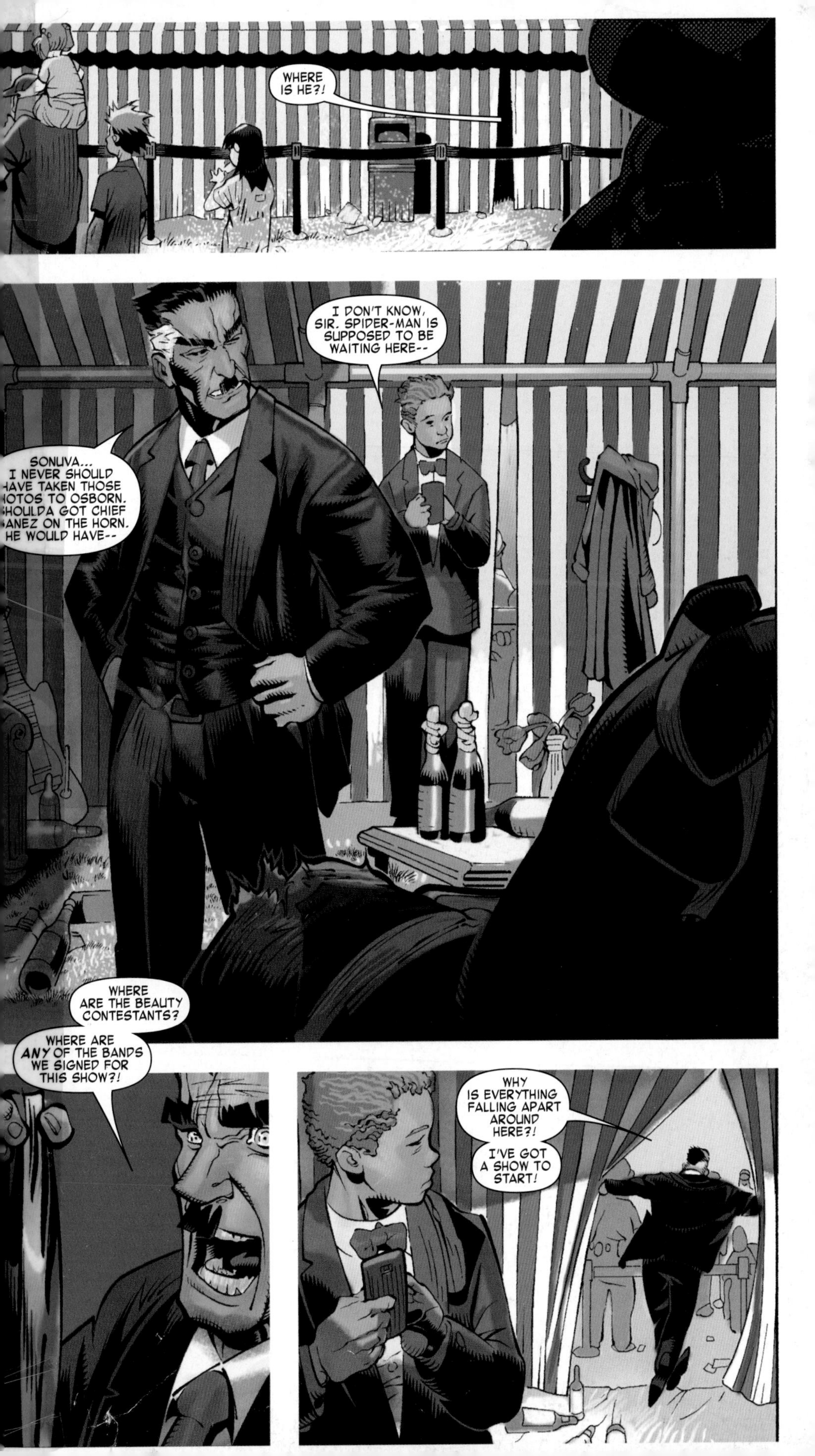
WHERE IS HE?!
I DON'T KNOW, SIR. SPIDER-MAN IS SUPPOSED TO BE WAITING HERE--
SONUVA... I NEVER SHOULD HAVE TAKEN THOSE HOTOS TO OSBORN. SHOULDA GOT CHIEF ANEZ ON THE HORN. HE WOULD HAVE--
WHERE ARE THE BEAUTY CONTESTANTS?
WHERE ARE *ANY* OF THE BANDS WE SIGNED FOR THIS SHOW?!
WHY IS EVERYTHING FALLING APART AROUND HERE?!
I'VE GOT A SHOW TO START!

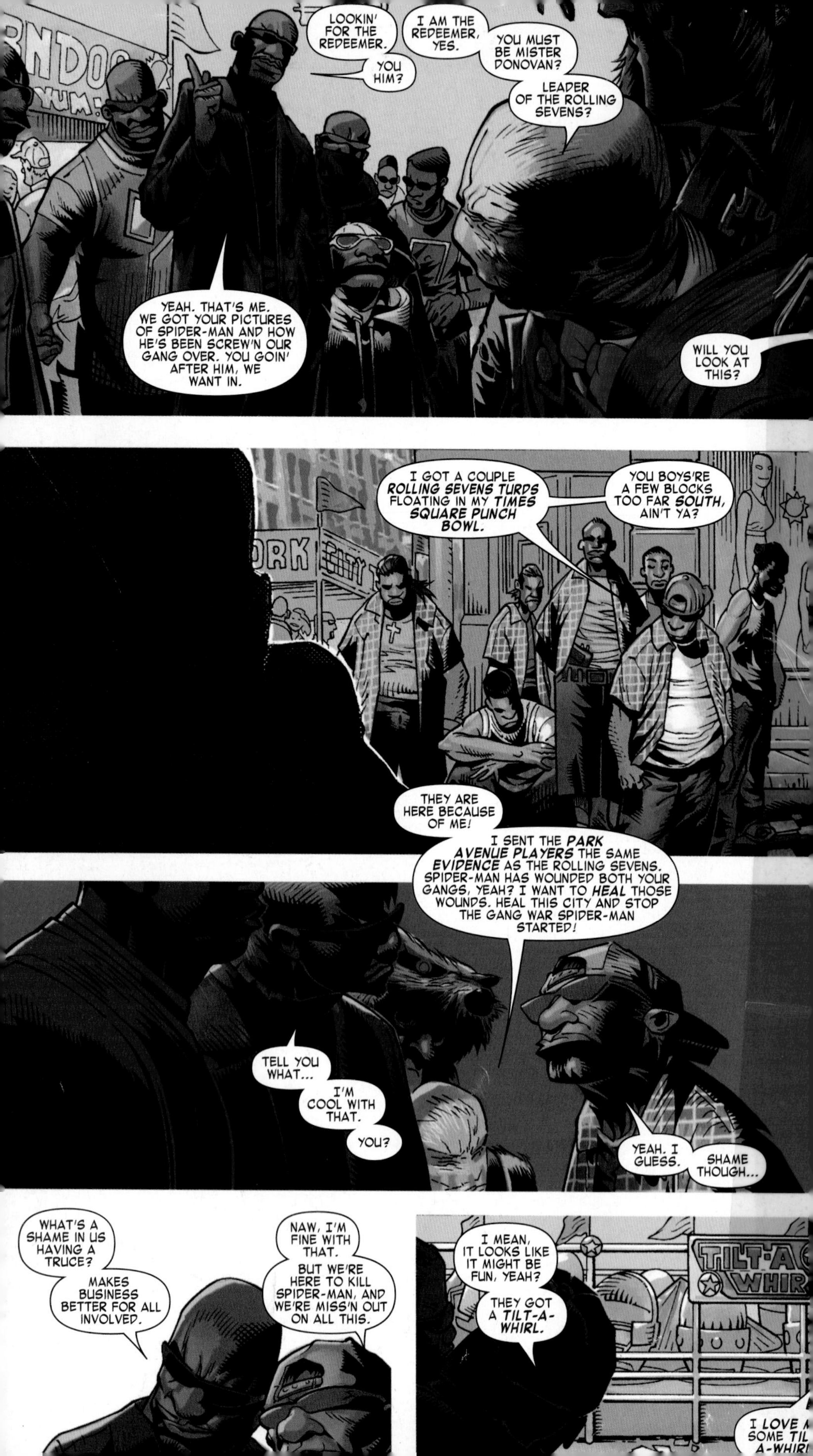
LOOKIN' FOR THE REDEEMER.
YOU HIM?
I AM THE REDEEMER, YES.
YOU MUST BE MISTER DONOVAN?
LEADER OF THE ROLLING SEVENS?
YEAH. THAT'S ME. WE GOT YOUR PICTURES OF SPIDER-MAN AND HOW HE'S BEEN SCREW'N OUR GANG OVER. YOU GOIN' AFTER HIM, WE WANT IN.
WILL YOU LOOK AT THIS?
I GOT A COUPLE ROLLING SEVENS TURDS FLOATING IN MY TIMES SQUARE PUNCH BOWL.
YOU BOYS'RE A FEW BLOCKS TOO FAR SOUTH, AIN'T YA?
THEY ARE HERE BECAUSE OF ME!
I SENT THE PARK AVENUE PLAYERS THE SAME EVIDENCE AS THE ROLLING SEVENS. SPIDER-MAN HAS WOUNDED BOTH YOUR GANGS, YEAH? I WANT TO HEAL THOSE WOUNDS. HEAL THIS CITY AND STOP THE GANG WAR SPIDER-MAN STARTED!
TELL YOU WHAT...
I'M COOL WITH THAT.
YOU?
YEAH. I GUESS.
SHAME THOUGH...
WHAT'S A SHAME IN US HAVING A TRUCE?
MAKES BUSINESS BETTER FOR ALL INVOLVED.
NAW, I'M FINE WITH THAT.
BUT WE'RE HERE TO KILL SPIDER-MAN, AND WE'RE MISS'N OUT ON ALL THIS.
I MEAN, IT LOOKS LIKE IT MIGHT BE FUN, YEAH?
THEY GOT A TILT-A-WHIRL.
TILT-A WHIR
I LOVE SOME TIL A-WHIR

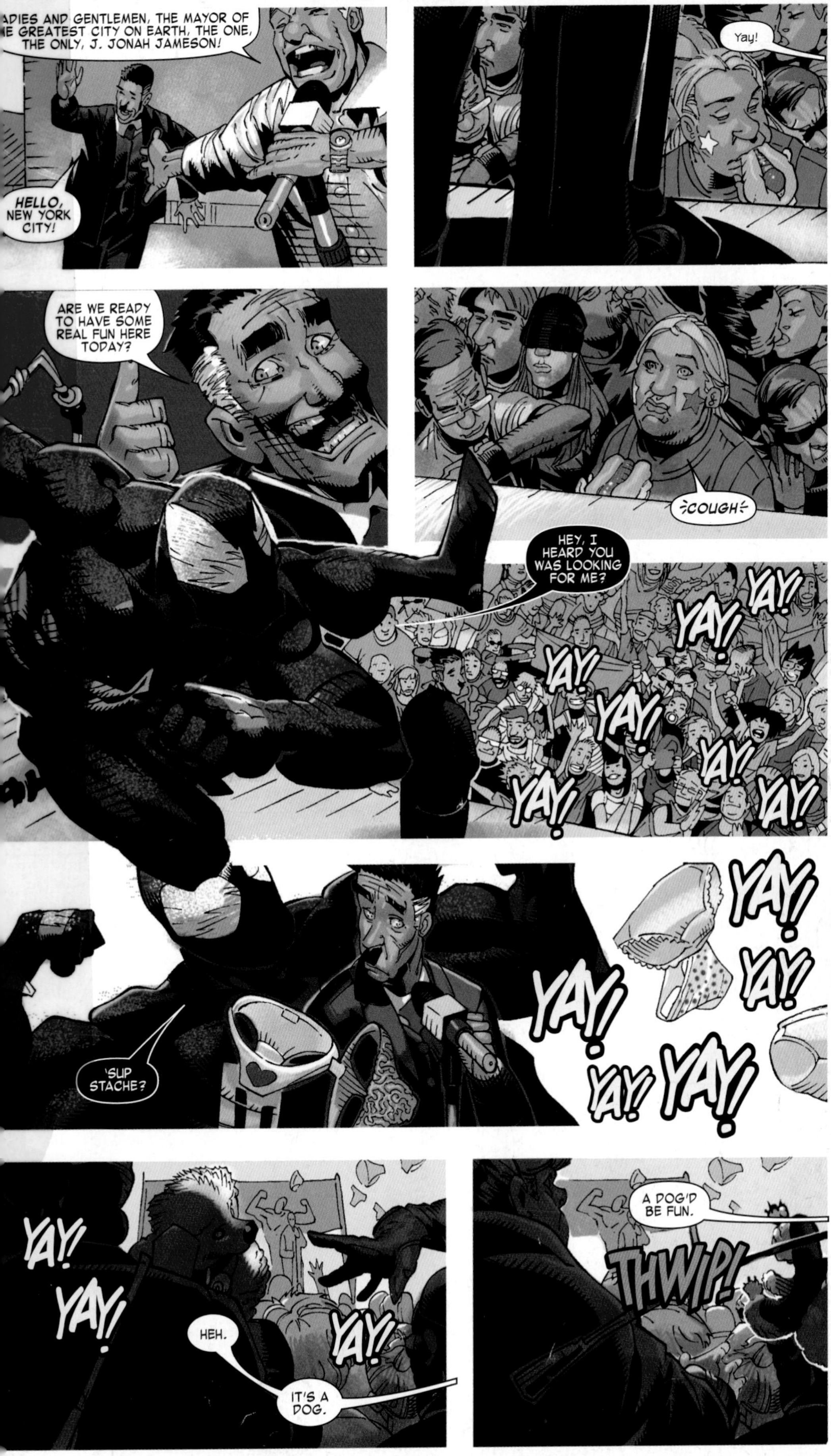
ADIES AND GENTLEMEN, THE MAYOR OF E GREATEST CITY ON EARTH, THE ONE, THE ONLY, J. JONAH JAMESON!
HELLO, NEW YORK CITY!
Yay!
ARE WE READY TO HAVE SOME REAL FUN HERE TODAY?
COUGH
HEY, I HEARD YOU WAS LOOKING FOR ME?
YAY! YAY! YAY! YAY! YAY! YAY! YAY!
'SUP STACHE?
YAY! YAY! YAY! YAY! YAY!
YAY! YAY! YAY!
HEH.
IT'S A DOG.
A DOG'D BE FUN.
THWIP!

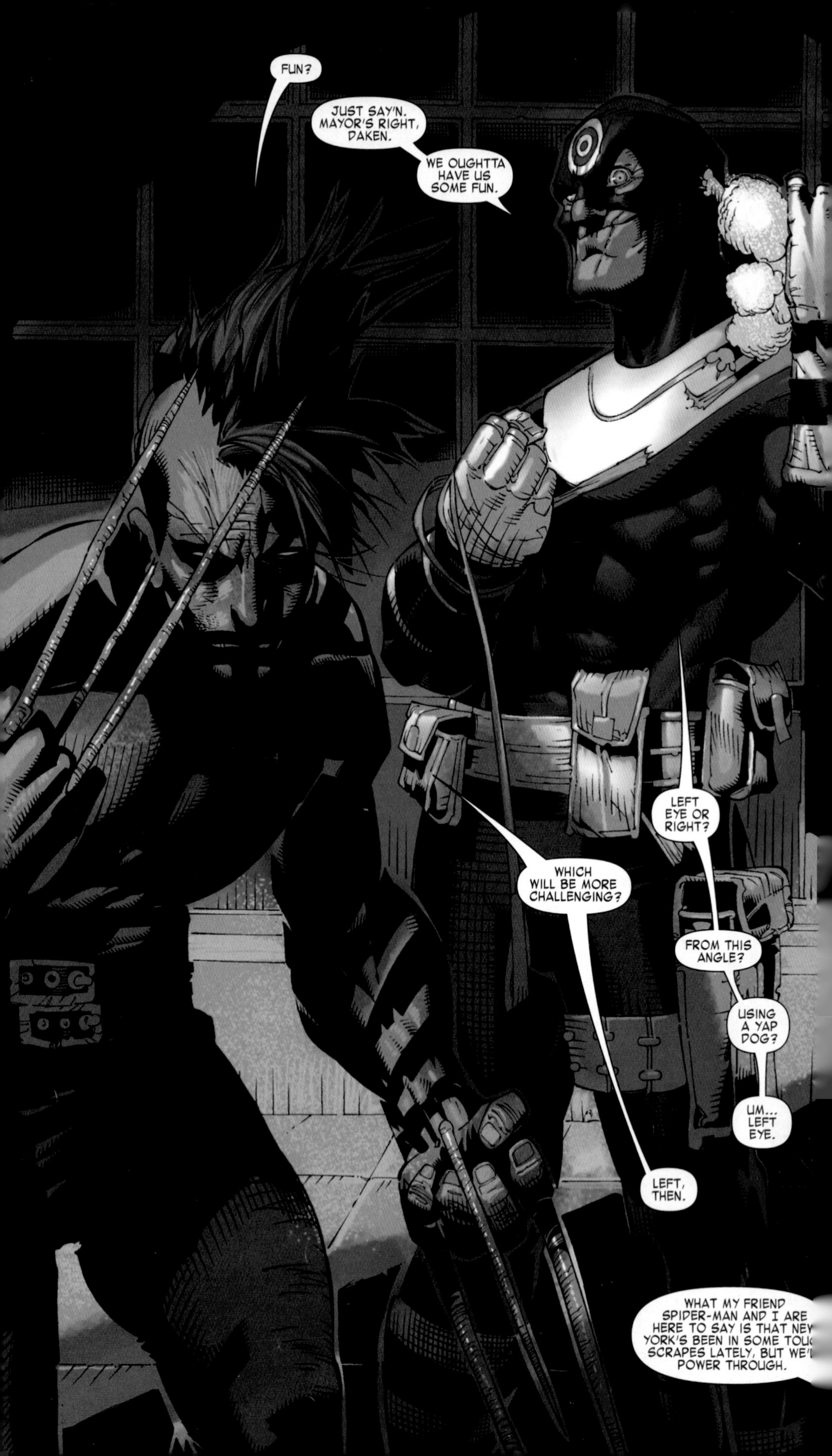
FUN?
JUST SAY'N. MAYOR'S RIGHT, DAKEN.
WE OUGHTTA HAVE US SOME FUN.
LEFT EYE OR RIGHT?
WHICH WILL BE MORE CHALLENGING?
FROM THIS ANGLE?
USING A YAP DOG?
UM... LEFT EYE.
LEFT, THEN.
WHAT MY FRIEND SPIDER-MAN AND I ARE HERE TO SAY IS THAT NEW YORK'S BEEN IN SOME TOUG SCRAPES LATELY, BUT WE'L POWER THROUGH.

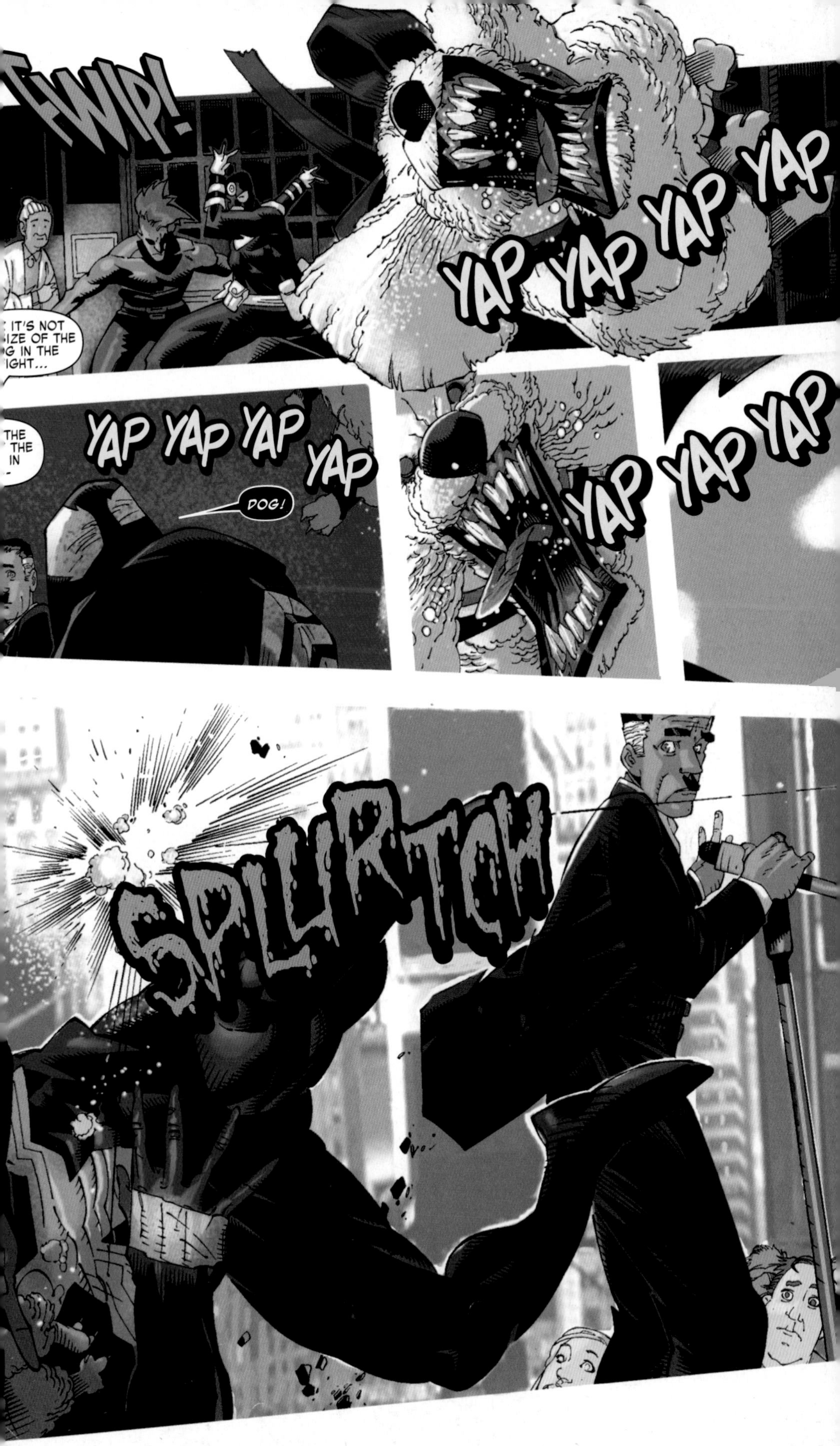
FWIP!
IT'S NOT
SIZE OF THE
G IN THE
FIGHT...
YAP YAP YAP YAP
THE
THE
IN
YAP YAP YAP YAP
DOG!
YAP YAP YAP YAP
SPLURTCH

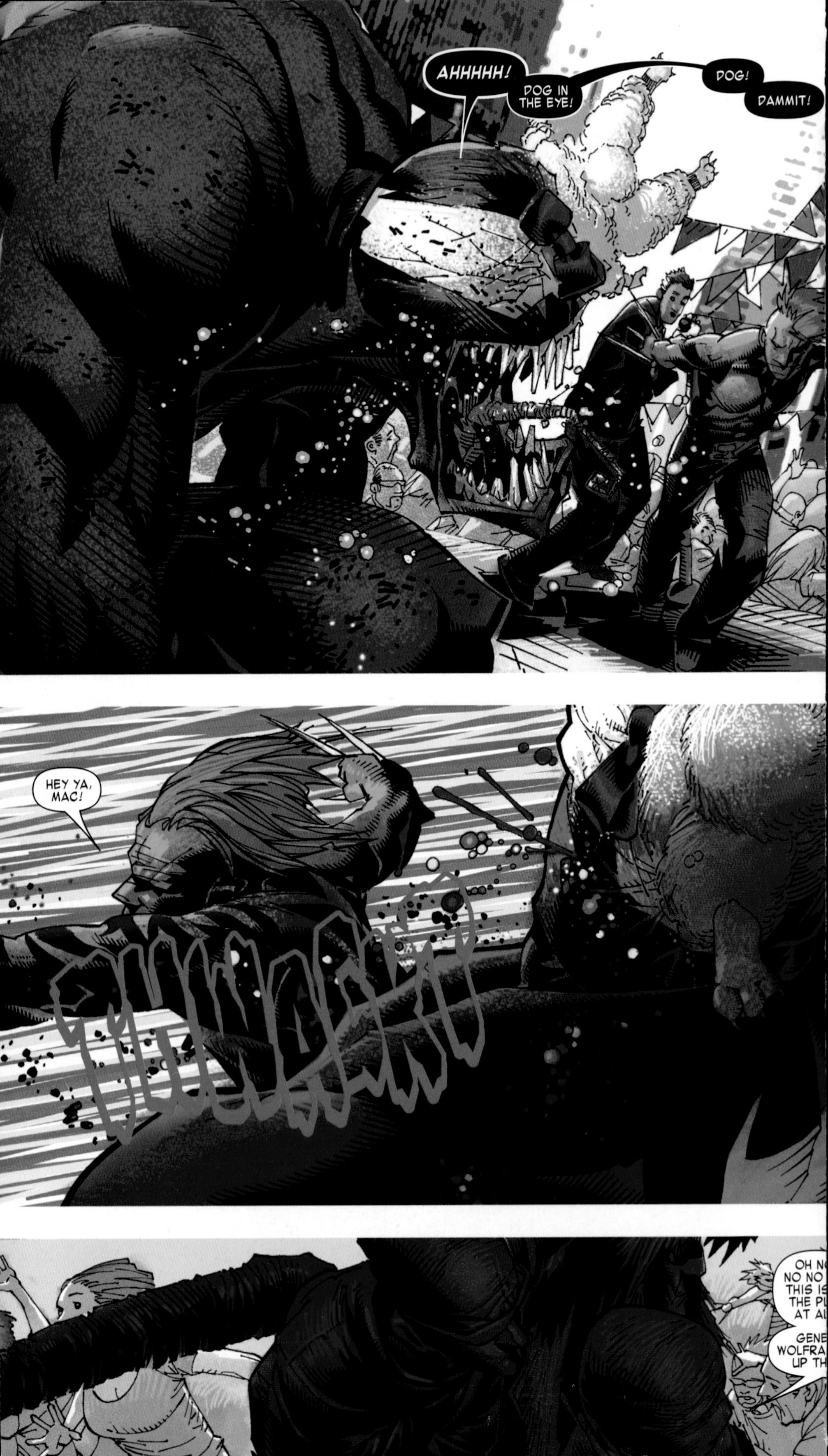
AHHHHH!
DOG IN THE EYE!
DOG!
DAMMIT!
HEY YA, MAC!
OH N
NO NO
THIS IS
THE PL
AT AL
GENE
WOLFRA
UP TH

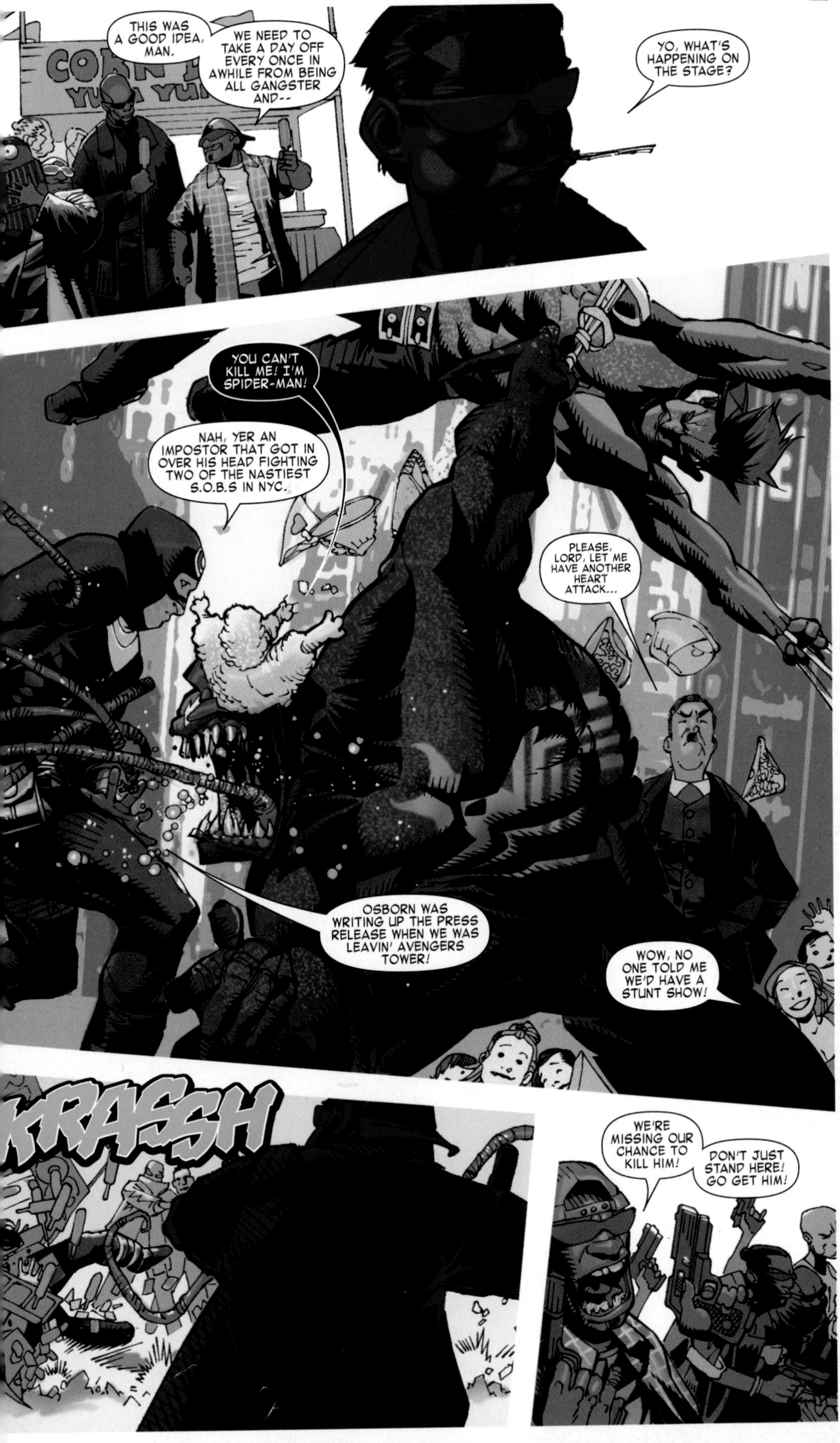
THIS WAS A GOOD IDEA, MAN.
WE NEED TO TAKE A DAY OFF EVERY ONCE IN AWHILE FROM BEING ALL GANGSTER AND--
YO, WHAT'S HAPPENING ON THE STAGE?
YOU CAN'T KILL ME! I'M SPIDER-MAN!
NAH, YER AN IMPOSTOR THAT GOT IN OVER HIS HEAD FIGHTING TWO OF THE NASTIEST S.O.B.S IN NYC.
PLEASE, LORD, LET ME HAVE ANOTHER HEART ATTACK...
OSBORN WAS WRITING UP THE PRESS RELEASE WHEN WE WAS LEAVIN' AVENGERS TOWER!
WOW, NO ONE TOLD ME WE'D HAVE A STUNT SHOW!
KRASSH
WE'RE MISSING OUR CHANCE TO KILL HIM!
DON'T JUST STAND HERE! GO GET HIM!

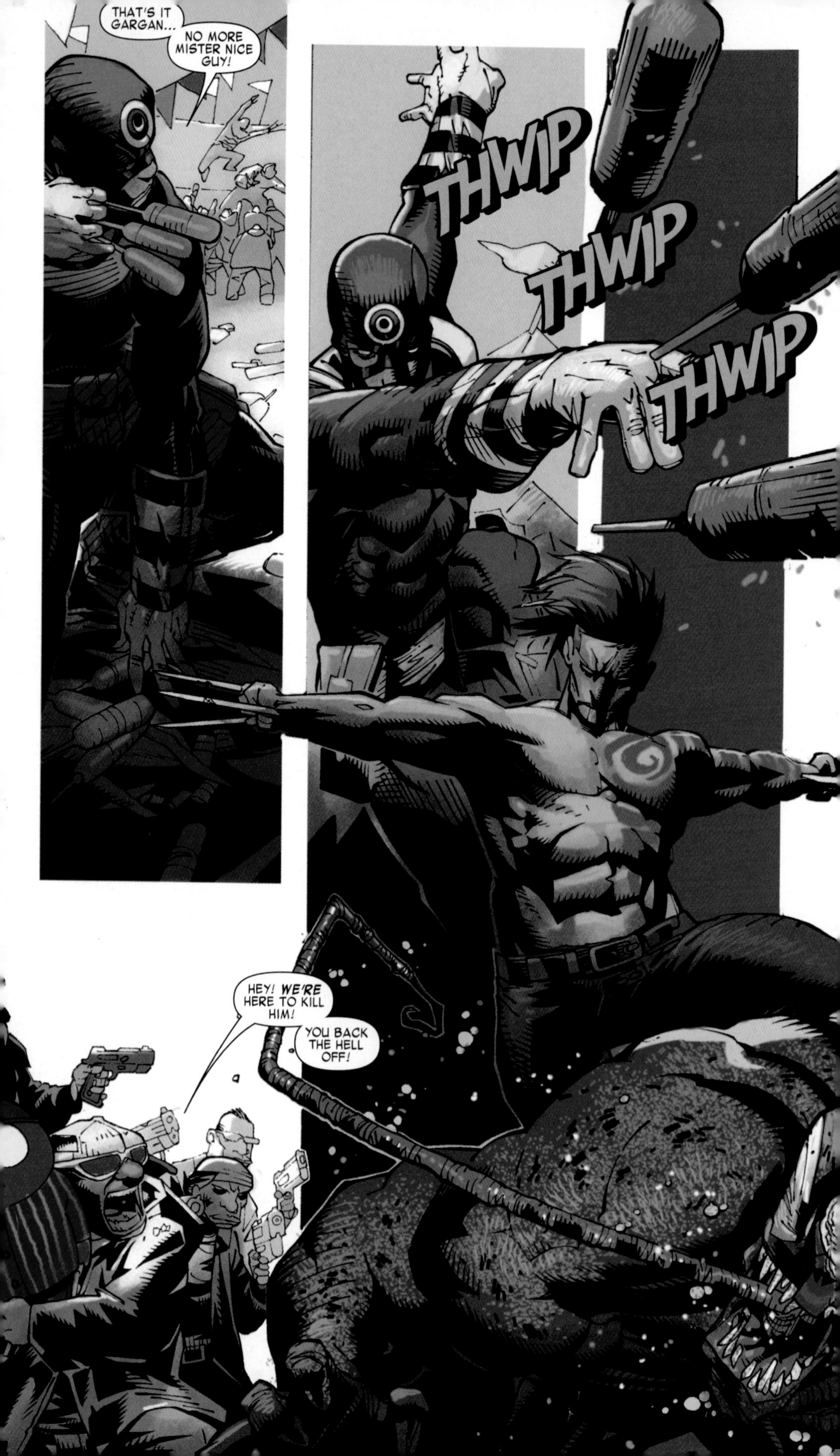
THAT'S IT GARGAN...
NO MORE MISTER NICE GUY!
THWIP
THWIP
THWIP
HEY! WE'RE HERE TO KILL HIM!
YOU BACK THE HELL OFF!

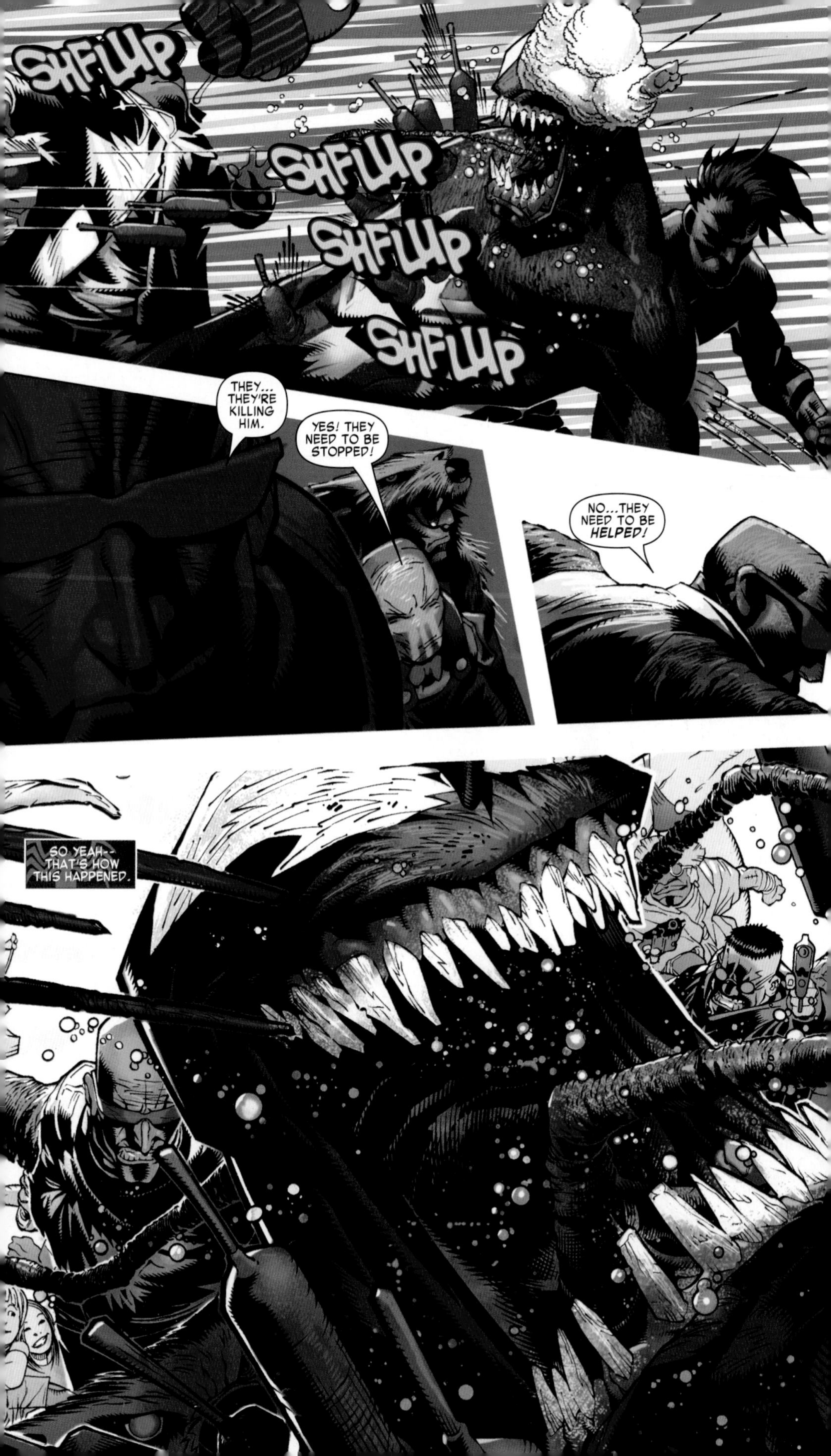
SHFLUP
SHFLUP
SHFLUP
SHFLUP
THEY... THEY'RE KILLING HIM.
YES! THEY NEED TO BE STOPPED!
NO...THEY NEED TO BE HELPED!
SO YEAH--THAT'S HOW THIS HAPPENED.

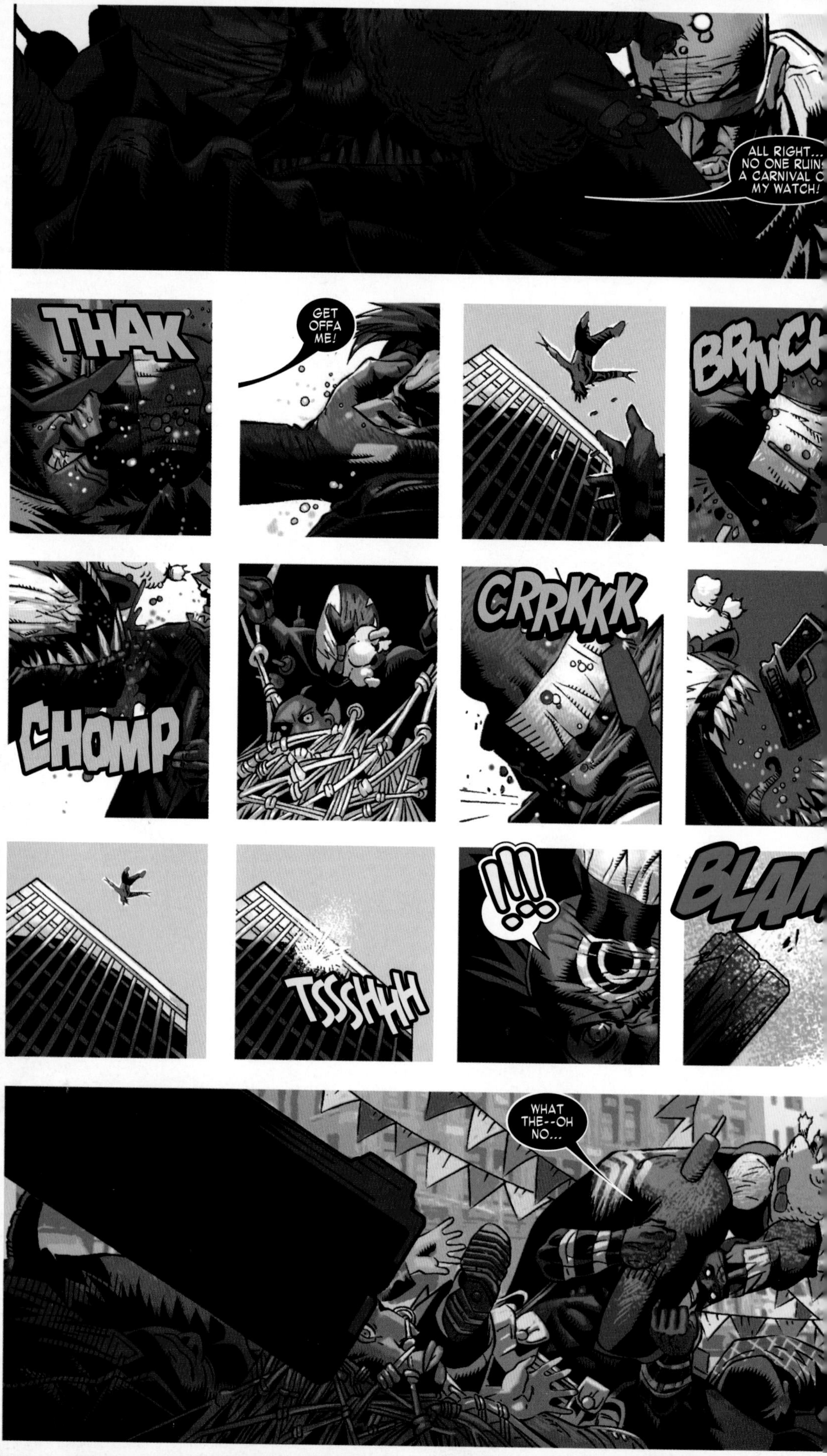
ALL RIGHT... NO ONE RUIN A CARNIVAL O MY WATCH!
THAK
GET OFFA ME!
BRNC
CHOMP
CRRKKK
!!!
TSSSHHH
BLA
WHAT THE--OH NO...

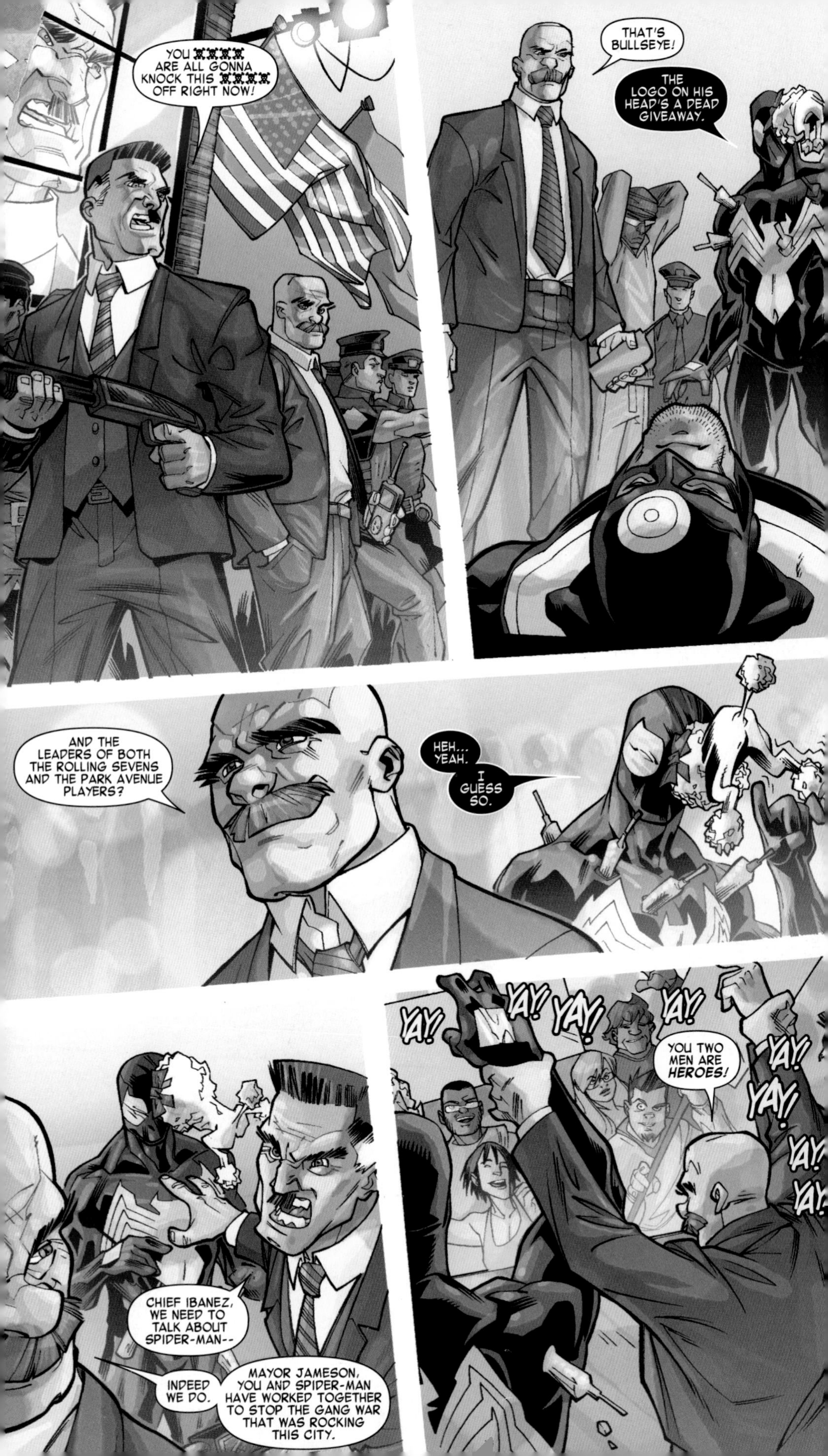
YOU ☠☠☠☠ ARE ALL GONNA KNOCK THIS ☠☠☠☠ OFF RIGHT NOW!
THAT'S BULLSEYE!
THE LOGO ON HIS HEAD'S A DEAD GIVEAWAY.
AND THE LEADERS OF BOTH THE ROLLING SEVENS AND THE PARK AVENUE PLAYERS?
HEH... YEAH.
I GUESS SO.
YAY! YAY! YAY! YAY!
YOU TWO MEN ARE HEROES!
YAY! YAY! YAY! YAY!
CHIEF IBANEZ, WE NEED TO TALK ABOUT SPIDER-MAN--
INDEED WE DO.
MAYOR JAMESON, YOU AND SPIDER-MAN HAVE WORKED TOGETHER TO STOP THE GANG WAR THAT WAS ROCKING THIS CITY.

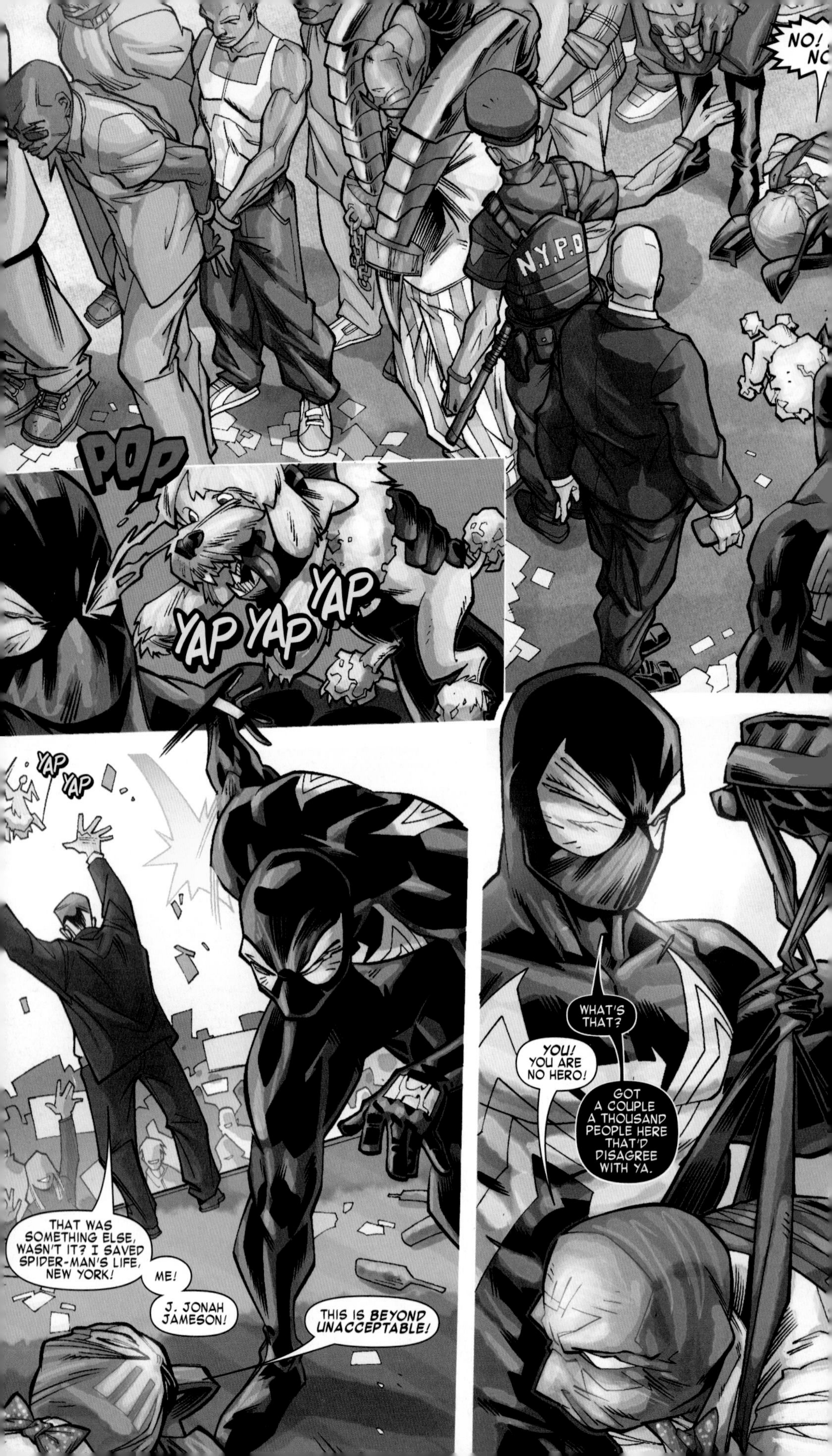

NO! NO
POP
YAP YAP YAP
YAP YAP
THAT WAS SOMETHING ELSE, WASN'T IT? I SAVED SPIDER-MAN'S LIFE, NEW YORK!
ME!
J. JONAH JAMESON!
THIS IS BEYOND UNACCEPTABLE!
YOU! YOU ARE NO HERO!
WHAT'S THAT?
GOT A COUPLE A THOUSAND PEOPLE HERE THAT'D DISAGREE WITH YA.

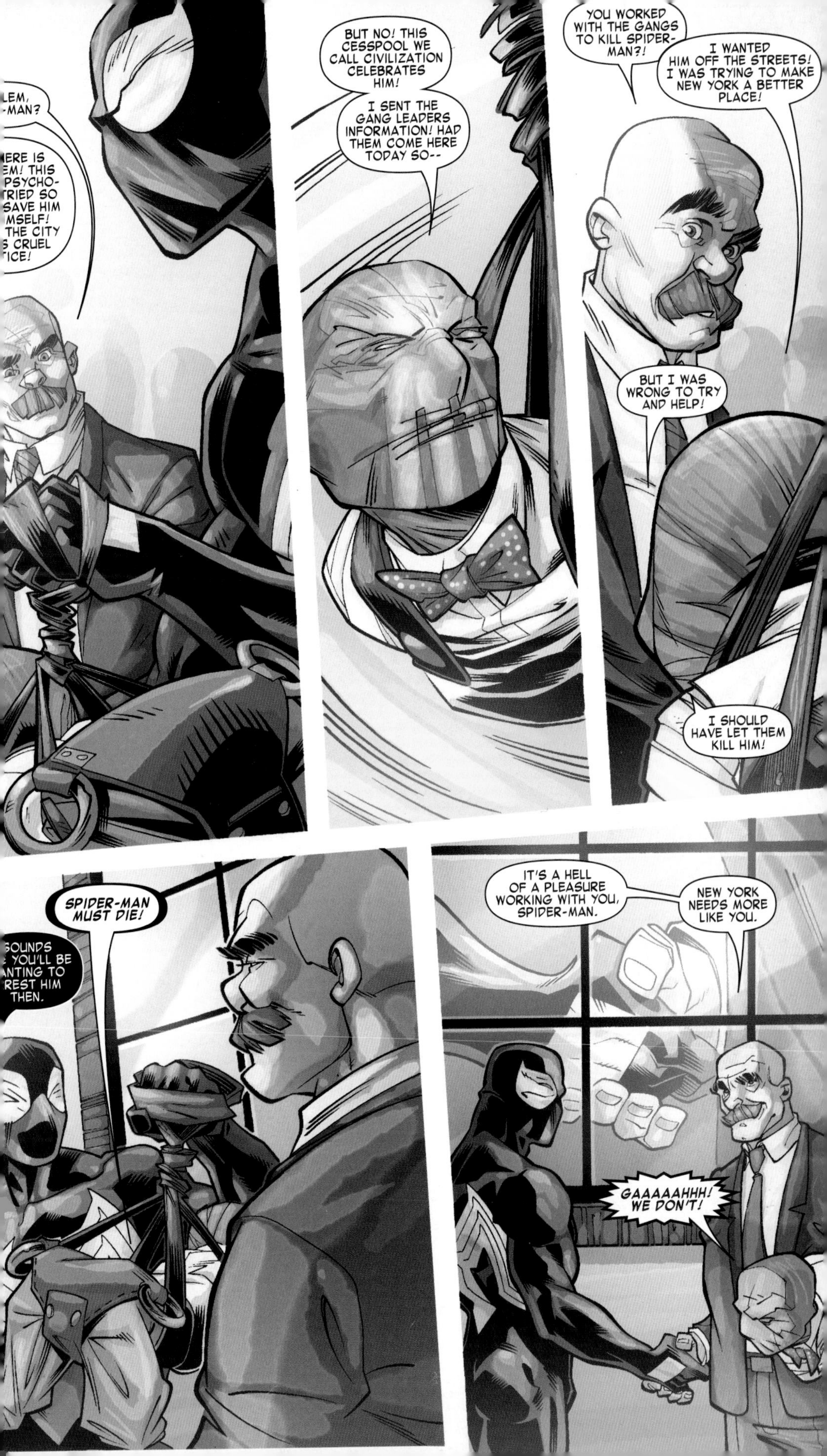

LEM, -MAN?
ERE IS EM! THIS PSYCHO- TRIED SO SAVE HIM MSELF! THE CITY S CRUEL TICE!
BUT NO! THIS CESSPOOL WE CALL CIVILIZATION CELEBRATES HIM!
I SENT THE GANG LEADERS INFORMATION! HAD THEM COME HERE TODAY SO--
YOU WORKED WITH THE GANGS TO KILL SPIDER-MAN?!
I WANTED HIM OFF THE STREETS! I WAS TRYING TO MAKE NEW YORK A BETTER PLACE!
BUT I WAS WRONG TO TRY AND HELP!
I SHOULD HAVE LET THEM KILL HIM!
SPIDER-MAN MUST DIE!
SOUNDS YOU'LL BE ANTING TO REST HIM THEN.
IT'S A HELL OF A PLEASURE WORKING WITH YOU, SPIDER-MAN.
NEW YORK NEEDS MORE LIKE YOU.
GAAAAAHHH! WE DON'T!

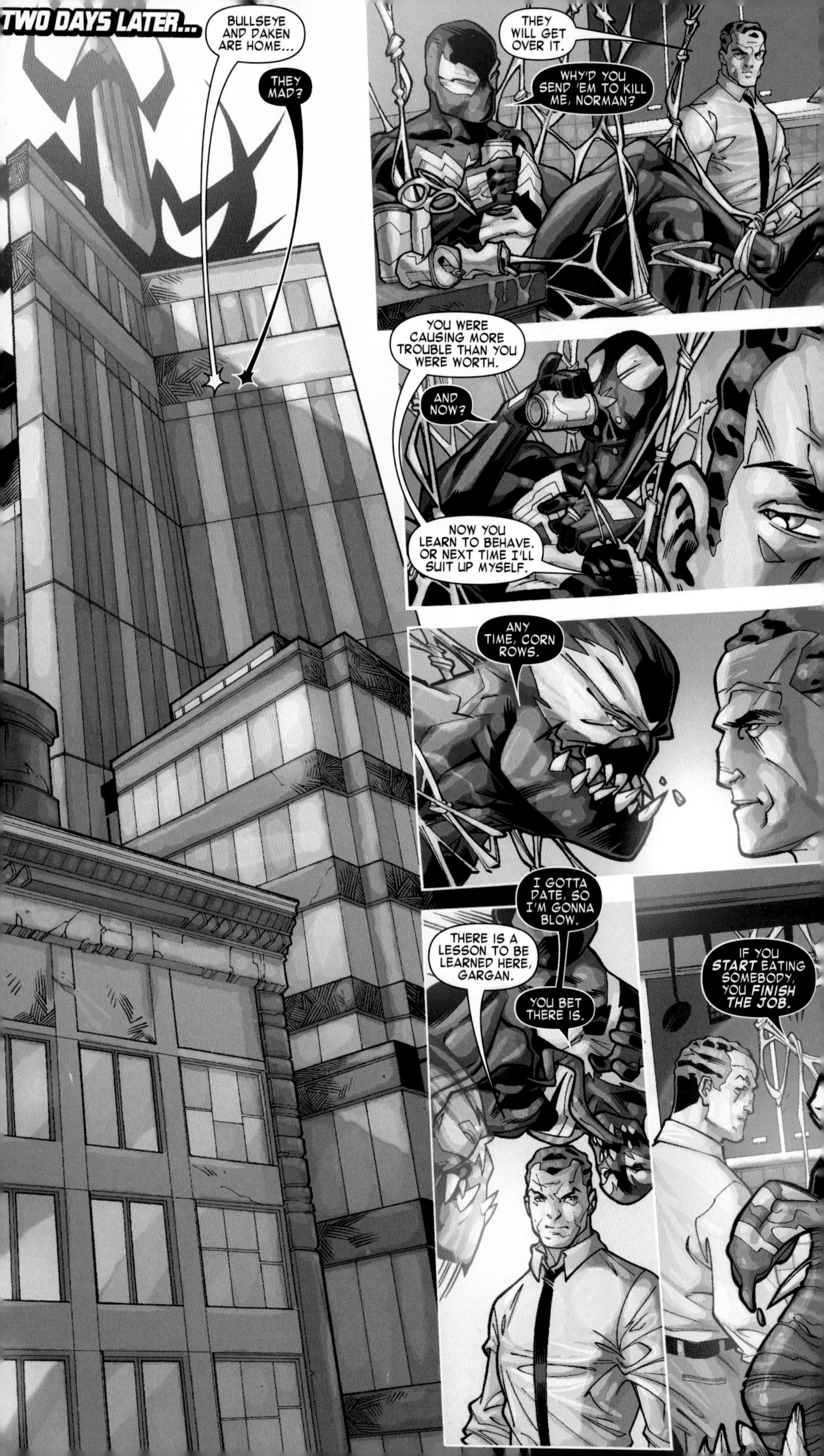
TWO DAYS LATER...
BULLSEYE AND DAKEN ARE HOME...
THEY MAD?
THEY WILL GET OVER IT.
WHY'D YOU SEND 'EM TO KILL ME, NORMAN?
YOU WERE CAUSING MORE TROUBLE THAN YOU WERE WORTH.
AND NOW?
NOW YOU LEARN TO BEHAVE. OR NEXT TIME I'LL SUIT UP MYSELF.
ANY TIME, CORN ROWS.
I GOTTA DATE, SO I'M GONNA BLOW.
THERE IS A LESSON TO BE LEARNED HERE, GARGAN.
YOU BET THERE IS.
IF YOU START EATING SOMEBODY, YOU FINISH THE JOB.

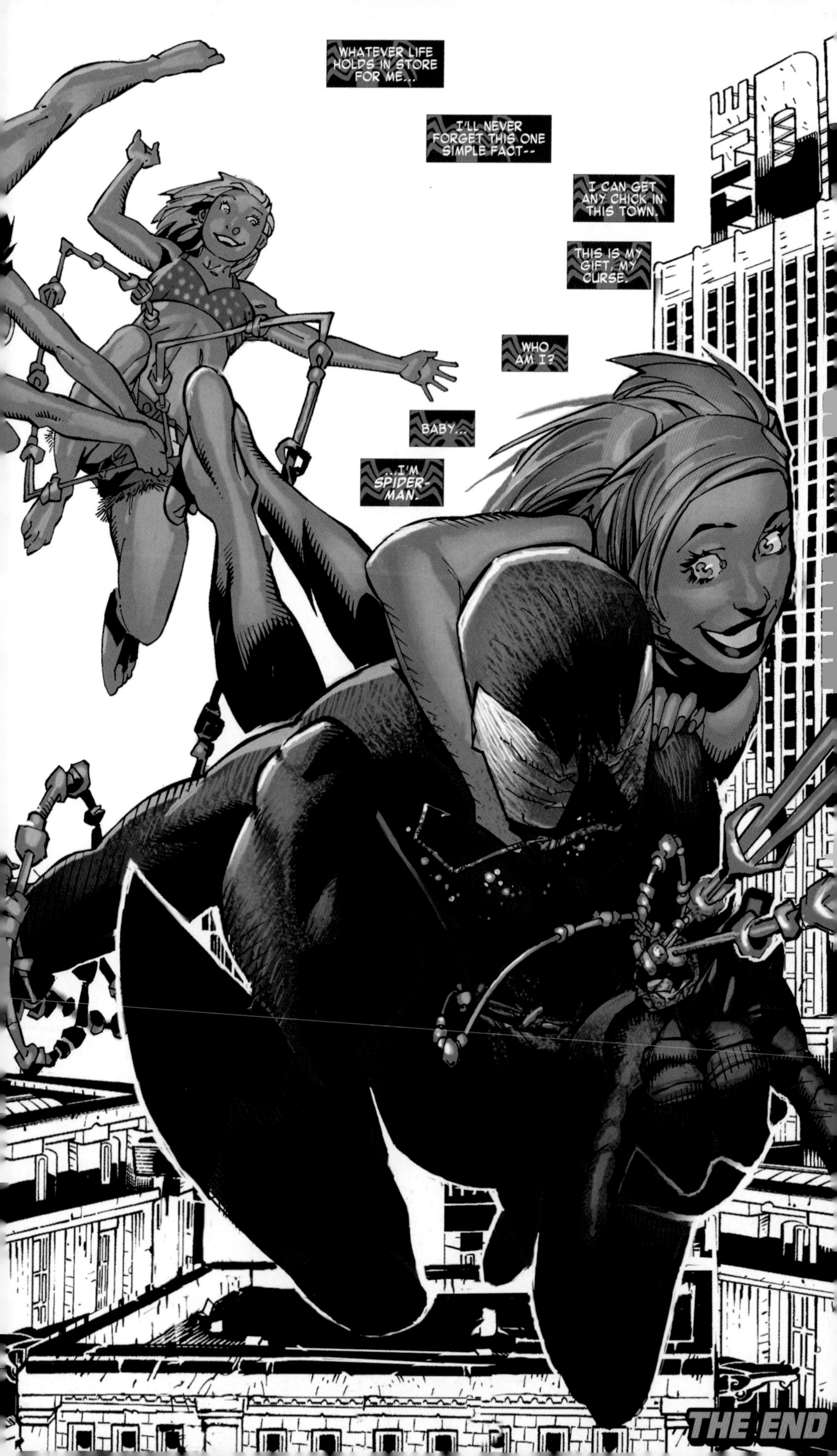
WHATEVER LIFE HOLDS IN STORE FOR ME...
I'LL NEVER FORGET THIS ONE SIMPLE FACT--
I CAN GET ANY CHICK IN THIS TOWN.
THIS IS MY GIFT, MY CURSE.
WHO AM I?
BABY...
...I'M SPIDER-MAN.
THE END

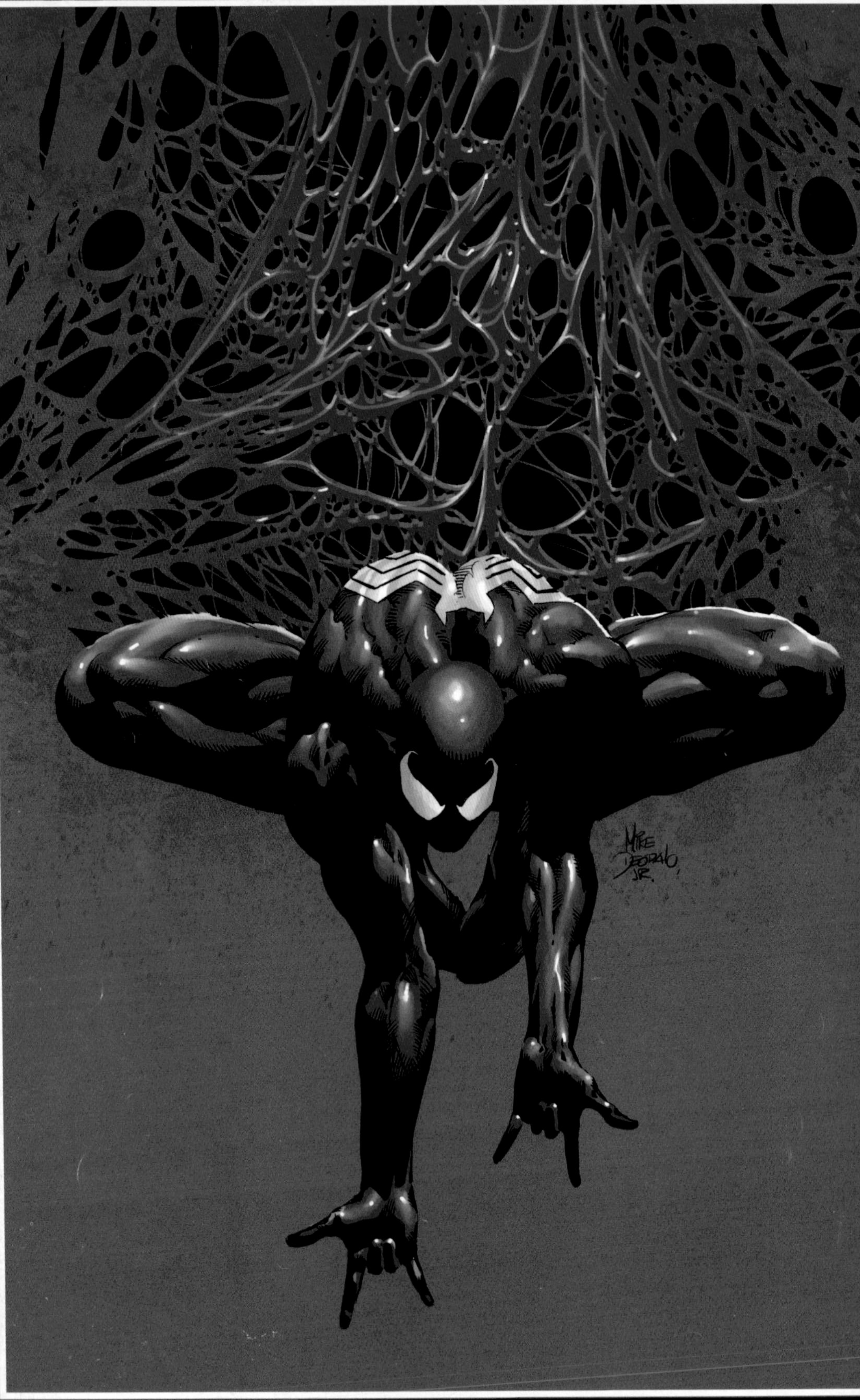

#1 VARIANT BY MIKE DEODATO

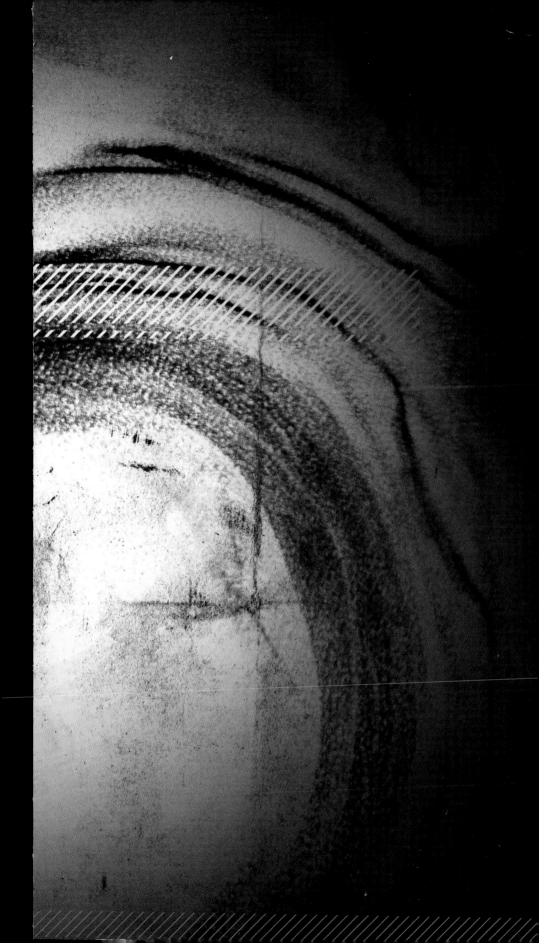

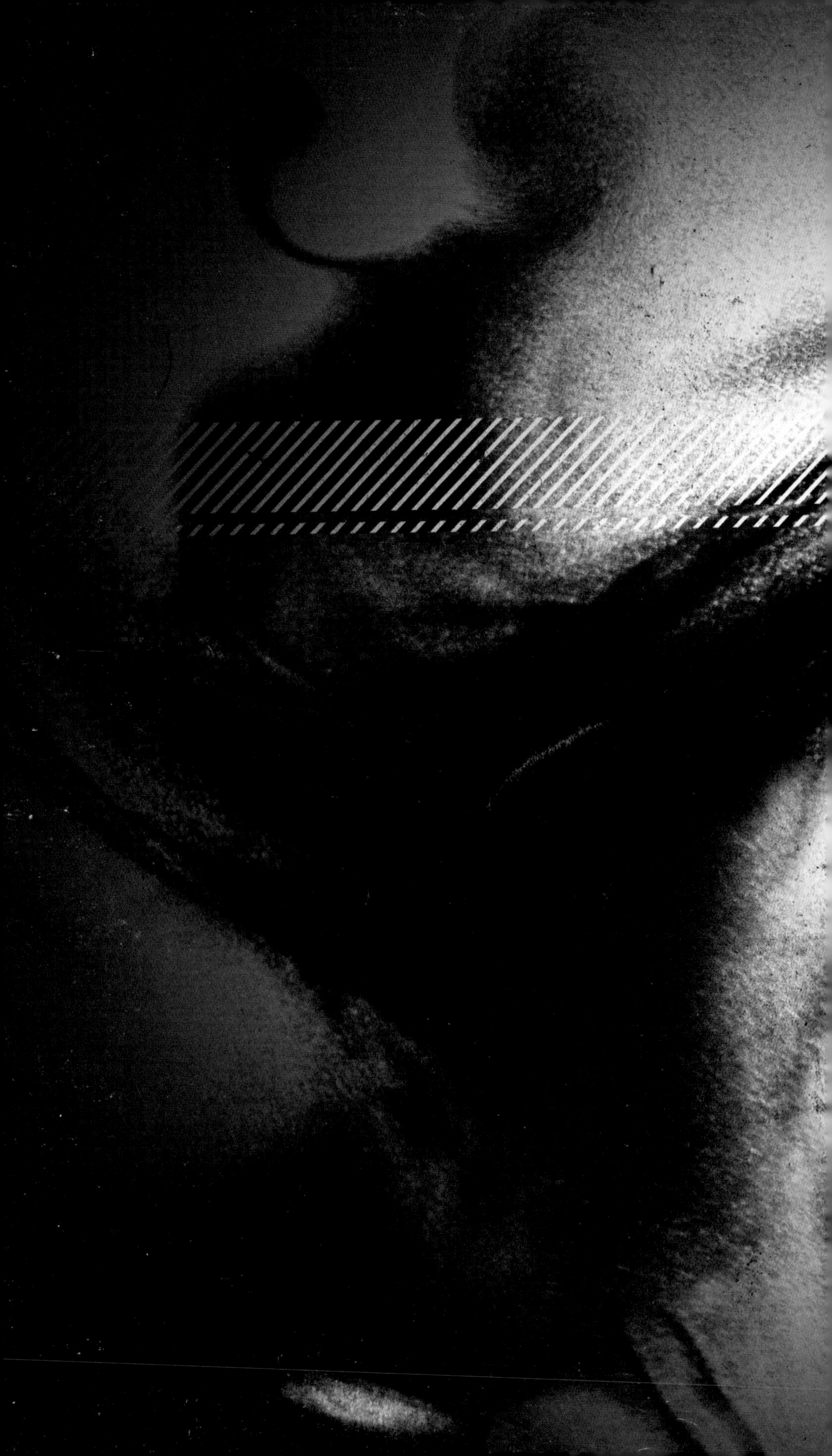